BILLY WATERS IS DANCING

BILLY WATERS ~IS~ DANCING

Or,
How a Black Sailor Found
Fame in Regency Britain

MARY L. SHANNON

YALE UNIVERSITY PRESS
NEW HAVEN AND LONDON

Published with assistance from the Annie Burr Lewis Fund.

Permission to reproduce lines from Rita Dove's *Sonata Mulattica* courtesy of Rita Dove.

For information about this and other Yale University Press publications, please contact:
U.S. Office: sales.press@yale.edu   yalebooks.com
Europe Office: sales@yaleup.co.uk   yalebooks.co.uk

Set in Freight Text Pro by IDSUK (DataConnection) Ltd
Printed in Great Britain by TJ Books, Padstow, Cornwall

Library of Congress Control Number: 2024932809

ISBN 978-0-300-26768-6

A catalogue record for this book is available from the British Library.

10 9 8 7 6 5 4 3 2 1

Contents

CONTENTS

Illustrations

Colour Plates

I. Robert and George Cruikshank, *Lowest 'Life in London', Tom Jerry and Logic among the unsophisticated Sons and Daughters of Nature at 'All Max in the East'*, from Pierce Egan, *Life in London* (1821). Author's collection.

II. T. L. Busby, *Billy Waters* (1819), later republished in *Costume of the Lower Orders of London* (1820). The Miriam and Ira D. Wallach Division of Art, Prints and Photographs: Art & Architecture Collection / New York Public Library.

III. John Philip Simpson, *Ira Aldridge (The Captive Slave)* (1827). Purchased with funds provided by Mary Winton Green, Dan and Sara Green Cohan, Howard and Lisa Green and Jonathan and Brenda Green, in memory of David Green / Art Institute of Chicago.

IV. Édouard Manet, *Portrait of Laure (La Négresse)* (1863). Pinacoteca Agnelli, Turin.

V. William Hogarth, *Captain Lord George Graham, in his Cabin* (c. 1745). © National Maritime Museum, Greenwich, London.

VI. William Elmes, *A Milling Match between Decks* (1812). © The Trustees of the British Museum.

Figures

Author's Note

There are historical images in this book that will sadden and even anger you; there is language used in nineteenth-century texts which many readers will find shocking and potentially upsetting. The outrages of the past should not be forgotten. But they also must not be reproduced: I have attempted to follow the expertise and guidance of scholars in African American and Black Studies by avoiding historically used terms (such as 'master'), which carry racist assumptions buried within them, in favour of terms such as 'enslaver' and 'enslaved'. I have reproduced the term 'Negro' where the source material demands it, but I have chosen to censor the more offensive 'N—er'. As Gretchen Gerzina explains in the Introduction to her book *Britain's Black Past*, 'the term "black" can refer to those from a variety of national origins' (5), hence I use it for Waters and others. Following the February 2021 version of the *Diversity Style Guide* (https://www.diversitystyleguide.com), I capitalise 'Black' but not 'white'.

At times I make use of the word 'we' to address the reader, and this is intended as an inclusive (not an exclusive) 'we' that reaches out to you, the reader, whoever you are and wherever you may be. Uncovering the past, however, cannot be a neutral act. I am aware that I have benefited from opportunities and assumptions that were denied to Waters; the last thing I want to do is to reproduce the exploitation of Waters all over again. What I aim to do is accord Billy Waters the critical attention he demands and deserves as an act of allyship.

As a white, able-bodied Londoner with an Anglo-Irish heritage, I first encountered Waters eight years ago in the same way many Regency readers did: in a colour illustration to Pierce Egan's 1820–1 book *Life in London*. At the time I was an insecurely employed young lecturer. I had recently finished my PhD and I was working three different short-term contracts at three different universities, hoping for a lucky break. My dream of being a writer and an academic seemed further away than ever. Many people asked me, gently, if it might not be better to get a *real* job. But there was Waters, balanced on the tightrope of truly precarious circumstances, struggling with challenges far worse than mine, with a family dependent on his ingenuity, and vulnerable in a way I would never be. And yet, in the picture I was looking at, still dancing. Waters' precarity caught my attention, but his ingenious resilience held it. In many ways his life was tragic. In every way, his life was heroic.

It is inappropriate for me to hog the stage, so I will close here and get out of the way. It's more than time for Waters to reclaim the limelight.

London, March 2023

⤳ ⤳

Prologue

'Enter BILLY WATERS, *dancing'*

The respect paid to Billy Waters amounted to a kind of hero-worship, heightened by the circumstance that he was a fact as well as a figure.

'N—er Minstrelsy' (1861)[1]

Some of us could confess with shame, that the feathered cocked hat and fiddle of Billy Waters had survived the memory of a thousand things of real importance: which could hardly be, were there not some psychological force in these street characters – an inexplicable interest and Attraction.

Alfred Gatty, 'London Street Characters' (1852)

London, 26 November 1821

There is a busy crowd outside the Adelphi Theatre tonight. Even though it's late November, the pavement of the Strand is jammed up with excited playgoers and assorted lookers-on. There is a new production at the Adelphi that *everyone* – rich, poor and middling – wants to see.

A new play by William Moncrieff is always going to create something of a buzz. He's written several popular plays already.[2] This one is different, however. This time Moncrieff's play *Tom and Jerry* adapts *Life in London* (1820–1), the phenomenally popular illustrated narrative released in weekly parts, a very modern publishing format. The serial has only just finished, and the whole of London has been talking about it.[3] All the boys now talk in 'flash slang' like the narrative's main characters, Tom and Jerry. The text was written by Pierce Egan, an energetic Irishman known for his sports writing, but the pictures are a major part of *Life in London*'s success. These were drawn and engraved by the famous artist brothers Robert and George Cruikshank, and they depict the worlds of London's rich and London's poor in vivid hand-coloured detail. The serial is ready-made for theatre. It's easy to imagine how the illustrations might come alive with actors, props and song. In fact, there have already been other recent stage versions of this literary phenomenon: William Barrymore's production at the Royal Amphitheatre in September went down well, and Charles Dibdin the Younger has a production at the Olympic Theatre.[4] But a new version on stage of the hit that is *Life in London* is guaranteed to make London's theatre-going population very excited. They know it will be crowd-pleasing, colourful and family-friendly. It's the kind of prospect that theatre managers drool over.

A few hundred yards away, another crowd has gathered. It's gathered around Billy Waters. Waters appeared in one of the illustrations to *Life in London* and he performs near the Adelphi most nights. He's part of the London streetscape in this burgeoning entertainment district between Charing Cross, Covent Garden and Fleet Street.[5] Look at him now, as he plays his fiddle and sings his trademark song 'Polly Will You Marry Me?'.[6] He's dancing too, balancing with amazing dexterity on his wooden leg and then kicking it out in time to the tune, the brightly coloured feathers on his hat capering along with him. It's a joyful dance, and an eye-catching one. It might make the well-travelled observer think of sailors' jigs and Mardi Gras revels. The crowd are enjoying it immensely. But if you look closely at his face, his skin shines with sweat. This is hard work. He has to keep it up, though. He has a family who rely on this income.

What he doesn't realise is that his task is about to get even harder. Inside the Adelphi, an actor called Signor Paulo is preparing to play 'Billy Waters' live on stage in a key scene of the play. It's a scene that will make Waters a household name across Britain and America. It's also a scene that will change the way the public sees him for ever.

Why have so few people heard of Billy Waters today? We seek figures of Black British history to restore to their rightful place in the

1. *Robert and George Cruikshank, Billy Waters in the pub, from* Life in London *(1821).*

narrative, but Waters with his ragged shirt and roving life has so far been largely overlooked. We focus increasing attention on the lives of the ordinary and the poor instead of on grand narratives of dukes and queens, but the many contradictions of Waters' life and his inability to write his own story mean he has been set aside for easier subjects. We explore the lives of people with disabilities from history, yet Waters the amputee with his triple threat of singing, dancing and fiddle playing has been ignored. How is it that Waters has been forgotten in a culture which now seeks to retrieve such stories, and celebrate so many of these elements in our histories? Why doesn't this sailor, performer, immigrant, father, lover, professional and extraordinary talent have his own biopic, his own documentary, or at the very least a cameo in every historical drama set in Regency London? Sometimes we are very bad at supporting the people who entertain us. As interest grows in recovering diverse histories, Waters and his world are starting to appear more prominently in museum collections, but hardly anything is written about him that is detailed, authoritative or even accurate. This book aims to set that right: it's not only the first full look at his life, it's the first proper reclamation of his place in literary and visual culture.[7] It's about how William Waters the man became first 'Billy Waters' the celebrity, and then 'Billy Waters' a well-known character who appeared as fictionalised versions of himself in books, plays, periodicals and images. How did the 'Dancing Fiddler' and celebrated 'King of the Beggars' become so important to nineteenth-century popular culture? Waters is a vital example of how Black performers were busily engaged in shaping Regency and early Victorian popular culture according to their own terms as well as the terms enforced upon them by white-dominated culture, not simply dancing on its periphery.[8]

Originally from the fledgling United States of America, William Waters ended up in the British Navy.[9] Later, performing on the streets of London was a vital supplement to his naval pension. Reliable and objective facts about his life are limited, but some things we do know for certain; we have his naval records which give his age and place of birth (among other things), and accounts of his life from the period, all of which can be cross-checked against other archival sources. He was an extremely striking figure, not just because he was a Black man in an era of enslavement.[10] Waters played the fiddle, sang, and danced – possibly all at the same time – a feat made all the more extraordinary by the fact that he did so balancing on a wooden leg. As if this wasn't enough, his costume was also designed to be eye-catching. Waters adopted a distinctive look of 'Cock'd hat adorned with various coloured feathers – Sailor's jacket – Canvas trowsers – wooden leg', which drew on numerous influences from across the Atlantic world:[11] naval and military, Caribbean and Dutch-American. Regency and early Victorian Londoners would have found Waters' absence from our stories about the city inexplicable: as Charles Hindley (the nineteenth-century commentator who reprinted much of the little we know about Waters' life) puts it, 'his ribbon-decked cocked hat and feathers, with the grin on his countenance, and sudden turn and kick out of his wooden limb, and other antics and efforts to please, excited much mirth and attention, and were well rewarded' with money from passers-by.[12] The popular broadside-publisher James Catnach declared that '[e]very child in London knew [Waters]'; author Douglas Jerrold, friend of Charles Dickens, asked 'who ever danced as he danced? Waters was a genius.'[13] Genius is a striking word to use by a nineteenth-century white writer about a Black performer. Jerrold demands that we wake up and pay attention to Waters' skills.

Waters and his fellow street performers were also categorised and patronised by well-to-do men like Thomas Lord Busby in the 1810s or Charles Hindley in the 1870s, who published books on London's street culture.[14] We should recognise the vulnerability of these people who didn't ask, or necessarily want, to be represented in text or image for the entertainment or instruction of others. As scholar Rosemarie Garland-Thomson has shown, there is an ethical dimension to how we look at people we encounter: this becomes more complex for encounters with people from the past who are no longer alive to engage with our reactions.[15] So I'm adapting an approach used by Oskar Jensen in his book *Vagabonds*, in which Jensen asks: how do we look *with*, not *at*, people? Jensen uses verbal testimony from the street workers and street sellers of Victorian London as one method; we have barely any reported words from Waters, so I must try something different. I'm going to use the images and texts produced about Waters to explore how a variety of people looked *at* him, but also to find clues about how Waters looked back. To look with Waters, rather than at him, is to use these sources to read past the narratives of nineteenth-century artists and commentators to see possibilities and perspectives that they missed. It is only through such representations and small archival traces that it is possible to uncover Waters' existence, seek to recover the richness of his world, and reassess how and why his image spread across so many nineteenth-century texts and images. To tell this story accords Waters the respect paid to other historical figures when we explore their lives and worlds to understand more about the cultures in which they moved. It's a story of exploitation: middle-class writers, illustrators, publishers and dramatists used Waters' image for their own ends (an exploitation which as a white able-bodied author I am striving not to reproduce). But it is also a story of agency: the first creator of 'Billy Waters' the performer was, after all, William Waters himself.

The people outside the Adelphi Theatre on that November evening in 1821 weren't just being entertained by a busker. They were encountering a well-known Londoner who was about to be made even more famous by the play many of them were hurrying in to see. Waters' instantly recognisable caricatured characteristics had already made him a striking part of an important picture in Egan's narrative *Life in London* (Figure 1).[16] This illustration shows Waters at the centre of a gathering set in a public house near Seven Dials in

St Giles parish where Waters was said to spend his spare time.[17] He is shown in the 'Holy Land' (the nickname for the area because of its large population of Irish Catholics) surrounded by the other beggars of St Giles, referred to as 'Cadgers', who proudly show off how they fake poverty to trick the unwary into giving them money. In this image Waters reproduces his street act indoors; it's part of *Life in London*'s insistence that London is not only a city of theatres but also a city where life itself is theatrical, because everyone is performing. To talk about performance is not always the same thing as discussing theatre: according to performance scholar Marvin Carlson, a busker is performing, but so is the passer-by who stops to watch and to listen and in doing so takes on the 'role' of audience.[18] Scholar Angela Esterhammer has suggested that 'performance', a term over which academics continue to argue, ought to be under-stood as a key word for the 1820s, and this could be said about the whole Regency period when understood in its broadest sense (from about 1790 to about 1835–40).[19] Waters was to be immortalised in Moncrieff's *Tom and Jerry* because of a scene based on this *Life in London* illustration in which 'Billy Waters' gets a significant speaking part.[20] It was a heavily fictionalised version of the street performer. The people crowding into the Adelphi might not have known it yet but in this play, street performance, illustration and popular culture were all about to collide. The fall-out was considerable.

In November 1821, Waters was on the cusp of becoming more widely known than ever before. He wasn't, however, about to become rich. Versions of Moncrieff's play were quickly staged around the British Isles and in the US, and its characters became household names on both sides of the Atlantic.[21] The Georgian and Regency periods experienced the rise of celebrity culture, but Waters saw none of the money from these performances.[22] There were many tales told about Waters, not all of them true. But in a period before modern copyright law Waters had no legal means of asserting his right to his own image, and no powerful patrons to defend him. The horrible irony was that to get inside the Adelphi to watch 'Billy Waters' the character on stage, the theatregoers had to jostle past William Waters the man as he sang and danced in the daily struggle to feed himself and his family. When they streamed out of the theatre at the end of the evening, many of the playgoers would inevitably have had their idea of Waters overlaid or even changed completely by what they had seen inside. How this happened and what it meant – for Waters and for others – is a story that deserves to be told.

Night after night, and year after year, Waters was turned slowly from a historical person into a fictionalised character who embodied the attractive possibilities of living on the edge of nineteenth-century society. While he was most famous in the 1820s and 1830s, even up to the 1870s you could make a reference to 'Billy Waters' in a periodical or newspaper and expect your readers to understand the connection, even if by 1870 the play *Tom and Jerry* was considerably old-fashioned.[23] In 1844 a man called Alfred Wyatt was hauled up before Bow Street Magistrates' Court on a charge of selling indecent pictures, but he managed to skip free of the charge by arguing (to 'loud laughter') that the images were nothing more than 'Billy Waters with his wooden leg' – a man with his leg in the air, rather than another part of his anatomy.[24] By 1887, however, Charles Dickens' protégé Edmund Yates wondered 'who is aware now that half a century ago Billy Waters was a well-known London beggar?', and a correspondent to the *Era* newspaper in 1884 was confused about whether Billy Waters and East-End street-singer Billy Barlow were the same person or different people.[25] Certainly journalist Alfred Gatty wrote in 1852 that Waters' image had 'survived' in Gatty's memory when other things 'of real importance' did not, but even he struggled to account for what he called the irresistible 'Attraction' of Waters as a performer and as a character.

How do we recover that attraction now and explain its 'inexplicable interest'? It's impossible to access Waters' performance directly now, of course; to think about performance always involves thinking about loss (the intangible moment that is forever slipping by into the past). In some ways Waters' world was not dissimilar from ours: the 1820s saw economic turmoil after a long period of conflicts on foreign soil, a complex relationship between Britain and America, technological changes sweeping through people's lives, forced and unforced migration, and a sense that the new generation felt at odds with the old. In other ways Waters' world is alien to us. Can Waters' life story be recovered when so many of the conventional tools of the biographer simply do not exist for him? Like so many socially marginalised people from the past, Waters left no papers, letters, or writings of his own. Most of his life is shrouded in mystery. From his birth in New York to his arrival in the British Navy in his mid-thirties, we cannot know for certain what he was doing. Yet it's my belief that this problem makes it more, not less, vital that Waters gets the full attention he deserves. A scarcity of evidence doesn't imply a lack of historical value: it reveals a great deal of historic neglect. Gaps in the archive for people overlooked by history mean that a more creative approach to reconstructing their lives and reputations is required.

This book, therefore, is a two-in-one biography of William Waters the man and 'Billy Waters' the character, or idea. The only way to understand one is to understand both. Waters occupied the unusual hinterland of being both a historical person and a street 'Character' that he *himself* first developed. So I have taken the innovative step of uniting the kinds of historical detective work done by Alain Corbin on a French clogmaker in his book *Life of an Unknown* – a man about whom Corbin had no more evidence than some entries in civil registries and knowledge of the nineteenth-century historical context – with Marion Turner's insight from her 'biography' of Chaucer's Wife of Bath that characters, too, can have a life. I also draw on Saidiya Hartman's technique of 'critical fabulation' that she develops across her multiple books on the history of enslaved Black people, a technique which enables her to present both a critical and a creative interpretation of gaps and silences in the archives.[26] I therefore include research-based imaginative passages at the start of each main section, which could be about Waters' life but don't have to be; they are designed to evoke the lives of ordinary people in the period. There were many disabled beggars and street entertainers in Regency London. There were other Black performers of various kinds, though none quite like Waters. None of these became quite such widely known fictionalised figures. There were many famous fictional characters who took on a life of their own in the nineteenth century (Dickens created a fair few of them), but though they had characteristics taken from life they were productions of imagination, not named historical figures.[27] Memories of Waters survived because he was fictionalised. My approach thinks through the implications of this.

In many ways the question 'Who was the real Billy Waters?' was not one in which the consumers of nineteenth-century popular culture were very interested. That this was the case tells us a great deal about the workings of that culture. *Life in London* led to a craze that spawned many imitations and spin-offs, typical in this period. Waters and other characters appeared in print and ballads, on tea trays and as ceramic figurines, in plays and in books. Scholarship still debates the proper language for this process: remediation; plagiarism; fan-fiction?[28] Perhaps there is a better analogy: the meme. With each stage production, each new image or periodical article, Waters became a kind of nineteenth-century meme: a portable idea of 'Billy Waters' for others to use.[29] Early modern literature scholar Helen Cooper developed this analogy for stock characters or motifs from the 200 years before Waters' birth, ones 'so useful, so infectious' that they might be said to have developed 'a life of [their] own', but Regency popular culture wasn't so different from its Early Modern roots.[30] Used mostly now for images that circulate on social media, memes are continuously being actively created as they spread and shift.[31] By the time we reach the early nineteenth century, where copyright was a bone of contention, debates between writers, illustrators and playwrights over who produced the 'original' idea were driven by economic considerations but ultimately missed the point about how their print and visual culture still functioned.[32] However, Waters was turned into a kind of nineteenth-century meme because he developed his own street performance from materials to hand, and made his own creative choices despite the constant vulnerability of his position.

Waters opens up other possibilities for understanding Black presences in nineteenth-century British culture beyond the lenses of abolition, blackface minstrelsy and the sentimentalism of Harriet Beecher Stowe's transatlantic bestseller *Uncle Tom's Cabin* (1852). As David Olusoga writes, Black British history is 'everyone's history', and 'divisions between so-called black history and so-called mainstream British history [are] unstable and unhelpful'.[33] In order to see how unstable these divisions really are we need to examine not just depictions of Waters himself, but of other kinds of performers and popular characters with whom his image became associated: sailors, veterans, street performers, disabled people and people of other ethnicities. We need to situate Waters' British celebrity within its transatlantic networks, and its connections to Frederick Douglass and William Thackeray. Olivette Otele writes:

> One could argue that given the low number of black Britons, they were likely to be excluded from grand narratives. Yet one could also argue that there was a relatively low number of white Britons in comparison to indigenous populations across the British Empire, and yet their stories have been widely researched and shared.[34]

A close focus on one person's world can be used to show the larger significance of small details, and bring individuals into dialogue with 'grand narratives'.[35]

What new insights are gained when we look at the nineteenth century from Waters' position, outwards? Quite a few, I suggest. The different portrayals of Waters – and their relationship to the cultures within which they were enmeshed – offer important new ways to reassess Regency and early Victorian notions of race, disability, performance, celebrity and the body. Waters opens up new perspectives on several other meme-like figures in popular culture: 'Jack Tar' the sailor and his girl 'Poll', the 'King of the Beggars', the 'Black crossing-sweeper'. Visual images of Black sailors are underexplored and while there are authoritative studies of disability and wooden legs in the long nineteenth century, Waters' life and afterlives demand we re-examine 'Jack Tar' the sailor in the light of new approaches to race and disability in the Regency and early Victorian period.[36] Thanks to the efforts of numerous scholars we know more than ever about the lives of Regency and Victorian street people, but Waters' story reveals the importance of the 'King of the Beggars' for understanding the place of well-known Regency and early Victorian street people in early celebrity culture.[37] Since the publication of Peter Fryer's *Staying Power* (1984), the link between race and class in nineteenth-century Britain has been widely discussed,[38] but Waters points us to the figure of the 'Black crossing-sweeper' as an idea around which these issues coalesced.[39] The transatlantic performance history of Moncrieff's *Tom and Jerry* with its role in the history of blackface has not been fully traced before, and its legacy for American and British Black performers has been overlooked. The story of Waters the man and Waters the character uncovers broader issues which help us to re-examine Regency culture.

My sources in this enterprise are rare books and archival materials, literary texts and fiction, newspapers, magazines, portraits, illustrations, prints, ballads and decorative objects. As a university researcher and teacher of nineteenth-century culture, I offer my training and expertise as tools for uncovering Waters' life and the larger cultural rhythms within which he danced. Twentieth-century scholars focussed a great deal of energy and attention on uncovering working-class reading, writing and other cultural work as a way of building class consciousness and demonstrating the agency of working-class people.[40] Such efforts, important as they were, implied the possibility of a quantifiable division between 'elite' and 'popular' culture. We should be wary of drawing any clear boundaries, though, when in fact the lines are blurred. After all, representations of lower-class people in caricatures or in street ballads shared imagery with so-called 'high art': with paintings now hung in major galleries, and novels now considered canonical. Middle-class children read cheap tales such as *Life in London*.[41] Characters from page and stage travelled between Britain and America, carried by transatlantic voyagers. We can think of nineteenth-century popular culture as a network because its texts, genres and influences were all so interlinked and ideas and characters circulated freely, meme-like: Waters' life and afterlives are a particularly complete demonstration of this.[42] But we mustn't think of it as some kind of closed system, or something that's simple to define. It defies simplistic categories of 'original' and 'imitation'. Its porousness challenges divisions between 'Black' and 'mainstream' British history. This is a story about Waters, who found fame during his lifetime in Regency Britain. But it's also a story about the development and circulation of popular culture in a globalised Atlantic world. It is therefore a story in which we are still participating today.

Why *did* Waters become such a recognisable figure of widespread interest, so much so that figurines of him were still being produced for sale almost forty years after his death? What does Waters' story reveal about how nineteenth-century transatlantic popular culture represented race, class, disability, masculinity and celebrity? How does Waters the Black disabled street performer add to our understanding of early Black writing, as well as the work of Dickens' first illustrator, and Dickens' circle? How *do* literary characters become so well known and circulate so widely, turning up in literature, magazines, pictures, songs and drama? And what did this all mean for Waters? These are some of the questions that struck me on my first encounter with Waters, and that I attempt to answer as we explore Waters' life and world.

This book, then, is not a conventional biography, nor is it only an act of historical recovery. It tells the story of 'Billy Waters' the character in Regency and early Victorian culture through the key events in the life of William Waters the man. Each section follows his life chronologically and is themed by the different parts of his costume: we follow his life to see how his performances developed and how others took them over. We'll see how Waters affected a bigger cast of people, from the Fitzgeralds of Church Street, London, to the actors of the African Theatre in New York. We will also see how fictionalised versions of Waters developed in ways beyond Waters' own control, and which anticipate our ambivalence about finding fame today.

✤ HAT ✤

In Which Waters Begins

New York City, May 17—

This is the favourite dancing-place in Catherine Market: a patch of cleared ground on the east side of the fish market in front of Burnel Brown's Ship Chandlery. Ned and Bobolink Bob (as Bob likes to be known) have already drawn quite a crowd with their shake-down. Ned has paused for breath so Bob has all the attention, which is just how he likes it. He's dancing away on a piece of raised board about six feet long (his 'shingle'), which he chose for its particular clatter and spring. Bob is fully immersed in his double shuffles and heel-toes, but he's able to glance across and smile at Jack who is beating his hands on the sides of his legs and making a loud noise with his heel. It's the Pinkster festival, and it's holiday time from the Long Island farms where all three men are enslaved. For now, the focus is on Bob's lightning feet.

Bob is too occupied to notice the small boy near the front who watches with all the rapt concentration of childhood. The woman next to the small boy claps her hands.

'They dance like the Pinkster King,' she says.

'Who is the Pinkster King?' asks the child.[1]

Childhood

New York, the early 1780s. It's an energised, exhilarated, shaken place. The British are gone, the Revolution is triumphant, and some kind of reconstruction is needed – and quickly. A diverse population of newly American citizens picks its way through a city ravaged by war and fire. Somewhere in that crowd of residents and visitors we should look for a small child named William Waters.

We don't know exactly when or where Waters was born, although his naval records list his name as William Waters and his place of birth as 'New York'. Despite the archival gaps where Waters' early years are concerned, we can make a case that the culture of the community into which he was born influenced the development of his act and his image. According to *Tom and Jerry* playwright W. T. Moncrieff, who claimed to have written 'an ample and interesting Biography' only to lose it while drunk, Waters was born an African Prince:

> BILLY WATERS, was born in the powerful African kingdom of TONGOCONGOTABOO, where he was a native Prince, and bore the name of POKIKOKIQUANKO; from this place he was at an early age, to the universal regret of his loving subjects, kidnapped, by

'an auld Quaker', who bought him from his treacherous attendants, for two axes, a frying-pan and a bag of nails. This *black*
piece of business made him a slave, in the French settlement, at
Demarara [*sic*], from whence however he speedily took *French
leave*, and entered, we believe, the British navy.[2]

This 'biographical sketch' is reprinted in Hindley's 1888 account of
the *Life in London* craze. But the fanciful and frankly racist language
here should immediately alert us not to trust this piece of Victorian
trivia. The attempted humour, such as it is, draws on stereotypes of
the 'comic'-stage Black character, and parodies the autobiographies
by those freed from enslavement (such as Olaudah Equiano and
Mary Prince).[3] The Waters presented here is very much a fictionalised character whose experiences are filtered through layers of
different voices.

The early years of William Waters are almost impossible to locate
– almost. The British Navy put him at thirty-five on 9 December
1811, and his burial record lists him as forty-five on 21 March
1823.[4] This suggests he was born somewhere around 1776–8. Early
nineteenth-century record keeping was not always precise, though;
these ages may simply be shorthand for 'mid-thirties' and 'mid-
forties'. Waters may never have known his own birthday. Frederick
Douglass could only guess at the year of his own birth, writing in his
autobiography that 'Like other slaves I cannot tell how old I am.'[5]
Based on those naval records it can be said with some confidence
that William Waters was born in New York State or New York City,
somewhere around the mid to late 1770s.[6] He was roughly the same
age as the newly fledged American Republic, and more or less
contemporaneous with the British occupation of New York City and
the foundation of the New York Manumission Society, an early
abolitionist group.[7] He was a young child when George Washington
entered New York City and drove the British from Manhattan Island
in 1783. He was Black or possibly mixed race. He and his family may

well have been among the so-called Black Loyalists who fled New York at the same time, having joined the British forces after the British promised freedom to enslaved people who fought for the Crown. Many such Loyalists ended up in London. Alternatively, he may have remained in New York or its surrounding ports beyond childhood and into adulthood; he does not appear on British naval muster lists (handwritten Navy personnel records) until 1811.

New York City in the 1770s and 1780s was not impressive. One disappointed traveller arriving in 1787 recorded their initial impression of 'miserable wooden hovels and strange-looking brick houses, constructed in the Dutch fashion'.[8] Merchants, labourers, and artisans lived awkwardly on the same street.[9] But by the 1790s things were looking up: money began to flow again, the lower West Side was rebuilt, so in 1797 a French duke travelling through North America declared that there wasn't 'in any city in the world a finer street than Broadway'.[10] A striking difference between New York and London for English visitors was the diversity of its population. William Strickland from England noticed the 'greater number of blacks particularly of women and children in the streets who may be seen of all shades'.[11] Waters was born in (or near) a city with a noticeable Black population.

For them, the Revolution had changed little: they still faced violence, cruelty, inequality and racism. Even if the young William Waters possessed free status due to birth or manumission (release from being enslaved), he was still reminded daily that his life mattered very little. Enslavement was critical to the economy of eighteenth-century New York City and its surrounding countryside. It began to be more peripheral to the economy by the turn of the nineteenth century but, despite New York State's 1799 gradual emancipation law, it was possible for someone to have enslaved status in the state until as late as 1848. There were some free Black families in eighteenth-century New York, but as historian Shane White puts it, 'probably there were no more than 100 free blacks in

New York City during the colonial period'. On the one hand, during the years after the Revolution and at the turn of the century New York City became 'the most important urban black center in nineteenth- and twentieth-century America'; on the other hand, 'even in 1790 about one in every five households in the city owned at least one slave'.[12] One new arrival to New York from England in the 1780s remembered that 'in the vicinity of New York, every respectable family had slaves – negroes and negresses who did the drudgery'.[13] Waters grew up knowing that at any moment he could be sold, or enslaved if he was born free. The constant awareness of life's precariousness was his from a young age. As flexible weapons against power he learned the charm and resilience that were to serve him well. He learned that a freedom which is given to you is never truly yours, and that true freedom has to be taken. Arguments about enslavement and abolition could be intellectual exercises for most members of New York's white population; for Waters they were a matter of life and death.

Enslavement ate through family life like gangrene. There were no large plantations in New York and its environs, and even in the countryside famers tended to have fewer than five enslaved individuals. Many families in the city owned only one enslaved person.[14] This meant that finding a partner and establishing a family – challenging anyway if you were enslaved – was made much more difficult. Maintaining that family was even harder: members of enslaved families might all be 'owned' by different people.[15] Families were not attractive prospects as goods for sale, and it was common for individual members to be sold and moved further away. In 1774 John Broome, a New York merchant, upended the usual practice when he put an enslaved member of his household up for sale: he requested that the buyer be 'of known sobriety and good character who lives not above ten miles from Staten Island' as the aim was to try to relocate the man for sale closer to his enslaved wife.[16] More usual, however, was the kind of horror that took place on a normal day in New Jersey in 1797, where an enslaver 'separated a child from its mother, his slave, the Mother by her cries has made the town re-echo & has continued her exclamations for 2 hours incessantly & still continues them'.[17] The endlessness of the mother's pain lays bare the vulnerability of New York's Black population. The unnamed mother has no voice or recourse but her 'cries', and even these are filtered through the lens of a white commentator. The New York Manumission Society, founded in 1785 in the decade after William Waters' birth, aimed more to reform the system of enslavement than to unilaterally disband it.[18] In this slave-holding society Waters learned young that family was a mirage if you could not defend it, and the price of freedom was sometimes the loss of all you knew.

The violence wrought on families is recorded in the work of early Black American writers looking back on their own childhoods, and implicit in depictions of Black families in nineteenth-century popular culture. In Frederick Douglass' *My Bondage and My Freedom* (1855), his second bestselling autobiography popular in both the US and Britain, Douglass describes powerfully how 'The practice of separating children from their mothers . . . is a marked feature of the cruelty and barbarity of the slave system' (37). Douglass depicts what he suggests was his relatively good fortune at being raised for a time by his 'dear old grandmother and grandfather' so that 'it was a long time before I knew myself to be *a slave*' (38). The descriptions of his early happiness and innocence, 'snugly in their own little cabin' (38), play upon the idealisation of the family unit by white-dominated nineteenth-century culture. This is intended to make the shock of the 'distressing revelations' that he will one day soon be forced to leave his grandparents by the 'old master' who views him as property pack even more of a punch (39). As Douglass writes, the fragility of his family structure 'haunted me' (39).

African American writer and abolitionist Harriet A. Jacobs, in her own 1861 memoir, writes movingly of her own childhood vulnerability. Like Douglass, in her earliest years she benefits from an extended family structure and writes that she was unaware of her own enslaved status. The process of disillusionment is similarly brutal and terrifying. The efforts of her enslaved grandmother to gain manumission for her family come to naught as, 'Notwithstanding my grandmother's long and faithful service to her owners, not one of her children escaped the auction block'. Jacobs writes that Black children 'are no more, in the sight of their masters, than the cotton they plant, or the horses they tend'.[19] Harriet E. Wilson's 1859 novel (based on her own life) about a Black girl in the Northern US is a fictional account of vulnerable childhood. Frado is abandoned by her white mother on the doorstep of a wealthy white family when she is around six years old. She becomes a kind of unpaid servant to the family, effectively enslaved, and suffers continuous neglect and abuse. Her despairing cry, 'I ha'n't got no mother, no home. I wish I was dead,' finds a heart-breaking parallel at the end of the novel when she is forced by poverty to leave her own baby with another woman as she travels in search of work.[20] All three writers were the generation after Waters, but it's unlikely that conditions were significantly better for him. They were likely worse. Wilson's novel was not uncovered until 1981, but the two memoirs were read in Britain as well as the US.

Two narratives closely connected with Waters, which contain mothers and their children, give an insight into how young Black children were perceived in Britain before the transatlantic abolition movement came to a head in the 1850s. In Pierce Egan's *Life in London*, the first literary text in which Waters appears, there is an episode set in a pub in what became known as the East End of London, where Tom and Jerry the protagonists find themselves in yet another racially diverse crowd. The Cruikshanks' illustration (Plate I) shows everyone dancing to the music of a different wooden-legged fiddler (a white man, this time, but another ex-sailor by his dress). In the accompanying text, Mrs Mace, an onlooker, introduces the characters in the scene:

that *are* black *voman*, who you *sees* dancing with *nasty Bob*, the coal-*vhipper*, is called *African Sall*, because she comes from foreign parts; and the little *mungo* in the corner, holding his arms out, is her child; yet I *doesn't* think *as how*, for all that, SALL has got any husband: but, *la!* sir, it's a poor heart that never rejoices, *an't* it, sir? (290)

'Mungo' was a nickname and a racist caricature for a young lower-class Black person, after the servant in Isaac Bickerstaff's popular play *The Padlock* (1768). This supposedly comic character, first played by actor, songwriter and manager Charles Dibdin (senior) in blackface, became a crude ethnic shorthand on stage and in satirical prints for the subservient, cheeky, dialect-speaking enslaved West Indian servant. In *Life in London*, the Black family is incomplete: Sall has no husband even though she has a child. Her yellow spotted dress indicates visually that she is a prostitute, and links her to other satirical prints that frame 'blackness as non-beauty and non-human'.[21] But of the possible reasons for this (the multiple potential challenges of maintaining family life in Sall's world), we hear not a word. Sall is poor, and foreign: that's enough. In another version of this image (Figure 2), Waters is added as the fiddler. This suggests that the scene in *Life in London* set in Billy Waters' pub and the scene set in African Sall's pub became linked in the public imagination. The fictionalised versions of Waters were seen as portable and adaptable right from the start.

In Douglas Jerrold's 1840s novel *St Giles and St James* (first published monthly in Jerrold's own magazine), we also find a mixed-race family. Jerrold knew both Waters and Moncrieff; he wrote a letter supporting Moncrieff's application for assistance from the Royal Literary Fund and it was he who declared 'Waters was a genius'. *St Giles and St James* is a novel very much in the *Life in London* tradition, drawing as it does a melodramatic portrait of both 'high' life and 'low' life in London, personified in its main

2. W. W., All Max in the East, a Scene in Tom and Jerry or
Life in London (1822).

characters St James and St Giles who are of course both named
after the affluent and poverty-stricken areas of 'town'. In the novel,
Kitty Muggs the maid (who is white) married the now-deceased
Cesar Gum the footman (who was Black). Their son Ralph 'when
scarcely six years old' was 'presented as a sort of doll footboy to
one of the Marquess's younger daughters'. Ralph must already earn
his keep and serve a wealthier child: 'like her pet pug, he was such
a curious little wretch – such a pretty little monster'. Ralph (who
turns out badly as he grows up) is in childhood just a dehumanised
background accessory to someone else's more privileged life.[22]

Texts and images published in London were influenced by texts
coming out of New York and vice versa. The Atlantic world, where
goods and people (and people as goods) moved around continuously, created a culture that blurred distinctions between the 'high'

and the 'low', the local and the global.[23] Although they were opposed in naval and military terms, Britain and the United States were about to get more culturally entwined, not less.[24] One of the paradoxes of the story of Waters' life and afterlives is that a truly transatlantic popular culture was emerging in a period when the political separation between Britain and the new United States had only just taken place. This transatlantic popular culture reproduced and created white attitudes towards Black children – Black people of all ages – in both Britain and America.

Violence done to family structures is matched by absences in surviving archives. Even when there are records and traces of Waters or other ordinary people from the past, historian Imtiaz Habib reminds us that 'it is the imprints that are visible and not their imprinters'; in other words, every historical record is little more than the footprints left by someone walking by, or a glimpse of their shadow on the wall. This becomes even more challenging when looking for archival traces of the very ordinary, the very poor and the enslaved. A lack of status in the past means that people can remain overlooked into the present; because it's challenging to locate Waters' early life, he has slipped from widespread knowledge and historical memory. As Habib points out, 'the documentary record is the plane of historical sight' and therefore that record is both 'passive and active': it reveals what a society sees as well as what it does not (choose to) see. Habib has called this the 'arc of invisibility' of ordinary Black presences in the historical record: ignored in documentary record-keeping and simultaneously stereotyped in literary culture, Black presences became obscured.[25] But it is possible to use the evidence of popular fiction, images and periodicals to try to make Waters' early life and influences visible once more. This evidence shows how transatlantic Black cultures were – in complex ways – actively contributing to the development and circulation of early nineteenth-century popular culture in ways that have still not been fully explored.

Community

In the midst of these horrendous circumstances, in his early years William Waters would have experienced a lively culture amongst the poor of New York, both Black and white. Children sang psalms by rote at church or at charity schools, if they attended them.[1] Lower-class New Yorkers of all races, whether enslaved, free, or indentured workers, often lived in cellars or basements of larger residences in the city. This was a brutal demonstration of social hierarchies; cellar dwellers were frequent victims of New York's numerous epidemics. But even here people found ways to grab back freedoms where they could. These cellar dwellings had separate access to the street and some were transformed at weekends into different worlds. By the 1790s Black-owned oyster cellars, underground dance halls and drinking dens were popular with New Yorkers from all kinds of backgrounds.[2] Of course, Waters may have been born on a farm outside the city of New York; in the countryside religious and secular festivals provided a respite and a chance to hear music, and dance, though often slave dances were driven by white slaveholders as yet another display of their power over Black bodies. He would still have had opportunities to come into New York itself, however; New York's lively waterfront markets were a huge draw, and 'during the day the black population of the city was swelled considerably by slaves from the surrounding area'.[3] These markets were known for their culture of performance, especially Catherine Market (in what's now the Catherine Slip Mall on the eastern edge of Lower Manhattan), where dance competitions offered prizes of money or dried fish.[4] William Waters may have witnessed such competitions during the festival of Pinkster, when enslaved people from the city and the countryside gathered to celebrate spring in a hugely important festival with roots in both African and Dutch culture. The festival's name came from the Dutch word for Pentecost. John J. Williams, a former enslaved man from Albany, observed that 'Pinkster Day was in Africa a religious day, partly pagan and partly Christian'.[5] Pinkster faded slowly as a festival after 1800, which was when it started to appear more in the written record. It made way for a new tradition of parades by Black New Yorkers.[6] The seeds of Waters' skills as a performer were no doubt sown in his early life in New York.

The Pinkster festival in particular offers the possibility of intriguing connections between William Waters as a young child in New York and his adult performances in London. The concept of the 'Black Atlantic' was defined first by Paul Gilroy; he argued that the Atlantic, with its surrounding landmasses, is 'a cultural and political system' all of its own, formed by the currents of migration (forced or otherwise) and trade. Paying attention to this, he argued, reveals how 'black settler communities have forged a compound culture from disparate sources' drawn from around America, the Caribbean and Europe. Gilroy's bigger, and much more significant, point, is that people of African descent in the eighteenth and nineteenth centuries lived between and across national boundaries, forced to engage with a transnational sense of the world, that developed out of the horrors and uprooting of slavery, the consequences of which are still felt today.[7] Pinkster certainly had multiple cultural roots. Elements of Pinkster celebrations took place across New

York and New Jersey in the late eighteenth and early nineteenth centuries, but the most elaborate were held in Albany on the Hudson River north of New York City. Dutch settlers of New Amsterdam (later New York) brought with them Pinkster when they arrived in 1624. From 1628 they also brought with them enslaved Africans, who gradually turned Pinkster into an event that celebrated the traditions of West Africa.[8] During the three or four days of celebration, which began on the Monday after Whitsunday, this festival involved the appearance of the carnival King dressed in finery and a series of dance performances (called in contemporary accounts the 'Guinea dance') where the dancers were costumed with feathers.[9] Many attendees camped out on Pinkster Hill for the duration of the festivities. King Charles (sometimes called King Charley in contemporary accounts) welcomed the revellers both Black and white, watched over the various sports and activities derived from West African traditions, and demanded a shilling fee from every tent, or two shillings if they were white. Accounts of Pinkster are few and sketchy, and mostly by middle-class white commentators (like accounts of Waters), but the major surviving sources agree on one thing: King Charles was in charge, his will was law during Pinkster in Albany, and his costume was spectacular.[10]

King Charles is described in an 1803 account published in a New York journal as 'an old Guinea Negro'.[11] In the 1860s, Dr James Eights – a white scientist and naturalist who recorded the history of Albany as he recalled it from his childhood – remembered back to 'sixty years ago' and described Charles as 'tall, thin and athletic; and although the frost of nearly seventy winters had settled on his brow, its chilling influence had not yet extended to his bosom, and he still retained all the vigor and agility of his younger years'.[12] According to Eights, Charles was originally from Africa, 'having, in his infant days, been brought from Angola, in the Guinea gulf; and soon after his arrival became the purchased slave of one of the most ancient and respectable merchant princes of the olden time, then residing on the opposite bank of the Hudson' (this merchant was from one of the Dutch settler families). It seems that rather than being a rotating position, Charles was King each year. Picture the scene: 10 a.m. on the first day of Pinkster, Charles rides in state to Pinkster Hill (Capitol Hill in Albany) on a beautiful cream horse led by two attendants, Dick Simpson and the fiddler Pete Hallenbeck (like Charles, enslaved Africans in the household of the Douw family).[13] He's preceded by his royal standard, and followed by a procession of 'distinguished and illustrious characters'. He's instantly recognisable by his outfit, topped off by a spectacular cocked hat:

> His costume on this memorable occasion was graphic and unique to the greatest degree, being that worn by a British brigadier of the olden time. 'Ample broad cloth' scarlet coat, with wide flaps almost reaching to his heels, and gayly ornamented every-where with broad tracings of bright golden lace; his small clothes were of yellow buckskin, fresh and new, with stockings blue, and burnished silver buckles to his well-blacked shoe; when we add to these the tri-cornered cocked hat trimmed also with lace of gold, and which so gracefully set upon his noble, globular pate, we nearly complete the rude sketch of the Pinkster king.[14]

This 'rude sketch' is in fact an extremely striking pen-portrait, which conjures up King Charles before us. But we should imagine King Charles in motion: dancing, music and song were key to the event. 'A Pinkster Ode' published in 1803 begs participants, 'While we have health, whence pleasure springs, / And peace to purchase fiddle-strings, / Let's with united voice agree / To hail this happy jubilee', and accounts claimed King Charles joined in enthusiastically with the dancing.[15] Dance was as much an expression of his authority as his hat: in West African traditions, authority figures had to dress well and dance well.[16] His tri-corn hat and colourful dress might have shared some cultural connections with the Afro-Caribbean figure of John-Canoe, or Jonkonnu, who led enslaved Jamaicans in dance and procession in a ritual of both licensed play and resistance.[17] Post-1776 it also suggested some kind of mockery of the defeated British. As the historian Shane White puts it, in a comment designed to emphasise the transnational elements of King Charles' many cultural influences, 'it appears, then, that the chief character in a ceremony on a Dutch holiday in America was an African-born black wearing a British brigadier's jacket of scarlet, a tricornered cocked hat, and yellow buckskins'.[18] This description calls to mind the illustration from *Life in London* with Waters at the centre of it in his own trademark hat (worn by naval officers), together with a sailor jacket and trousers (Figure 1). Perhaps Waters' bicorn headgear levelled its own mockery at both British officers and (more safely) Britain's defeated enemy, Napoleon.

Alongside costume, dance was an especially important element of the Pinkster festival and something that Waters must have experienced as a young child. Drumming, dancing in a circle, and some kind of shuffling quality to the steps were all key features of Pinkster dancing, as well as being 'so characteristic of much of African dance', as historian Sterling Stuckey points out. Stuckey argues that dance subtly perpetuated values and culture under the very gaze of affluent white Americans.[19] The language of the white sources on Pinkster displays a kind of fascinated bafflement towards the dancing, veering sometimes into angry disgust: as the anonymous A. B. saw it in the 1803 *Albany Centinel*, 'the whole consists in placing the body in the most disgusting attitude and performing, without reserve, the most lewd and indecent gesticulation'.[20] Eights recalled 'couples joining in the performance at varying times, and continuing it with their utmost energy until extreme fatigue or weariness compelled them to retire and give space to a less exhausted set'.[21] The music or beat was provided by drums made from eel pots with sheep skin stretched over them, or banjos played percussively like drums.[22] Age was no barrier to participation: King Charles 'generally led off the dance', then other dancers, 'juvenile and antiquated, would put in the double-shuffle heel-toe breakdown'.[23] There was also little distinction between audience and performers: those watching clapped and sang in time until it was their turn to join the dance. Dancing at Pinkster did far more than make holiday, as Stuckey has powerfully argued. It retained community and even religious values against the odds. It passed on tradition. It was 'the most dramatic and powerful manifestation of African sensibility'.[24] King Charles' participation had a symbolic power of which the young Waters would have been aware.

How likely is it that Waters would have seen, or heard about, Charles the Pinkster King? Pinkster was first recorded in print in 1789 and last recorded in Albany in 1822, but Pinkster was not confined to Albany alone.[25] Thousands gathered at what is now City Hall Park for Manhattan's three-day Pinkster festivities.[26] The dancing competitions in the New York City markets involved Black New Yorkers, as well as those visiting from upstate: accounts of Charles would easily have spread by word of mouth.[27] It's even possible that New York City had its own Pinkster king at one point. In the so-called 'Negroes Burial Ground' uncovered in Lower Manhattan in the 1990s and dating from the eighteenth century, archaeologists discovered the skeleton of a Black man 'buried in a British marine officer's coat'.[28] Only King Charles is recorded as wearing such a uniform; was the dead man a Pinkster king? Pinkster was noted in the press: the fullest contemporary account of the ceremony was published in the *Albany Centinel* in 1803 and reprinted in the *New York Daily Advertiser* almost immediately afterwards, with a note claiming that Pinkster was essentially an old-fashioned festival and now 'entirely abolished in this city'.[29] But it wasn't so old-fashioned that it couldn't make the jump from festival and outdoor space to the stage: on 21 May 1804 the *New York Evening*

Post advertised a special performance of a 'pantomime interlude' called 'Pinxter Monday or Harlequin's Frolics'.[30] New York City Pinkster festivities on Whitsun Monday were also known as the 'Sweep-Chimney's Holiday':

> Whitsun Monday called by the negroes of Long and Staten Island 'PINGSTER HOLIDAY' is also known as sweep-chimney's holiday. On this day, all the negroes of Long and Staten Island obtain permission from their masters to visit New York to participate in the 'amusement of the day'. On their arrival in the city, they immediately repair to the Park, which is the general rendezvous, where they meet their friends the sweeps – after reciprocating the usual congratulations, they divide into different groups, some of these engage in pitching and tossing coppers, others in leaping, jumping and a great variety of extraordinary feats of agility to the no small delight of the most worthless part of the community.[31]

Pinkster here is associated with the so-called 'worthless' of the city, the poor chimney-sweeps and the poor Black New Yorkers.[32] Despite the snide tone of this anonymous journalist, we should be alert to the sounds of an active and potentially multi-racial culture involving Pinkster in the parks and streets of New York City. If Waters did not leave New York for good until long into adulthood, then it's even more likely that Pinkster was a key part of his cultural heritage.

Like Waters, King Charles may not have been on a theatre stage but he was celebrated for his performance skills. 'A Pinkster Ode', published in 1803, conjures up an idealised pastoral scene where King Charles is 'known' by the various qualities of his performing body:

> All beneath the shady tree
> There they hold the jubilee.
> Charles, the king, will then advance,

Leading on the Guinea dance,
  Moving o'er the flow'ry green,
 You'll know him by his graceful mien;
You'll know him on the dancing ground,
  For where he is folks gather round;
  You'll know him by his royal nose,
You'll know him by his Pinkster clothes,
  You'll know him by his pleasant face,
  And by his hat of yellow lace;
You'll know him by his princely air,
  And his politeness to the fair;
And when you know him, then you'll see
A slave whose soul was always free.
  Look till the visual nerves do pain,
 You'll 'never see his like again'.[33]

King Charles' 'hat of yellow lace' combined with other elements of costume, countenance, dancing and behaviour are all part of the effect; the 'Ode' claims that when combined they allow both the reader of the 'Ode' and the participant in the festival special access to Charles, to 'know' him. The boundaries between physical bodies and bodies brought to life on the page through words are blurred so that all is just 'jubilee'. But this performance reveals, even as it seems to conceal behind its idealisations, the harsh realities of life as an objectified slave; because he is enslaved, only King Charles' 'soul' can be 'free'. Albany passed a law banning its large Pinkster processions in 1811, perhaps because of fears about the kinds of agency it encouraged, although Pinkster celebrations persisted: an advert in the *Albany Gazette* in 1815 offered a $50 reward for the return of Caesar, a 'black man' who was allowed to attend a Pinkster celebration but did not return to his 'master'.[34] King Charles' behaviour at Pinkster seems to have persuaded the poet of 'A Pinkster Ode' of the evils of enslavement and the dignity of Black agency.

Perhaps Waters also learned something from stories about the Pinkster King.

At the very least, the history of Pinkster shows that music, dance and costumed performance occupied an important cultural place in the lives of the Black inhabitants of New York State during Waters' earliest years. The festivities are evidence of the survival and circulation of elements of West African culture in New York State.[35] It is into this cultural melting pot that Waters was born. Pinkster suggests that New York State's Black population also had an understanding of the European festive mode that is now (following cultural theorist Mikhail Bakhtin) called the carnivalesque, a circumscribed moment within which topsy-turvydom reigns, the 'low born' are in charge and the normal rules temporarily do not apply.[36] Although Pinkster allowed space for free expression by enslaved New Yorkers, 'the point of reference for this bacchanalian interlude was always the order and certainties of the "normal" social structure', as White points out.[37] 'A Pinkster Ode' presents Pinkster as a multi-racial holiday; while it lasts, 'every colour revels there, / From ebon black to lilly fair', but the revellers are enjoying what they know full well is 'their short-lived liberty'.[38] James Eights' account ends with the words: 'our ancient city was at length again left to its usual quietude, and all things within its confines soon became properly restored to its accustomed routine of duty and order'.[39] For white commentators, Pinkster exists within the contained time and space of the carnivalesque; it therefore can only exist temporarily. But for Black New Yorkers, dance was much more than carnivalesque: it could be a site of resistance, a spiritual statement and a strategy for cultural endurance against overwhelming odds.[40] In New York Waters learned that performance – however it was used – had power. The limited space for freedoms allowed by Pinkster still resonated throughout late eighteenth- and early nineteenth-century New York State, and this raises the possibility that William Waters created his famous act partly from materials gathered during his early life.

The prevalence of Pinkster celebrations in New York State during Waters' early years influenced Waters' own creative choices. The Pinkster costumes are visible in the extravagant costume and performing style which he adopted in London, that was of such interest to the first illustrators of Waters, and which first made him famous. It was Waters' unique performance that earned him attention. Early nineteenth-century commentators focus on his sailor jacket and trousers, wooden leg, his fiddle, his wig and especially his striking feathered hat. The successful publisher of broadsides (a form of cheap print that carried news or topical subjects, often as a page of verse or ballads) James Catnach made it clear that it wasn't just 'every child in London' who knew Billy Waters; 'his hat and feathers with his peculiar antics attracted much mirth and attention'.[41] In Figure 3, which comes from a children's picture-book, Waters is described as 'that jovial blade' (slang for a man) whose 'fame' is known through 'all the town' because 'he plays on his fiddle and capers so well'.[42] Six-year-old Londoner Edward William Cooke, later a celebrated marine painter, drew Waters' picture in one of several childhood sketches (Figure 4).[43] Moncrieff adds Waters' wooden leg to the list of eye-catching elements and again the emphasis is on jollity:

Billy was an accomplished cadger [fake beggar], a skilful musician, and adroit dancer (doing more on one leg than others can do on two) and possessed abilities that as an actor would have rendered him an ornament to the stage.[44]

Douglas Jerrold adds Waters' skin colour as a crucial part of the performance:

Can we close this paper, without one word to thee, O, William Waters? Blithest of blacks! Ethiopian Grimaldi! They who saw thee not, cannot conceive the amount of grace co-existent with a wooden leg – the comedy budding from timber. Then Billy's

3. *Waters in a children's book,* The Cries of London (1824).

complexion! We never saw a black *so* black: his face seemed polished, trickling with good humour.[45]

Calling Waters 'Ethiopian Grimaldi', Jerrold emphasises the carnivalesque aspect of Waters' act because Grimaldi was famous for pantomime (and was Dickens' favourite clown). The rhythms of the Pinkster dances fed into Waters' creativity. As with the Pinkster King, music, dance and reappropriated imperial uniform played a part in creating a unique performance experience.

Waters was unique even in a street culture that often involved elements of performance. Sellers of printed ballads debuted new songs in the street to entice customers and teach purchasers the tunes. Girls selling milk or matchsticks cried out their wares, as did chimney-sweeps looking for new customers. Famous beggars were pictured in books and in prints, their clothes and manners dissected.[46] But of all of the street people of London, perhaps only one person came close to the originality of Waters, and that was Joseph Johnson. Johnson was another Black ex-sailor from the Atlantic world who found his way to the London streets. Johnson also relied on key props: his crutch and stick, and his extravagant hat (Figure 5). A ballad singer by trade, Johnson travelled around villages and towns as well as London, and specialised in popular

4. *A drawing by Edward William Cooke (aged six).*

maritime songs such as 'The Storm', 'The British Seaman's Praise', and 'The Wooden Walls of England' (although he was reputedly a merchant sailor not a naval one). His hat was his best idea, however:

> . . . novelty, the grand secret of all exhibitions, from the Magic Lantern to the Panorama, induced Black Joe to build a model of the ship Nelson; to which, when placed on his cap, he can, by a bow of thanks, or a supplicating inclination to a drawing-room window, give the appearance of sea-motion.[47]

Joseph Johnson's amazing hat probably had its roots in Jonkonnu celebrations. Charles' and Waters' hats also link – albeit more subtly – to the elaborate headwear worn by enslaved Jamaicans during the Jonkonnu festivals.

Like King Charles' tricorn, headgear in early nineteenth-century communities with African heritage carried connotations of authority as well as performance; indeed the performance of authority. The leader of the African American sailors held in Dartmoor prisoner-of-war camp in 1814 was Richard Craftus, 'King Dick', whose authority was symbolised by his bearskin grenadier's cap.[48] White eyes read Black headgear differently. Sam Springer (supposedly escaped to England from enslavement in St Kitts) was said, in the wonderfully named *Streetology*, to have been exhibited on the streets as 'The Black Giant' in what seems to have been some kind of feathered headdress to advertise 'a collection of living curiosities' on show for the delight of the public.[49] Springer performs the presence of the 'exotic' on the streets of London; his image in *Streetology* also shows him advertising the text itself (Figure 6). Springer's image is being used by others on multiple levels here.

5. *Joseph Johnson, showing his hat* (1817).

Slightly earlier, in 1810, Sarah Baartman, a Khoikhoi woman, arrived in London from the Cape and was exhibited at 225 Piccadilly for 2 shillings' entry as the 'Hottentot Venus'. This was one of many exhibitions of people with bodies deemed 'foreign' or 'curious'. Excited attention focussed on her buttocks and Baartman quickly became a demeaning meme-like image in popular culture, which racialised Black female sexuality.[50] She was sometimes depicted with feathered or embroidered headdresses. To what extent was she able to consent to these entertainments? The vile prurience with which she was poked, prodded and illustrated shows the dangerous ways in which white viewers stared at Black bodies. In the early nineteenth century, popular plays created the stereotyped figure of the 'stage Black', who was either comic or vengeful; later in the century, so-called human zoos and freak shows objectified non-white people as exhibits

6. *Sam Springer* (1837).

of 'savage' cultures.[51] These kinds of entertainments helped to define what 'civilisation' meant to their audiences by deliberately exhibiting people who supposedly embodied its opposite. They also offered spectators the potential thrill of identifying with people who seemed to stand outside the rules and requirements of 'respectable' society. Gretchen Gerzina argues that much of nineteenth-century understanding of 'Blackness' was based upon plays, exhibitions and other forms of spectacle.[52] In New York, Waters may have been someone else's property by law, so any interpretation of his performing body is shaped by a context of objectification and exploitation.

Waters stood out, however, because he was neither a street vendor nor a ballad singer nor an exhibit; he exceeded the categories of 'exotic' performer, itinerant musician or beggar. He brought together many different skills. He was notable because of his race, but he did not rely on race alone to generate novelty. The different pictures and descriptions show that Waters' hat made him stand out and enabled him to be understood as a carnivalesque character. It's the unique combination of music, dancing, song, race and, importantly, costume, that meant Waters was discussed, depicted and, eventually, fictionalised. It's a combination that emerged from his own creative choices, though it was eventually taken from him by white artists and writers. The particular attractions of this combination to multiple audiences and to white commentators are something a young Waters might well have learned at Pinkster time.

The most reproduced picture supposedly of Waters has no hat (Figure 7). The celebrity portrait was a well-established genre by the late eighteenth century, and the portrait of the celebrity actor was especially popular.[53] Waters' own portrait in oils hangs in the National Maritime Museum in London and is attributed to Sir David Wilkie, a hugely successful artist with the coveted status of Royal Academician, though not especially celebrated for portraiture. This is the image of Waters with which modern summaries of his life tend to begin, perhaps because the portrait has a quiet, grave dignity about it. Waters stands with his wooden leg thrust slightly forward, wearing a red waistcoat that we see again in some later images, but without the extravagant cocked hat. He's not holding a fiddle and he's not dancing; it's as if the removal of his hat has removed his public persona. He gives the viewer a wary yet direct look, biting his lip as if uncertain, though his stance is tall and open.

But although this is probably the most commonly used image of Waters, of all the images that survive this is the one we can be *least* certain actually depicts him. In fact, almost everything known about the picture is disputed. The painting itself offers no positive

7. *Billy Waters – or is it? Attributed to Sir David Wilkie (c. 1815).*

identification: without key elements of his costume it's possible that this is William Waters, but Waters would not have been the only Black man with a prosthetic limb visible on the streets of nineteenth-century England and of interest to artists.[54] It's as likely to be a portrait of a man known only as 'Old Commodore', who lost his right leg (Figures 19 and 58), as William Waters, who lost his left (though images of Waters frequently shift the position and extent of his wooden limb).[55] Despite the painting's attribution, one Wilkie expert went so far as to say to me that this painting 'certainly has nothing to do with Wilkie'.[56] Even the date of the painting is uncertain.[57] There is no hint of his New York origins here. Just when it seems we have a glimpse of the historical William Waters, he dances out of view.

Or does he? This rather beautiful little painting doesn't present either the carnivalesque caricature or picturesque street character who appears in other images of 'Billy Waters'. Nor does it conform to any of the representational stereotypes of submissive enslaved figure, orientalised 'other', or 'scientific' ethnography that appear in many contemporary images of Black men or Black women. The tentative date of the painting places it at a significant moment in the history of Black people in Britain; in the 1810s the very fact of this painting's existence meant that it engaged with abolitionist debates. Yet *Billy Waters* defies the abolitionists' common representation of the abject and theatrically posed enslaved figure (calculated to allay white fears about Black agency); if it is set alongside the painting of another black man in red from around the same time, John Philip Simpson's 1827 *Ira Aldridge* (*The Captive Slave*), which was posed for by the actor and New Yorker Ira Aldridge, the difference becomes clear (Plate III).[58] The subject of Simpson's painting is seated, chained and passively gazing up to the heavens for help; the subject of *Billy Waters* looks out of the canvas square-on. Black models were in demand in the nineteenth century; popular models (like Wilson, another ex-sailor, in the 1810s, and Fanny Eaton in the 1850s–60s) worked for several different artists, helped by the fact that the art world was a small one involving circles of interlocking networks.[59] This is mocked in an 1807 caricature *A Meeting of Connoisseurs* (Figure 8), where visitors to an artist's studio cluster round the athletic figure of a Black male model, possibly meant to stand for Wilson. *Billy Waters*, however, steers resolutely clear of the muscular stereotypes (for example in Figure 9) that are satirised in Boyne's caricature.

It instead invites comparisons with Manet's 1863 *Portrait of Laure* (Plate IV), a work that has been newly contextualised (and renamed) by art historian Denise Murrell. Murrell describes *Portrait of Laure* as an insistently modern painting, which, by depicting a non-white subject as just another citizen (in contrast to the highly exoticised and sexualised representations of Black women common in earlier Western art), directly engages with the conditions of modern city life.[60] In *Billy Waters* we are being asked to face up to an individual rather than a caricature. His facial expression is guarded, however, and carries with it the suggestion that this sitter may be uncomfortable in this new role. It is certainly not a role with which the nineteenth-century viewer would have most readily associated Waters.

Yet if Waters' childhood memories of the kinds of music, dance, and performance practised by Black people in New York State find echoes in his own act, then by stripping all of that away the oil painting also strips away those layers of personal cultural engagement. It isolates Waters. If Waters' own act was influenced even slightly by childhood memories of Pinkster, Waters was drawing on a complex web of African, European, and North American influences. There's a lively critical debate over whether Pinkster was a festival primarily European or African in origin. Most recently Jeroen Dewulf has argued that 'Pinkster should be understood as an Atlantic Creole festival in a Dutch-American context, rather than a Dutch-African festival in an American context', suggesting it has Afro-Portuguese roots alongside its vocabulary drawn from Dutch settlers.[61] Either way, the key point is clear: Pinkster was a mixture of all kinds of festivals from around the Atlantic world, passed from group to group around the network of popular culture. It proves the wider point that forms of West African culture existed in New York, New Jersey, and the Hudson Valley during the late eighteenth and early nineteenth centuries. The picture of Waters in his hat from the children's book (Figure 3) depicts Waters as a childlike and racialised oddity, but it also advertises Waters' own creative choices. Yes, it presents him as an individual who stands out for being exceptional in certain ways. But it also shows someone who was able to draw upon multiple cultural influences from the range of different communities of which they were a part. This is not to suggest that the anonymous illustrator fully understood the complex influences behind the scene they drew and engraved. But Waters brings with him his own experiences and his own ideas about culture and performance, even as he is turned into a fiction-alised image of himself for the publisher's own purposes and for the entertainment of others. What this illustrator might have (unintentionally) represented is the influence of the cultures of the 'Black Atlantic' circulating before their (and our) very eyes.

Because of the very absence of Waters' trademark professional costume signalled by his hat, it is not the oil painting that fixed the

8. *Thomas Williamson,* A Meeting of Connoisseurs (1807).

9. *Benjamin Robert Haydon,* A nude male figure, study of the black
sailor Wilson (*1810*).

image of 'Billy Waters' within the nineteenth-century imagination.
It was within popular culture that Waters gained fame. Nineteenth-
century popular culture was always looking backwards, sideways
and across the way. It engaged with complex global influences
alongside the newly commercialised mass market and so-called
'elite' cultural forms.[62] It was full of complexity and cultural
exchange in ways that could be seen as exciting, troubling, or
subversive, depending on who you were. Romanticism's insistence
on the power of original genius is one lens through which to look at
early nineteenth-century creativity, but the network of popular
culture offers another. Waters' talent lay in bringing lots of different
elements together in his performance. Waters' image was appropriated for the gain and interests of others; we must never downplay
that fact. But it is also true that Waters himself put together the

germ of an idea so powerful that it was considered well worth appropriating, it lived on for decades, and it brings him back to our attention now. Waters' early years in New York were one rich source of ideas. His time at sea was the next important influence on his life and on his act.

~ SAILOR ~
JACKET

In Which Waters Goes to Sea

HMS Ganymede, off the Portuguese coast, 11 January 1812

From here, halfway up the mainmast of the Ganymede, Cadiz Bay lies spread out before him like a seabird might see it. It's a chilly day, but there is enough sunshine to glint off church towers in Cadiz itself, and to dance along the white-capped breakers of the bay.

Voices on the main deck below remind him that his shipmates are always present. Beside him, his messmates perch on the ropes. He mustn't allow himself to get too distracted as they are in the middle of a sail drill. They must coordinate their movements together, like dancers do.

He's had a wandering career. Now he finds himself on a British man-o'-war. Sometimes the gunner's mate imitates his American accent.

He breathes in the fresh air, tanged with salt. So far I've survived, he thinks. So far, I've survived.

Going Aboard

Compelling and remorseless, the sea rolled through Waters' life like the constant tide. Once he left childhood behind, Waters spent a significant portion of his life as a sailor before he became a performer. He spent a very short but important part of that time in the British Royal Navy. Black mariners traversed the Atlantic world, and the sea is a crucial part of masculine identities in work by early male writers of the Black Atlantic. From the moment he first donned the blue jacket and white trousers of a sailor (and perhaps before) it was a crucial part of Waters' own sense of self. Fifty years before Waters joined the British Navy, Olaudah Equiano wrote of personal bravery under fire when he worked on a British warship as an enslaved servant and 'powder monkey' in 1759. For Frederick Douglass, posing as a free sailor to escape enslavement in Baltimore in 1838, his performative disguise in 'sailor's "rig"' was the only thing standing between him and recapture.[1] Going to sea as a Black man in the late eighteenth and early nineteenth century took courage, and came with added layers of danger and risk.

Understanding Waters' maritime world in the years between 1775 and 1815 – one of the most significant wartime periods in British naval history – is crucial to understanding both his performances and their survival in nineteenth-century accounts and images. Waters' naval service was critical in his transition from America to Britain. If we explore this nautical world we see the ways in which Waters navigated the hazards, as well as the opportunities, of his experience of being a Black sailor. This allows us to appreciate Waters' skills at the same time as his extreme vulnerability. It shows the importance of Waters' British naval service for his later perform-ances: how he created them and how they were received. It reveals how Waters sailed in a 'visual Atlantic' of vivid images, which enabled ideas about sailors to circulate around the Atlantic world. These images celebrated, but in some instances undermined, the actual mariners like Waters, upon whom the Atlantic world depended.[2]

Moncrieff, in the dubious 'Biographical Sketch' which Charles Hindley reprints, claims that Waters was born in Africa but went to sea because of a nefarious kidnapping, which:

> ... made him a slave, in the French settlement, at Demarara [*sic*], from whence however he speedily took *French leave*, and entered, we believe, the British navy as a cook *par excellence* on board the Ganymede sloop of war, under the command of Sir John Purvis.[3]

This ponderously playful account makes heavy use of the kinds of puns beloved by a certain type of nineteenth-century comic writer. It makes no mention of Waters' New York origins, but it's not implausible that at some point in his youth or early adulthood he could have ended up in Demerara. His advanced seafaring skills by the time he joined the Royal Navy (downgraded rather predictably by Moncrieff into servant-like cooking skills) might have been acquired on deep-sea voyages aboard merchant shipping, and Demerara was an important sugar colony in (first Dutch, then British, then French, then British) Guyana. However, it is also possible that this account of Waters as an unruly 'slave' stems from memories of the 1795 and 1823 rebellions by enslaved people in Demerara, which caused shock waves around the Atlantic world.[4] Yet again Moncrieff resorts to racialised cliché.

As a poor Black man in this period, Waters had limited freedom of choice: but he made his own decisions where he could. We may not know when Waters first went to sea, but there might be a clue in his name. Names matter to anyone, but to enslaved or newly freed Black Americans, names carried deep layers of significance.[5] The renaming of newly arrived enslaved people was part of the process of turning people into goods. Names were chosen by slave-holders, as were the names of children born into slavery. African identities were erased. People who were newly released from enslavement were suddenly able to choose their own first and last names. That choice could involve acts of assimilation or defiance. William Waters may have been named by a slaveholder because of his maritime training; he may have inherited the surname from his father; he may have chosen the surname himself. Whatever its origin, it's significant that Waters gave that surname when he joined the British Navy as 'black seamen took advantage of sailors' anonymity to name themselves at will'.[6]

In his autobiography the enslaved Equiano objects to being renamed Gustavas Vassa – saying 'that I would be called Jacob' – but is ignored; twenty years later Congo-born Thomas Arbuthnot of HMS Galley *Arbuthnot* chose a surname that proclaimed his allegiance to his ship.[7] Waters could have given any name to the weary officer charged with filling in the muster book, but the surname he gave, and the surname he stuck with (at least officially) from that point onwards, announces the importance of a watery world to his sense of identity. Seafaring offered young Black men a chance of greater freedom of movement and professional validation than might otherwise be allowed them on land. It also carried reminders of personal or familial Atlantic journeys into enslavement. Going to sea could be viewed as a heroic bid for self-determination or a tragic reminder of the brutal inequalities of the Atlantic world; perhaps Waters' chosen surname commemorated both perspectives.

When Waters first appears in naval records he was immediately 'rated', or categorised, as an able seaman. This suggests he was already an experienced sailor who had been to sea from a relatively young age. The rank of able seaman meant he was much more skilled than a landsman (who had probably never been to sea before) and even than an ordinary seaman (who might have experience on small boats or other craft but only be semi-skilled). Able seamen 'were the most skilled of seamen, and had mastered the ability to reef, knot, splice, man a ship's wheel, as well as work aloft in the ship's rigging, among other duties'.[8] The ability to work efficiently at all of these 'sea skills' took five or more years of experience, making able seamen the most valued and valuable of 'hands'.

Growing up in New York Waters would have had ample opportunity to learn such sea skills. As Leslie M. Harris points out, once the process of emancipation began around the turn of the nineteenth century, 'Perhaps the most steady and highest paying work available to black working-class men, and to a few women, was maritime work.' A full picture of the numbers of Black seamen in late eighteenth- and early nineteenth-century New York is not easy to come by, but Shane White uses census data for New York City in 1800 and 1810 to estimate that at least 40 per cent of male Black New Yorkers were involved in either labouring or maritime work.[9] This did not necessarily mean going to sea: between the Revolution and the turn of the nineteenth century, New York City saw over a third of all US trade pass through its ports, creating work in the many dockyards and warehouses as well as on the ships themselves. Many Black crew members were stewards or cooks on inland or coastal voyages; some Black women were chambermaids on steamboats. But there were also opportunities – not all of them voluntary – for Black New Yorkers to find themselves actually sailing an ocean-going vessel. Perhaps as many as one-fifth of New York City's maritime workforce in this period was made up of Black New Yorkers.[10] One of them was John, charged with theft in 1801, who pieced together employment as a sailor on a voyage to Cadiz, Spain, with work back in New York as a labourer; his wife, meanwhile, was only able to find work by moving to Newark.[11] As maritime historian W. Jeffrey Bolster puts it, 'Characterised by long male absences and female-headed households, maritime rhythms became inextricably entwined in the family life, community structure, and sense of self-expression of northern blacks in the early republic.'[12] Waters may have been drawn to the sea for reasons of circumstance, practicality, and expectation.

Seafaring did not necessarily imply freedom or free status for Waters. Bolster has shown that in the American South, 'Mariners constituted about 9 per cent of South Carolina's skilled slaves in the eighteenth century, and a full 25 per cent of skilled runaways.' Furthermore, most enslaved mariners in late eighteenth-century South Carolina were sailors rather than fishermen or boatmen: 'men who either crossed oceans or sailed extensively coastwise'.[13] In major American ports such as Philadelphia or the Chesapeake Bay area of Maryland, merchants and sea captains were frequently slaveholders even though they owned no land: they must have employed enslaved mariners. A successful Maryland businessman and merchant called Robert Carter had two Black captains skippering his schooners: William Lawrence was master of the *Harriet* in 1774 and so-called 'negro Cesar' was in charge of the other. A man called Ishmael, who fled enslavement in Maryland in 1778, 'had been bred to the sea by Mr Cornelius Calvert of Norfolk'.[14] It's not inconceivable that William Waters' first training in maritime work came from working for a slaveholder as a boy or a young man. Perhaps he followed on from his father's work. Waters may not have been allowed much, or indeed any, free choice over his introduction to maritime life.

Waters may also have been drawn by the sea's watery pull: maritime work was full of dangers but offered the tantalising possibility of heroic adventure. In the pubs and homes of a port city like New York, there were plenty of sailors both Black and white ready to spin a yarn and regale an adventure. Black seamen from the Caribbean, the Americas and Europe criss-crossed the Atlantic as enslaved mariners or as free men, with many voyaging to and from London and other major ports. They carried with them news and opinions from around the Atlantic world, spreading word of abolitionism, freedom, and flight. Enslaved mariners were still enslaved. But some managed to use their elite skills – and the considerable responsibility these skills afforded them – to escape, even for a short time, the particular sufferings meted out ashore. There were other threats: free Black men at sea were at constant risk of becoming enslaved or re-enslaved through capture, kidnap, or imprisonment (so much so that maritime historian Charles Foy calls it 'an Anxious Atlantic' for Black sailors).[15] As late as 1841 a New York abolitionist newspaper reported on 'The Imprisonment of Colored Seamen' who went ashore in Southern ports.[16] Shipboard life for any sailor was frequently a hellish one, full of the dangers of accident, tyranny, and disease. It offered no halcyon respite from racist attitudes or actions. As historian Nicholas Rogers points out, we should be wary of such redemptive narratives that posit straightforward 'multi-ethnic alliances among servants, slaves and seamen'.[17] But it did offer a route to a certain kind of mobility that was denied to Black Americans ashore. One man who felt this was Joshua Blue, an enslaved New Yorker who ran away in 1800 perhaps to sea, because he had frequently said that 'if free, he should prefer that mode of life'.[18] Ships carried enslaved Africans to their doom. By the time he was old enough they also offered Waters a way to reassert his right to self-determination.

At some point in his adolescence or early adulthood, Waters made the transition to deep-sea sailing, and the musical skills he used later in London may have played a part in this. Whether Waters learned the fiddle to improve his chances of employment, or picked it up in New York or during maritime work, is unknown, but music was a crucial part of shipboard life in both American and British ships. US naval surgeon Edward Cutbush wrote in 1808 that every American man-of-war should be provided with two violins for the healthy exercise of dancing, and assured readers that 'There will be no difficulty in procuring a "fiddler", *especially* among the coloured men in every American frigate, who can play most of the common dancing tunes.'[19] For a Black man in Waters' world, musical skill could be as much a curse as a benefit, as the American and British navies were ready to seize musicians from better-paid merchant shipping or elsewhere. This happened to John Marrant, born free in New York City around twenty years before Waters and author of *A Narrative of the Lord's Wonderful Dealings with John Marrant, a Black* (1785). Marrant was 'master both of the violin and the French horn' and during the American Revolution 'was pressed on board the *Scorpion*, sloop of war, as their musician as they were told I could play on music'.[20] It also happened to violinist Joseph Emidy, who learned his skills after being brought to Lisbon from a Brazilian plantation as a boy. Emidy was kidnapped from the stage door of the Lisbon Opera House on the order of Captain Sir Edward Pellew of the British ship *Indefatigable* (immortalised in *Hornblower*). Impressed into Pellew's crew to 'furnish music for the sailors' dancing', Emidy spent four years entertaining them with 'hornpipes, jigs, and reels'. Emidy was clearly a resilient adapter to circumstance, as Waters also had to be.[21]

Nevertheless, many Black seamen between 1750 and 1850 first voyaged the ocean not as valued hands but as servants, as Moncrieff's account of Waters' life assumes. The young man in the sailor jacket in Plate V is both musician and servant as he plays for the Captain in Hogarth's painting *Captain Lord George Graham, in his Cabin* (c. 1745), while in Francis Allyn Olmstead's *Incidents of a Whaling Voyage* (1841) it is Mr Freeman the Black cook who 'with many demisemiquavers strikes up the song, while all the rest join in the chorus' as the crew work.[22] A Black servant features in George Cruikshank's satirical caricature *Mr B. on the Middle Watch* (1835, Figure 10), part of a series based on drawings done in 1820 by his friend and collaborator Captain Frederick Marryat that are now in the British Museum.[23] Mr Blockhead is hunched against the terrible weather and this image is intended to be comic, but there is not much for the servant to laugh at: he has been called out on deck in scanty clothing to provide the sodden officers with warming wine. Waters' voyages may not have offered him many freedoms.

Music was not something necessarily forced upon Waters, however. It wasn't forced on the Black American sailors in Dartmoor Prisoner of War camp in 1814, who used music and dancing to stave off boredom and despair. They regularly filled their dismal captivity

10. *George Cruikshank,* Midshipman Blockhead, Mr B. on the Middle Watch, 'cold blows the wind & the rains coming on' (1835).

'with the sound of clarionets, flutes, violins, flageolets, fifes, and tambourines, together with ... whooping and singing'.[24] Admiral Collingwood in the Royal Navy wrote of his fleet that 'Every moonlight night the sailors dance,' and one Private Wheeler recorded that 'Two evenings a week is devoted to amusement ... The hands instantly distribute themselves, some dancing to a fiddle, others to a fife.'[25] Robert Hay, in his memoir of life in the Royal Navy during the same period as Waters, records how, 'In the evening the instrument of black Bob, the fiddler, was in almost constant requisition.'[26] Black military bandsmen were common across the British and American armed forces, including Black American fife-and-drum bands, and sailors both Black and white looked to fiddlers to enliven repetitive days at sea.[27] Music was integral to military life and Black musicians were integral to it. Practitioners and scholars today increasingly believe a large portion of surviving sea shanties have Black American and Caribbean origins. Black dock labourers and shanty-men sang songs which sailors picked up and developed. Musician Jim Megeean describes sea shanties as '"world music" with a multi-ethnic origin'.[28] Much of Waters' song repertoire would have been such sea shanties.

Black musicians at sea were not mere passive producers of white-sanctioned music, but active co-creators of a shipboard musical culture that merged influences and traditions. Bolster asks us to imagine popular culture as a river:

> picking up contributions from contacts along-shore and feeder streams, relegating parts of itself to back-eddies, losing yet others to silent evaporation or stranding, and constantly mixing its elements, even while it moves inexorably along a course that it continually redefines.[29]

Oskar Jensen characterises popular culture with another watery metaphor of the 'mainstream', suggesting that London popular culture in particular might be characterised as 'a great river delta of disparate cultural influences' which became 'the common repertoire of all types of audiences'.[30] Ships, however, enabled sailors from different places to share skills and knowledge within their oak walls. This cultural mix was then carried from port to port in a pattern which is much more like a network than the linear movement of a river. Life at sea was another place where we see the network of popular culture at work.

Ships are not neutral spaces, as cultural historians agree. For Christina Sharpe, the ship is both a symbol and a fact of how the effects of the Atlantic slave trade continue to be played out in the present. Sharpe suggests that the Atlantic world still experiences what she calls 'ship time', where the present day is enfolded into a 'past that is not past' because of the traumatic consequences of enslavement.[31] Perhaps rather optimistically, Linebaugh and Rediker see the ship as 'both an engine of capitalism . . . *and* a setting of resistance' where radical ideas circulated among multi-ethnic crews.[32] For Paul Gilroy, the ship – 'a living, micro-cultural, micropolitical system in motion' – is also an important site and symbol of the circulation of people and ideas around the Atlantic world. Gilroy places more emphasis on the cultural effects of this circulation: ships, he argues, and the sailors that they carried, participated actively in the creation of what we now call 'modernity';[33] tragically, via the slave trade, and heroically, via the circulation of cultures and ideas. Many sailors felt deep love for their ships, assigning them nicknames and personalities. Black history in the eighteenth and nineteenth centuries is one of forced and some unforced circulation of bodies, cultures and identities. Questions about originality in culture are perhaps already missing the point. From enslaved Africans carrying West African dance traditions with them across the ocean, to mariners like Waters adding European fiddle music to their knowledge of African American music rhythms shared during Pinkster, the enforced mobility and circulation of Black cultures was part of the ways in which nineteenth-century popular culture functioned as a network. This maritime world flowed through Waters' life and his London performances.

In his participation in maritime life, Waters was contributing to something much larger than himself. The world of the mariner was one that opened up beyond one particular continent and one particular culture. Bolster has argued that it's possible to map not only the exchange of people as commodities during the transatlantic slave trade, but also the 'currents of black people in motion carrying and exchanging ideas, information, and style'. These currents include 'the out-and-back daily voyages of slave fishermen', 'the inter-island voyages of black and white crews and runaway slaves', and lines to and from African, American, and European ports, 'international voyages on which blacks sailed'. Bolster presents what he calls a 'dynamic graphic of black seafaring', one which emphasises Black agency within white-dominated society.[34] Tiffany Lethabo King uses the image of the shoal, a shifting sandbank that is neither land nor sea, to suggest that oceanic metaphors for Black history and experiences reveal 'Black thought, movement, aesthetics, resistance, and lived experience' constantly 'chafing and rubbing up' against 'flows of Western thought'.[35] Waters may have had no choice but to go to sea, his actions constrained by the history and consequences of the Atlantic trade in human beings. But it is possible to emphasise this terrible fact whilst also recognising the courage and resilience of young men like Waters who defied the limitations placed upon them and carved out a life for themselves using the sea.

Press'd?

On 5 October 1811, William Waters from New York was entered into the muster book of HMS *Ceres*, a 'guardship' or receiving ship for new recruits permanently moored off the Great Nore (a deep channel off the Nore anchorage – the site of a notorious mutiny in 1797 – where the Thames Estuary meets the North Sea). We don't need to follow Waters across his whole maritime career to understand one of the most significant periods in his life for his later performances and afterlives: the few months he spent in the British Navy between October 1811 and May 1812. If we focus on this episode in Waters' life, and engage in what writer Robert Douglas-Fairhurst has called *'slow biography'*, we will find other ways of looking *with* Waters, rather than *at* him.[1] This shows how Moncrieff's version of events is not to be trusted, but also how Waters' naval career, as for so many sailors before and after him, was a fateful turning point in his life. It led to one of the greatest traumas he experienced. It also demonstrated his capacity for survival against the odds. It was crucial in shaping how his act was understood and represented both during and after his life.

It's unlikely that Waters joined the British Navy entirely out of free choice. He was constantly vulnerable to the whims and priorities of others. He was caught in the cross-currents of much bigger political tides and had few resources with which to navigate them. In autumn 1811 the issue of the impressment (forced naval conscription) of sailors was increasingly critical to the buildup of tensions between Britain and the US. It was becoming clear that war was brewing yet again between the Old World and the New. The major issue at stake was the perceived violations of American neutral trade rights as the Napoleonic Wars rumbled on, and behind this lay the frictions and anxieties caused by the political adjustments required now that the new United States of America had entered the international scene.[2] The impressment and recruitment of American sailors by British naval vessels (to feed the endless demand for more personnel in a time of war) was just the tip of a massive diplomatic iceberg. It was, however, what caught the public attention. It also helped to place Waters on the deck of HMS *Ceres* that October.

The British Navy had a mandate to seize men in times of war and, contrary to many depictions of the press gang, what they most wanted were experienced hands.[3] Since 1776 American sailors were technically the citizens of another country, but in 1811 many had still been born subjects of the British Crown. This made usefully murky waters for the Impressment Service to exploit, despite the US government issuing so-called protection certificates to mariners as they tried to shore up their own stocks of manpower. Press gangs were not choosy about who they grabbed, and Americans were more similar in dress and manners to British men than Danish or Swedish or Italian ones who also found themselves taken by the press.[4] Black American sailors were even more vulnerable, as they were much less likely than their white counterparts to have a paper trail of citizenship documentation, or a network of supporters. One man took no chances when sailing between Providence and New York during the War of 1812: Noah Brown, a free Black man who had once been impressed, carried a bottle of rum laced with laudanum to offer to any British press gangs who boarded his vessel, 'for he had no notion of going back again into English servitude'.[5]

A 'free Mulatto man' and 'native of the City of New York' named William Waters made sure to get a seaman's protection certificate in Philadelphia in 1798. He stood before a notary public (a type of lawyer) called Clement Biddle to swear an oath and make his claim. Biddle carefully recorded that Waters was 5 feet 6¼ inches tall, a good height for a sailor, with a scarred left hand (accident?) and the mark of a sore on the left side of his head (disease?). A Mary Waters stood next to him and supported his US citizenship claim. Was he the William Waters we are tracking? It's a common name; this man was mixed race and knew his age to the exact year (twenty-nine), which doesn't match other sources. But Philadelphia was an important sea port and a likely destination for Waters, and the certificate is fascinating evidence of the lengths to which sailors had to go in order to protect themselves from enslavement and impressment.[6]

Nevertheless, William Waters arrived on HMS *Ceres* in 1811 with around a hundred other men via the *Tower* tender, a smaller boat used to transport recruits from its base near the Tower of London to waiting ships. If it was anything like the tender in which his fellow-American Jacob Nagle was kept when grabbed by a press gang near Tower Hill, it had a dark, barred hold lit by one candle and 'large Norway rats that ware so numerous and ravenous you could get no rest for them'.[7] Perhaps Waters was already settled in London and signed up to earn money or escape a problem. Perhaps he was nabbed between voyages as he left an east London pub. Press tenders also would lie in wait for shipping as they headed into British ports, so Waters might have been picked up from a vessel in the Port of London.[8] If so he was probably on a merchant ship, as during the early nineteenth century, 'African Americans took advantage of gradual emancipation in the northern states to fill nearly a fifth of all American merchant sailing berths.'[9] But it did not necessarily have to have been an American one: British law granted naturalisation to foreign sailors who had served two years aboard any kind of British ship, though this was unevenly applied, and as British subjects this meant they could be legally impressed.[10] Waters may have come straight from a US warship, but because he entered the Navy in British waters rather than out at sea this seems less likely. He was entered into the muster book as 'vol' for volunteer, but given the high number of pressed men on board the *Ceres*, this seems dubious.[11] Pressed men were given the chance to 'volunteer' and collect the 'volunteer's bounty': many a seaman must have cast a glance at the press gang or the British warship training its guns at his own vessel, accepted the inevitable and taken the bounty money as the least worst option available, as Jacob Nagle did.[12] Waters represented an attractive prize: an able seaman was 'a competent and versatile sailor, accustomed to meeting challenges and facing danger'.[13] Waters' own British naval service demanded his separation from any family and friends in America. But it also offered an escape from the dangers of American attitudes towards enslavement. Waters' exposed position meant that he was an easy target for impressment, but his ability to respond to circumstance is evident in that word 'vol'.

Entering the British Navy meant a new kind of life. In the fifty years before and after Waters' own naval service, sailors were thought of as both fundamentally different to other men and examples of a desirable 'manliness' for others to emulate. They were 'Jack Tar'. This figure began as a white Englishman but was quickly adopted in the United States, as Paul Gilje has shown, and the same maritime songs, images, and plays were popularised in America, sometimes with the words changed to reflect their new context.[14] There was no official uniform for non-officers in the Regency or Victorian periods, but caricatures and images created a more or less standard sailor costume: some combination of white (possibly striped) canvas trousers, blue waist-length jacket, striped shirt and red neckerchief loosely knotted immediately signified a mariner to all who saw it.[15] Waters advertised himself as a Tar with his blue jacket and sailor trousers.

Tars were seen as different to other people, as belonging to the sea, partly because this was the only way in which the tension between 'impressment and British rights and freedoms' could be resolved.[16] Dress, language and manners, real or imagined, helped to place sailors as 'a distinctive subcultural group . . . as strange as the shark's teeth or shell that they carried with them as mementoes of their voyages'.[17] Yet 'Jack Tar' was a paradox: he also united different traits considered increasingly desirable for landlocked men. 'Jack Tar' covered different 'manly' life stages: youthful sexual adventurer, brave and skilful patriot, faithful sweetheart, emotional family man, self-controlled professional and idealised veteran. Famous Tars were celebrated in pictures, trinkets and teapots: like Jack Crawford, who nailed his admiral's flag to the mast under heavy fire when it was shot down.[18] Familiar and exotic, 'Jack Tar' could be comic and grotesque, heroic and laughable, sentimental and self-sacrificing; the figure encompassed ambiguity and complexity.[19] Once the US was independent from Britain there was some divergence between the two national images of the sailor; by the mid-nineteenth century the mariner was taken more seriously as a symbol of the vigorous American Republic or the sentimentalised loyal British subject. During Waters' lifetime, popular culture delighted in 'stereotyping sailors as bluff, good-natured, rough-hewn patriots who have their own dialect, costume, and moral compass: the Stage Tar'.[20] The hornpipe, for instance, was first linked to sailors on the eighteenth-century stage: from the 1740s onwards male and female performers in Britain and America would 'dance the hornpipe in the character of a sailor'. Although sailors enlivened leisure time with dancing, it was just as much the popular stage that taught sailors that 'Jack Tar' danced the hornpipe.[21]

Sailors, however, co-created ideas about 'Jack Tar'. Frederick Douglass knew how to perform 'sailor style' and 'sailor talk' to escape

Maryland for New York.[22] Naval service meant different things to different sailors: surviving sailor autobiographies that cover the late eighteenth and early nineteenth centuries show us this. But sailor autobiographies tend to emphasise the world of the sailor as very different from that of land-based society. For example, Robert Hay first joined the British Navy in 1803, and his account of the guardship he joins at Plymouth presents a cornucopia of all the world's people that, paradoxically, renders his new shipboard world a strange one: 'complexions of every varied hue, and features of every cast', from 'the African' to 'the Asiatic', the 'English swain' and 'the sunburnt Portuguese'. Sailors participated in popular culture by conforming to the costume, language, and rolling gait of the mariner. A sailor himself, Waters would have been well aware of these conventions and the ways in which being a sailor was already a kind of performance.

For Waters the position was even more complex. As a Black mariner, Waters suffered a double stereotyping in his white-dominated world. Rowdy, joyful, and active, elements of 'Jack Tar' in British and American popular culture were not unlike descriptions of enslaved Africans in the period.[23] Waters was 'read' through these kinds of dangerous ideas: for example, in the frontispiece to Egan's sequel to *Life in London*, *The Finish to Life in London*, Waters loses his personal name and becomes simply a representative of 'Folly' (Figure 11). Waters' blue sailor jacket, wooden leg and dark complexion are very prominent in this image. Black sailors sat at the intersection of ideas about race, class, and 'manliness'. They lived with the daily awareness of what critics now call 'intersectionality', or the understanding that 'gender cannot be fully extricated from race, or race from class, or class from sexuality'.[24] An intersectional approach to cultural history means recognising and highlighting such connections. This allows us to explore the multiple ways in which early nineteenth-century society designated people as 'different', and to recognise the arbitrariness of these categories and not reduce them to tidy lists or neat definitions. It also underlines yet again the challenges of Waters' position.

11. *Waters as 'Folly', from Pierce Egan's* Finish to
Life in London (1889).

Transatlantic writers and journalists did not hesitate to blur their categories in defence of 'Jack Tar', but they did so in ways that complicated white perceptions of the Black mariner still further. Sailor rights and slave rights were often aligned rhetorically in Britain and the US, as part of a perceived resemblance between impressed sailors and the enslaved African, though no one has yet connected this to visual representations of Black mariners.[25] Before Waters was even born, as early as 1728, abolitionist campaigner James Oglethorpe wrote in his pamphlet *The Sailor's Advocate* that:

How comes it then that so very useful a part of his Majesty's subjects as the SAILORS are, should be prest into the Service, denied their liberty and turned to slaves? For SLAVERY is nothing more than SERVICE by FORCE. The PREST PERSON is assaulted and seized on the King's highway, and hurried into a floating prison, without being allowed to speak or write to his friends.[26]

This kind of rhetoric proclaimed the evils of impressment by suggesting not that enslaved people deserved liberty, but that impressed sailors deserved it more. *The Sailor's Advocate* was reprinted throughout the eighteenth century, and the language used within it persisted in public debates on both abolition and impressment on each side of the Atlantic. The issue of impressment was accessible to non-seafaring Americans after the Revolution via a transatlantic popular culture shared in songs, periodicals and pamphlets. For example, the *Western Eagle* newspaper in 1814 claimed that Britain 'press'd the brave seaman, and made him a slave'.[27] Nautical plays emphasised the comparison on the London stage in the 1820s–40s, while a New York abolitionist newspaper teetered on the brink of this kind of unpleasant idea when it declared in 1841 that 'Poor jack-tar' is 'an *old salt*, poor creature! As unfitted for human life as sea brine is for drink. How can we forget him while we are abolishing slavery?' In this article impressed sailors are not only like enslaved people because of their treatment on board ship and their restricted personal freedom (although that's an important part of the article's argument), but also because they are outcasts in society, 'these *poor, cast-away, wrecked* brethren'.[28] The forced labour of the impressed sailor and of the enslaved African mark them both out, in this article, as figures of tragic misfortune who need the white abolitionists' special attention and care, but not, perhaps, the freedom of self-determination. Waters' status as both a sailor and a man of African heritage meant that his vulnerability to the control of others was that much more enhanced; his resilience is therefore that much more impressive.

White mariners frequently evoked the language of enslavement themselves to depict their impressment, but this does not mean they felt an especial sense of connection with Black shipmates. On the contrary, such images are used to proclaim the special status of the free-born white Englishman and therefore the utter horror and implausibility of keeping him enslaved to the Navy against his will. There have been several scholarly attempts to argue for working-class interracial solidarity during the Regency period, but this is to underplay the amount of working-class racism prevalent in the early nineteenth century even amongst radicals.[29] We cannot know what Waters felt on arriving on HMS *Ceres*, but remarkably we do have Robert Hay's account of being pressed on to the *Ceres* in October 1811, exactly the same month as Waters. In it, Hay implicitly sets the white Englishman above the enslaved African. Hay's tale, set in 1811 but written from the perspective of the 1840s, follows the narrative structure of capture, suffering and escape that had become the generic standard for narratives of enslavement (by then intertwined with other kinds of narrative writing, as Julia Sun-Joo Lee has shown).[30] Hay loses no opportunity to equate the impressed sailor with the enslaved captive, declaring, 'A few hours before I had entered London possessed of Liberty and buoyed up with animating hope. Now, I was a slave immured in a dungeon and surrounded by despair' (220); he uses the same language of 'dungeons' and 'slavery' as *The Sailor's Advocate* did over a hundred years before. Hay immediately dreams of escape, as 'Our distance from the shore being only about 6 or 8 miles, the land was seen clearly and many an anxious, earnest look did I take of it' (223-4). He recruits another impressed sailor and the eventual success of their escape over the side of the *Ceres* into a rowing boat and then onto shore is described in idealised terms of absolute joy:

We had just escaped from thraldom and were beginning to taste the dawning sweets of that blessing so highly valued by Britons.

Everything around us tended to exhilarate our spirits and we gave unrestrained scope to our feelings . . . We leapt, we ran, we rolled, we tumbled, we shouted, we gamboled in all the excess of joy and exultation . . . (232–3)

Their delight comes from their physical freedom but also their re-entry into British national life, which means they 'taste the dawning sweets of that blessing so highly valued by Britons', something that their 'thraldom' in the Navy prohibited. Did Waters see the Kent coast from the *Ceres*' deck and dream of freedom too? Or did the Navy seem to him a chance for freedoms denied to him elsewhere?

Hay's autobiography differs from most sailor memoirs by ending on escape: in his use of form as well as language Hay links the impressed sailor and the enslaved African, but only to celebrate 'Jack Tar' as implicitly more entitled to freedom than the escaped slave. By contrast Robert Wedderburn – son of a Jamaican planter and an enslaved woman, and Regency radical – and Frederick Douglass (both ex-mariners) make the point in the other direction. Wedderburn in his short-lived periodical *The Axe Laid to the Root* (1817) presents rebellions by enslaved Africans as examples of a commitment to liberty that is far more impressive than that displayed by so-called free-born Englishmen, while in Frederick Douglass' *The Heroic Slave* (1841), Madison Washington leads a party of fellow enslaved Black men to capture a sailing ship, winning the respect of the white sailor in the final chapter, who recounts the events.[31] As Daniel James Ennis points out, it is writers such as Douglass who are 'the only ones who can speak with authority on the connection between slavery and impressment', yet again and again white sailors and journalists and campaigners used the language of enslavement to differentiate 'Jack Tar' implicitly from Black people, seen as synonymous with the enslaved African.[32] Waters did not publish his experiences, but every time he performed whilst wearing a blue sailor jacket his costume would have evoked this complicated web of ideas in the minds of his audiences – whether white or Black – who would have understood him through them.

Waters' first hours and days in the Navy involved not adventure but confinement and monotony: Robert Hay wrote of his own experiences aboard a guardship, 'Though the duty in this ship was merely trifling no person was fond of staying on board.'[33] Life on the *Ceres* was dull, not unlike the autumnal weather. Lieutenant Commander G. A. Orton had to keep the men occupied with mundane tasks such as cleaning, painting the officers' wardroom, and stowing away supplies. Every Sunday, Orton read his skeleton crew and their 'supernumerary' new recruits the Divine Service and the Articles of War, and 'broached a cask of red wine' as a treat. Sometimes Orton was called upon to receive and discharge prisoners-of-war. Meanwhile the *Tower* tender skipped back and forth bringing more men to fill the Navy's bottomless need (about seventy or eighty each time, roughly twice a week). Twice a week the ancient battleship HMS *Namur*, the very same one on which Equiano served as a 'powder monkey', collected men from the *Ceres* to distribute them around the fleet. On 23 November 1811, the *Namur* collected Waters.

The *Namur* was a special ship that had enjoyed a heroic past; it had taken part in some of the most significant sea battles of the eighteenth century, and played a key role in the aftermath of the Battle of Trafalgar. That autumn, however, it was based near the Great Nore, off the coast of Sheerness, with a crew of 250, including ten boys, and a vast quantity of rotating 'supernumeraries'. It was under the command of Captain Alexander Shippard, but the following month would be taken over by Jane Austen's brother Captain Charles Austen as the flagship of Vice-Admiral Stanhope; it would also shortly become home to the ten-year-old Douglas Jerrold, later to become a playwright, journalist and notable fan and chronicler of Waters' performances.[34] But all this was in the future. Waters had what was likely his first taste of British naval discipline on board the *Namur*: on Friday 6 December, the day before Waters left, Shippard 'at 10.50 Executed Thos [Thomas] O'Hara late belonging to the *Neireide* per sentence of a court martial'.[35]

On 7 December, Shippard noted in his log that HMS *Ganymede* had anchored nearby. The warship that was to change the course of Waters' life had arrived, and it was in need of experienced men.

Life Aboard

If sailors were frequently understood and represented as fundamentally different from people ashore, then 'Jack Tar' was just as
frequently celebrated for his manly skill and patriotic heroism.
Waters' service in the British Navy demonstrates that he was a
skilled and resilient man, trusted by the ship's officers as part of an
elite portion of the crew. These qualities would not have deserted
him once he left the Navy. Waters would have been well aware of
the stereotypes of 'Jack Tar' that were all around him – playbills,
pictures, songs, even jugs, quilts, and toys[1] – driven by the network
of popular culture. He was also perfectly capable of both using and
resisting them in his own performances.

Waters' qualities were rewarded with speedy promotion, which
suggests that his skills were an important part of his sense of identity. Waters entered into the *Ganymede*'s muster as an able seaman
on 9 December 1811, and received two months' allowance as his
volunteer's bounty, 16 shillings' worth of Navy-issue prefabricated
'slop' clothing (perhaps including his blue jacket and canvas trousers), a hammock, and an allowance of tobacco.[2] The *Ganymede* had
a full complement of 175 men and was classed as a sixth rate post
ship: in other words, it was smaller than a fifth rate frigate because

it carried fewer than twenty-eight guns, but because it carried at least twenty guns it was suitable to be in the charge of a captain, rather than a lieutenant or commander. Its gun deck, which was 126 imperial feet long, carried twenty British 9-pound guns, with additional 6-pound guns and a carronade on the quarterdeck and forecastle. HMS *Ganymede* became an official British warship in June 1809, a few months after it was captured from the French and renamed from *L'Hébé*.[3] The previous Captain, Robert Preston, had been court-martialled that summer for the cruel treatment of his crew, so the freshly installed Captain John Brett Purvis had something to prove.[4] The ship's muster tables from November to December 1811 reveal that the ship was at Spithead in late November, then headed to the Nore to find additional crew. It was at this point, on 8 December 1811, that Waters found himself transferred over to an active British warship. By 29 December the *Ganymede* was at sea.[5] After a brief stop at Plymouth, *Ganymede* was ordered to head to Gibraltar (transporting eight prisoners there) and then on to Cadiz as part of a convoy. Waters was now part of a group of able seamen selected by the *Ganymede* to crew its tour of the Atlantic's European coastline.[6]

Waters' capabilities were quickly recognised. The crew in which Waters now found himself was both experienced and international (*Ganymede* had collected only able and ordinary seamen at the Nore), making it pretty representative of the Royal Navy as a whole. There were numerous seamen hailing from the major port cities London and Liverpool, the fishing areas of the West Country, Ireland, and Scotland. Alongside them were a smattering of Italians as well as men from Sweden, Brazil and Spain. Besides Waters, there were three men from America: Thomas Brown, from Providence, an able seaman who at twenty-seven had already served on the British warships *Thisbe* and *Devastation*; John Henderson, newly pressed, who was forty-one; and thirty-eight-year-old James Humpheries, a prisoner of war who chose service in the King's Navy over incarceration. Waters, at (roughly) thirty-five, was among the older crew members but by no means the oldest: that honour went to William Morgan from Birmingham, who was fifty-six and also rated 'able seaman'.[7] When the *Ganymede* paused at Plymouth in early January 1812, the captain and first lieutenant were able to assess their new crew properly, and made a spate of promotions on 2 January. Waters and his fellow-American Thomas Brown (who may also have been of African heritage) were both made quarter gunner, along with Robert Foreman, a pressed man from Berwick aged twenty-three. This promotion was significant: quarter gunners were petty officers, and assistants to the gunner. They were therefore part of what was known as the gunner's crew, comprising one or two gunner's mates, an armourer and one quarter gunner to every four guns. The gunner on the *Ganymede* was Noah Bakes, who passed his two oral examinations in time to receive his official warrant on 16 November 1811. Under Bakes' supervision were Gunner's Mate John Smith, and Yeoman of the Powder Room John Ferguson, both newly promoted. At a stroke these skilled men became central to Waters' daily life and world. He worked with them, ate (or 'messed') with them, even slept alongside them, hammock to hammock, sharing the ship's roll.

The gunner's crew were elite, able seamen chosen for their experience, skill and initiative (without quite the same level of youth and agility as the topmen, who did the toughest parts of sail drill). On HMS *Unite* they were considered 'the best seamen in the ship'. They got an extra shilling per month than any other able seamen but, with their workload and the level of skill required, it was felt that they earned it.[8] *Ganymede*'s Noah Bakes was responsible for the maintenance of the guns and all related equipment, and for the supply of gunpowder (firing the guns was supervised on the gun deck by the lieutenants). To manage all this he needed his quarter gunners, so Waters' days were full: checking and maintaining the guns and gun carriages in his section, making sure they were always ready should an enemy ship creep over the horizon, and helping Bakes wherever needed.[9] In addition, he and his colleagues performed duties as an elite division of seamen – keeping watches and setting the sails. Waters learned the way the *Ganymede* juddered under full sail, and how to make his messmates laugh. Music wasn't Waters' only skill.

The responsibilities of Waters' role are a window into his character. Waters' duties (indeed the duties of the entire crew) were recorded in the ship's *Watch, Station, and Quarter Bill*, a handwritten booklet kept on ship for reference. He only needed to remember his number – 125 – and he could check where he was supposed to be and what he was supposed to be doing when the ship was setting sail, tacking, or cleared for action; whether he was part of a boarding party, and if so what weapons to carry. The document for *Ganymede* hasn't survived, but one for a similar-sized ship, HMS *Pomone*, is safe in the archives of the National Maritime Museum. When the ship cleared for battle, Waters was trained for the vital job of preparing and distributing gun cartridges in the claustrophobic powder magazine on the lower deck. In battle this was dreary, monotonous and nerve-jangling – as John Nicol of the seventy-four-gun *Goliath*'s gunners crew found out – with no way of seeing how the battle was progressing apart from snatched news from the women and boys who carried the cartridges to the guns, and the cries of the wounded from the sickbay nearby.[10] It took a calm temperament and a steady hand. When the ship tacked or reefed, Waters was to be found high up in the rigging, assisting with the staysail sheets or the topsail. He took his turn on watch, beneath starry skies, as part of the shift patterns of a sailor's life. As he settled into these rhythms, Waters saw how necessary he was to the teamwork that enabled the *Ganymede* to power through the waves.

Sailors prided themselves on their skills; in John Singleton Copley's study of sailors at work we glimpse their strength and elegance, skilful as dancers (Figure 12). The *Ganymede* spent a great

12. *John Singleton Copley,* Study of Sailors Raising a Flag (*undated*).

deal of time in sail drill and gun exercises during the first few weeks of 1812; Waters and his shipmates were gradually being honed from a disparate collection of experienced men into a practised team who could work together efficiently under pressure. Ex-sailor John Bechervaise described a list of sailor qualities that would have seemed alarming to a seasick novice: 'a man, who, if placed in difficulty, will have the presence of mind to overcome it; if placed in danger, will possess the necessary courage to meet it; or if presented with an object of beauty, will regard it with all the enthusiasm of genuine admiration'.[11] Experienced mariners like Waters were expected to set an example. All of this suggests that descriptions of Waters as a genial comic buffoon by Moncrieff and others were astonishingly wide of the mark. Instead we should picture a skilful and athletic performer.

A Veritable Jack Tar

W hen Waters donned a sailor jacket he was doing something more than putting on a useful piece of work clothing. He was staking a claim, in the face of multiple assaults upon that claim, to his active and dignified citizenship of the Atlantic world. In the magazine *The Mirror of the Stage* in 1823, Waters was contrasted with the popular white singer and ex-sailor Charles Incledon. Incledon, who had spent time in the Navy in the 1780s, was celebrated as a patriotic ballad singer and a Regency showman who made the ballad 'The Storm' famous (this song was also sung by Joseph Johnson):

> 'To Correspondents' . . .
>
> 'LATITAT,' in speaking of advertisements, setting forth Mr Watkins Burroughs' *attempt* to sing 'The Storm', asks, if in histrionic practice, the *attempt* is to be received as the *deed*? – We answer, all depends on the audience – if they conceive so, 'The Storm' of Mr Watkins Burroughs might pass off a la Incledon – if not, a la Billy Waters.[1]

The joke here is about whether Mr Watkins Burroughs, a popular actor who played the lead in a stage adaptation of *Life in London*, can perform 'The Storm' well or badly. Will he be able to personify the manly Tar, and wring the hearts of his audience like Incledon? Or will his performance be more like that of that other famous musical ex-sailor, Billy Waters? The implication is that Waters cannot be other than a comic joke, not a heroic Tar. But assessing Waters' performances differently shows that he used his sailor costume deliberately to claim his own 'Britishness' alongside his African American heritage.

Waters' promotion suggests that his skin colour did not single him out as any less skilful than any of his fellow crew members. On the contrary, he was made a petty officer. This does not mean his shipboard life was free from racial tensions. Black sailors actively chose to represent themselves in print culture as dedicated, skilled and heroic Tars in order to combat those very problems. The first autobiographies by Black writers published before 1800 were all by mariners, and they used their experiences to fire up the abolitionist cause and to demonstrate in print that Black men were the antithesis of the racist stereotypes attached to them.[2] These autobiographies predate Waters' own experiences by a generation; nevertheless their accounts of battles are significant for the ways in which the authors choose to emphasise their participation as part of trained and skilful crews. Sailor and writer Briton Hammon was:

> order'd on board the Hercules, Capt. John Porter, a 74 Gun Ship, we sail'd on a Cruize, and met with a French 84 Gun Ship, and had a very smart Engagement, A particular Account of this Engagement, has been Publish'd in the Boston News-Papers in which about 70 of our Hands were Kill'd and Wounded, the Captain lost his leg in the Engagement, and I was Wounded in the Head by a small shot.[3]

Hammon's use of 'We' emphasises that he is just as much a part of the *Hercules'* extraordinary crew as any other mariner, including the captain: Hammon was 'Wounded' just like Captain Porter and the seventy other Hands. Hammon's reference to the articles 'Publish'd in the Boston News-Papers' is provided to support the legitimacy of his own account and the legitimacy of the heroic bravery in which he himself participated. The role of Hammon as a heroic Black Tar is not just one that he claims for himself: it is backed up, he tells us, in reputable print.

Similarly, Equiano's autobiography emphasises his thirst for action and longing to engage with the enemy. He describes a fierce sea fight in 1759 on board the *Namur* when he was only fourteen years old:

> The engagement now commenced with great fury on both sides: the Ocean immediately returned our fire, and we continued engaged with each other for some time; during which I was frequently stunned with the thundering of the great guns, whose dreadful contents hurried many of my companions into awful eternity. At last the French line was entirely broken and we obtained the victory, which was immediately proclaimed with loud huzzas and acclamations . . . My station during the engagement was on the middle-deck, where I was quartered with another boy to bring powder to the after most Gun. And here I was witness to the dreadful fate of many of my companions, who, in the twinkling of an eye, were dashed to pieces, and launched into eternity . . . We were also, from our employment, very much exposed to the enemy's shots; for we had to go through nearly the whole length of the ship to bring the powder . . . [but] cheering myself with the reflection that there was a time allotted for me to die as well as to be born, I instantly cast off all fear or thought whatever of death, and went through the whole of my duty with alacrity.[4]

Like Hammon before him, Equiano's use of 'we' and graphic description of courage under fire makes the point (without having to directly say it) that he may be an enslaved African, but he is every bit as essential, as brave and as skilled as the white crew members he calls 'companions'. Similar techniques are used in John Marrant's autobiography when he records his sea service later in the eighteenth century. Marrant served in HMS *Scorpion* for nearly seven years after his initial impressment, between 1775 and 1782. Marrant writes that:

> I was in the engagement with the Dutch off the Dogger Bank, on board the Princess Amelia, of 84 guns. We had a great number killed and wounded, stationed at the same gun with me; my head and face were covered with the blood and brains of the slain: I was wounded but did not fall, till a quarter of an hour before the engagement ended, and was happy during the whole of it.[5]

Marrant's bravery is recorded by him here as both exceptional and common: he is part of a collective heroic 'we'. These authors defiantly claim their status as heroic Tars because of the prejudice with which they were surrounded. Several decades later, though the slave trade was now illegal in the British Empire, Waters was still in a precarious social position.

This was despite the fact that Black sailors were highly visible in the British Navy during the eighteenth and nineteenth centuries. Ray Costello lists numerous sailors of African heritage found in the muster books of Nelson's fleet at Trafalgar in 1805, and makes the point that Anglophone names (such as the one Waters adopted) may hide the presence of many more. Costello suggests that 'what is interesting about these stories and the roles each of these black sailors played at Trafalgar is that it would seem that by this time seafarers of African descent were notable, if anything, for their ordinariness'.[6] Shipboard culture, however, was likely more complicated than this. Black sailors are depicted as unremarkable and indeed able members of a British man-of-war in several caricatures from the period of Waters' own naval service. Ray Costello suggests that 'Nineteenth-century artists such as Daniel Maclise, Denis Dighton and Andrew Morton show sailors of African descent engaged alongside their shipmates in the everyday shipboard toil, in a way that many historians do not', but it is in nineteenth-century popular culture that we see most representations of Black sailors such as Waters.[7]

Amateur caricaturist Lieutenant John Sheringham drew a Black sailor in his group of elite mariners discussing a heroic naval action while relaxing around their mess table (Figure 13). Sailors could change their mess if they were not happy; to be included in this image means social acceptance. Yet we should note that he is positioned at the back of the group, furthest away from the focal figure of the main speaker. William Elmes' 1812 *A Milling Match between Decks* shows a Black sailor and a white sailor competing in a boxing match on equal terms while crewmates and women relax below deck and some dance to the music of a one-legged fiddler (Plate VI).[8] However, for all this seeming equality, in Elmes' caricature it is the white sailor who is called 'Jack', while the Black sailor is called by the name of 'Mungo', which has migrated to attach itself to Black mariners. Into the nineteenth century it remained true that Black sailors could be petty officers but probably not warrant officers, and Waters was never going to have the chance to be a commissioned officer and follow the route up to captain. Black sailors were seen as obviously lower class and not captain material, with only a few exceptions notable for their rarity.[9]

The figure of the white sailor, by contrast, was used as a heroic emblem of national pride in Britain and also in the fledgling United States. The context of this was a period of grave political unrest and economic upheaval leading up to and following the American and French revolutions. Alongside strong loyalist sentiments in Britain during and after the war years was deepening political and economic turmoil and rising class militancy, which eventually culminated in the 1848 Chartist protests. A system of harsh prisons, new military barracks in cities and draconian press and theatre regulations helped to keep the population in fearful check, but popular culture helped too.[10] One epitome of this in Britain was the celebrated actor and ex-sailor T. P. Cooke (1786–1864), who was seen as the embodiment of tender yet 'manly' masculinity. As a white, able-bodied man, Cooke had options open to him that were not open to Waters. Audiences took pleasure 'in characterizing the nation through Cooke's performances of stage sailors', pleasure heightened by their knowledge that Cooke had been an actual, as well as a stage, Tar.[11] In *The Nautical Tom and Jerry; or Life of a True British Sailor* (Theatre Royal, Liverpool, 1843) – a comic play by C. A. Somerset, which rather shamelessly plays off the popularity of *Life in London* by naming its sailor leads Tom and Jerry – Tom arrives on stage crying patriotically, 'Old England forever, Hurrah!', alongside such nautical exclamations as 'Snap my mizzen in a gale of wind, what do I see?'[12] Charles Dibdin (father of Charles Dibdin the younger, who wrote an adaptation of *Life in London* for stage) used his government-commissioned patriotic sea songs to create an image of jolly 'Jack Tar' as carefree, singing, dancing, but also fiercely patriotic.[13] Dibdin's popularity extended to the US and continued into the 1840s and 1850s. The *New York Herald* in May 1837 advertised an evening's entertainment at the Franklin Theatre consisting of the play *Tom Bowling* (a version of one of Dibdin's most popular 'Jack Tar' songs adapted for stage), followed by *The Shipwrecked Tar*.[14] 'Jack Tar' permeates Dibdin's nautical repertoire and Dibdin's true 'tar' may be as poor as a 'beggar' but he is still ready to 'sing like a mermaid, and foot it [dance] so lightly' ('Bill Bobstay'). In this way he always wins the love of his messmates, his girl, and, crucially, his country. Dibdin's song 'All Girls' is set below decks when a ship is in port and expresses how all 'Jack Tar' needs to be happy is 'a lass and a fiddle' and to take up 'the sprightly jig'. George Cruikshank's 1841 illustration to this

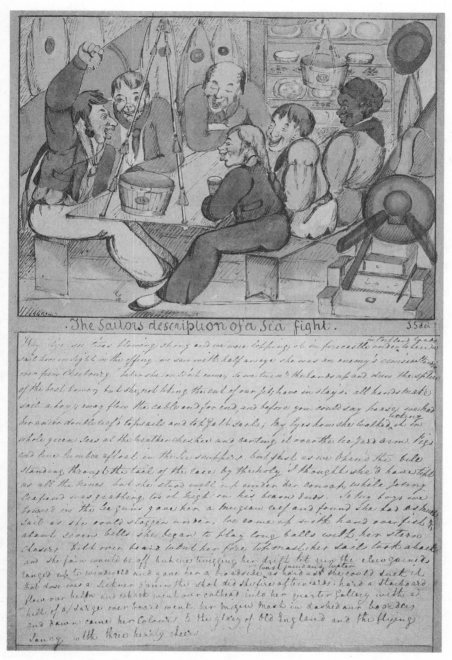

13. *Lt John Sheringham,* The Sailor's Description of a Sea Fight
(c. 1819–25).

song includes a Black fiddler in a supporting role (Figure 14) and draws on the same kinds of visual vocabulary as the Billy Waters picture from *Life in London* (Plate XII).[15] Sailors were associated with music and dancing which celebrated patriotism and national pride.

Yet Waters was forced by history and circumstance to experience a complex relationship with nationality. For Black mariners – whether American like Waters or from elsewhere in the Atlantic world – service in the British Navy carried different meanings than it did for their white British counterparts. They were already forced to accept the kind of treatment that their perceived racial differences entailed. Scholars have suggested that impressment in the British Navy for Black sailors entailed a new kind of freedom and identity as a British subject, although this says something about how challenging conditions were for people of African descent on shore.[16] Surviving memoirs of Black sailors certainly suggest a level of strategic acceptance of their position: Equiano writes that he 'became inured to that service', even 'began to consider myself as happily situated', and

14. *George Cruikshank,* Tars Carousing (1841).

'now not only found myself quite easy with these new countrymen, but relished their society', but this is not exactly a ringing endorsement of his experiences as an enslaved mariner. American mariner Briton Hammon ended his naval career with a pension paid because his arm was disabled by injuries incurred during battle; Hammon was 'acknowledged not as a passenger or chattel, but as a member of the Royal Navy'.[17] Nevertheless, Hammon's narrative is an account of one adaptation to injustice after another.

A significant irony for African American sailors lay in the fact that they could be described as free sailor-citizens (compared with British sailor-slaves) because they were American, but were thought of as barely entitled to citizenship because they carried the legacy of enslavement. Several decades later there were signs of change: Henry Jackson, a free Black man who called himself 'an old salt', was described deliberately by a reporter for New York's abolitionist *National Anti-Slavery Standard* as 'a veritable Jack Tar'. Jackson had been a sailor for twenty-three years, 'a hard life at best', and in the war of 1812 was made a gun captain on the USS *Ohio*:

'Lieutenant Miller, this ain't right', said I – 'in times of peace, I'm nothing but a poor black n—er, and wherever I go they ask me for my *free papers*; but when war comes, nobody asks for a n—er's free papers then – he'll do to fight, as well as a white man – but no matter, I'm captain of this gun, and you'll find me at my post.' It was funny to see how some of the men tried to get clear of the fighting. One was a Dutchman – another was an Englishman – and another was something else. But the black n—er was made Captain of the Gun!

'But, my friends . . . although the whole human tribe is against us, let us bear it all, for our children's sake. You may be assured, the fire is most burned out. The time is coming on, when our cause will be vindicated, and Ethiopia shall spread aboard her wings.'

The speaker sat down amidst loud cheering.[18]

Jackson has no doubt that the true heroic Tar, indeed the true heroic revolutionary, is a Black man. Abolitionist Robert Wedderburn was himself an ex-sailor, as were several of his radical comrades, 'moving to and fro between nations, crossing borders in modern machines that were themselves micro-systems of linguistic and political hybridity'.[19] Paying attention to this Atlantic circulation of culture allows us to see how popular culture created both repressive images and ideas and the desire to challenge them: it is with this in mind that we should return to Waters.

Waters' sailor jacket demonstrated to white eyes (albeit less obviously than Joseph Johnson's ship-shaped hat) his British loyalties and his place, as an ex-Tar, in the development of Britain's maritime empire. But he also laid claim to a wider Atlantic sense of cultural identity in ways that Black audience members might have read very differently. His song repertoire may well have included Black-inspired shanties like 'Oh, Huro, Me Boys' and 'Grog Time of Day', heard by Robert Hay in 1811.[20] His dancing combined hornpipe and Pinkster influences. His jacket and trousers cheekily referenced new fashions in officer uniforms and elite menswear as well as ordinary sailor clothes.[21] Moncrieff claimed to remember 'toasting *Emancipation* to the *blacks!*' in a London public house with Waters.[22] As James C. Scott points out, using an appropriately maritime metaphor, it is unhelpful to think that there is a binary between resistance and non-resistance, especially when, in most times and places in human history, resistance is 'dangerous, if not suicidal':

Everyday forms of resistance make no headlines. But just as millions of anthozoan polyps create, willy-nilly, a coral reef, so do the multiple acts of peasant insubordination and evasion create political and economic barrier reefs of their own. It is largely in this fashion that the peasantry makes its political presence felt. And whenever, to pursue the simile, the ship of state runs aground on such reefs, attention is usually directed to the shipwreck itself and not to the vast aggregation of petty acts that made it possible.[23]

For Scott, small acts can add up to large changes, or go nowhere at all, but they still count as resistance (he uses the potentially objectionable term 'peasantry' as a shorthand for politically disenfranchised ordinary people). Understood in this way, elements of Waters' performances take on added significance. He irreverently adapted the figure of 'Jack Tar' to express his Black Atlantic identity.

Anglo-American popular culture created a range of visual material that shaped the image of 'Jack Tar' and restricted Black mariners' place within that ideal. Julia Sun-Joo Lee suggests that there was such a thing as the 'textual Atlantic', a mixing and remixing of texts, genres, writers and cultures where Black and white authors alike borrowed and reused and reformed each other's ideas and materials. We might also call it a 'visual Atlantic', where popular imagery was generated, used, adapted and changed by many different kinds of writers and performers from many different backgrounds.[24] Visual imagery circulated between the UK, the US, the West African coast and the Caribbean, meme-like, picking up additions and rebellions as it went. This visual Atlantic was used against Waters but also used by him. No fool, Waters knew the world in which he danced, and shaped his rhythms accordingly. He was about to need all the courage and ingenuity he could find.

~ WOODEN ~
LEG

In Which Waters Becomes a Disabled Sailor

Haslar Hospital, near Portsmouth Harbour, 6 May 1812

The sky above the Patient's Airing Ground today is magnificent: wide and open with only faint clouds. A brisk southerly wind ruffles the skirts of his jacket. He lifts his face to the sun and feels it, warm, on his skin.

Beyond the brick wall roll the choppy waters of the English Channel. He knows that warships are moored at Spithead anchorage. Small boats scud to and fro from Portsmouth and from Gosport. The wind carries the smell of salt and tar, and the snatched sounds of slapping rope and men's shouts from the distant ships at anchor.

He will not climb a rigging again. He will not haul a rope again. He will not clean a gun again.

He must begin, again.

It is a long, slow walk from the Airing Ground back to the Hospital wing with only one serviceable leg.

Crisis

O
n Tuesday 3 March 1812, Captain John Brett Purvis sat in his cabin aboard HMS *Ganymede* while it was moored in Cadiz Bay and recorded the following events of the day in his Captain's Log:

> Am. Moderate Breezes and cloudy, loosed sails
> Wm. Waters fell from the main yard and broke both his legs and otherwise severely wounded him
> Received eleven Carpenters from the squadron to assist fitting up cabins for the reception of the Spanish Ambassador
> Opened cask of Beef and Pork[1]

The crew were employed in the rigging, the armourers were at the ship's forge, and the sailmakers were also busy. For most of the *Ganymede*'s crew this was a routine day in the Mediterranean squadron. For William Waters it was the day that would transform his life for ever.

Waters' accident was a traumatic event which left him not only with a lasting impediment but also with continuous discomfort, if not pain. It also left him with one of the defining elements of his act: the wooden leg. This wooden leg was a part of what made Waters entertaining for white middle-class commentators, both during his lifetime and when they remembered him after his death.[2] In the years following the Napoleonic Wars, wooden legs 'meant' the tragic consequences of war and the heroism of the ordinary combatant. They also were understood as comic: Adam Smith insisted in 1759 that it would be 'ridiculous' for a man with a wooden leg to be a tragic hero and some of this feeling persisted.[3] The wooden leg was a symbol as well as physical evidence of vulnerability, but also of survival and endurance against the odds. It was also a new fact of Waters' life.

Exploring the ways in which Regency and early Victorian visual culture depicted wooden-legged sailors shows us Waters' tenacious courage when faced with all-too-real issues of precarity, movement and balance. He was forced to navigate life as a disabled sailor so he used existing ideas and motifs in his act. Popular culture not only created the ways in which disabled sailors were viewed but also had tangible effects upon their actual bodies in ways which were nuanced and complex. This was especially true for Waters.

Moncrieff presents Waters' accident in a comic tone which deliberately undercuts any sense of Waters as a skilled or heroic 'Jack Tar':

> . . . during a fierce engagement, he lost a leg, some say gallantly fighting the enemies of old England, though others insinuate it was through falling down the cockpit ladder, in his hurry to hide himself; we cannot pretend to decide which was the fact, it however occasioned his being sent to England, as unfit for service.

Thomas Busby comes close to the truth, informing his readers that Waters 'lost his leg by falling from the top-sail yard to the quarter-deck, in the Ganymede sloop of war, under the command of Sir J.

Purvis' (although *Ganymede* was larger than a sloop). Hindley claims Waters' 'own version was that he fell from the top-sail yard to the quarter deck during a storm', but we should note that there is no mention of a storm in Purvis' Captain's Log.[4] Perhaps the accident was a dreadful outcome of a sail drill gone wrong.[5]

After the initial shock of seeing him fall, and the amazement that he was still alive, Waters was carried below to the sickbay (known as the cockpit). This was usually on the Orlop deck, a dark, dank and stuffy area below the waterline where the air smelt foul from the bilges (Figure 15). But this was a relatively safe area of the ship in battle (sometimes the sickbay moved to a higher deck when the ship was not in action). Waiting for him was the ship's surgeon, Felix Delany, who was well aware that swift action resulted in better patient outcomes. Delany combined the knowledge of physician (the only medical professional entitled to call themselves a doctor), apothecary (dispenser of medicines, more like our general practitioner) and surgeon, and had passed an examination by the College of Surgeons to get his warrant.[6] Waters' right leg must have suffered a clean break but the left must have been a compound fracture; the only treatment for severely broken limbs was immediate amputation to save the patient from putrefying to death. The operation was performed on board: Waters' hospital entry log reads 'Wound' rather than, like sailor John Lewis who arrived from HMS *Rover* two days before Waters, 'compound fracture'. Perhaps Delany was a rather better surgeon than his equivalent on the *Rover*.[7] Nevertheless, without anaesthetic or antiseptic apart from strong alcohol or syrup of poppies, amputation was a dangerous and agonising experience. Compound fractures were especially nasty and unpredictable. Sometimes patients died days after amputation and no one knew why. Waters was now in a race against time, shock, and blood loss. But he was lucky: Delany knew his stuff.

Speed was crucial. The goal was to remove the shattered limb in less than a minute (celebrated surgeon Robert Liston reportedly

15. Scene below decks showing man having leg amputated (c. 1820).

took twenty-eight seconds). The combined horrors of the increase in machinery accidents during the Industrial Revolution and a period of almost continual war between Western powers from the mid-eighteenth century meant that surgery had improved, but not by much: Delany would not necessarily have seen the need to sterilise his blades. As six or seven untrained surgeon's assistants, known as 'loblolly boys', held Waters down, Delany got to it. After applying a tight tourniquet to reduce blood loss as much as feasibly possible, with sharp knives he flayed open the skin to expose muscle, bone and nerves (leaving a flap of skin to cover the stump), and then cut the muscle with a special curved blade. Only once the muscle was held aside by his assistants did he reach for a saw to cleave the bone. Delany balanced speed with care not to splinter the bone, and tied the arteries and veins with ligatures as he went. There was blood everywhere. Blood loss could kill a patient quickly; shock could kill them if they survived the operation; infection was likely and another potential death sentence. The death rate for thigh-level amputations after the 1815 Battle of Waterloo was 70 per cent.[8] Some were able to make light of their ordeal: sailor William Richardson recounted how after a fierce battle with the French in 1796 he saw a man whose leg had been shot off 'hold up the stump . . . crying out, "Hurrah, my boys! I shall now get to old England again, and see my mother!"'[9] Such tales of bravado fuelled the Napoleonic War-era mythology of the heroic ordinary soldier and sailor. After the operation Waters was likely in shock, with his body traumatised and in excruciating pain; but, crucially, he was still alive.

It says a great deal for Waters' physical strength and resilience that he survived the fall, and the subsequent operation, at all. The Amputation Foundation explains that 'the emotional effect of limb loss can be traumatic'.[10] We should note, though, that things could have been even worse: Waters broke both legs in the initial accident, but (thanks to the skill of Delany as well as his own constitution) only lost one. Waters' wooden leg could be seen as a symbol of tragic misfortune; it could equally be read as an astonishing story of survival. The *Ganymede*'s masts were over 100 feet tall. The deck was solid oak. As Waters came crashing down he knew that his chances of surviving were limited at best. His days should have ended right there. That they did not must have placed a whole different meaning on existence for him. The resilience displayed in his performances and his life looks different when placed against that flightless fall, and the surgeon's knife.

On Tuesday 7 April, just over a month later, the *Ganymede* was back home at Spithead and moored up near Haslar Hospital. This was where Waters and two other crew members were headed: Alexander Cable, able seaman, suffering from rheumatism and Jos. Simpson, who like Waters had some kind of 'Wound'.[11] Waters was still alive; at this point his prognosis was looking much better, although post-operative problems were not yet understood. He was now in the care of an expensive modern facility which the Navy provided for the repair of its vital assets: its sailors. Begun in 1746 and completed in 1762, Haslar was a state-of-the-art medical institution housed in an imposing building four storeys high, with a main building, two wings, and several roomy wards (each capable of accommodating ninety patients), as well as rooms for the nurses and a system for providing clean water and removing sewage. During war it could hold upwards of 2,000 patients at one time. With a magnificent entrance, a large dining hall, a lawn for exercising or sitting outdoors, and surrounded by views and sea breezes, the hospital was a veritable 'palace' for injured mariners (though there was also a guardhouse for the prevention of 'riots and desertion'). In view were Spithead, Gosport and the ships in Portsmouth Harbour. Waters' feelings on arriving at this place are unknown, but a visitor in 1860 declared that 'this national institution cannot be inspected without the most satisfying and gratifying emotions . . . at mealtimes a more pleasant sight than these brave defenders of our country cannot be seen elsewhere'. One wonders if Waters would have agreed.[12]

In late spring 1812 there was a steady headcount of 300–400 patients at Haslar, suffering from complaints recorded as Catarrh, Consumption, Debility, Fever, Idiotism, Measles, Syphilis and Paralysis. Slightly fewer than forty patients died across April and May; four or five each month were already dead when they arrived. Patients were drawn from all ranks of the Navy: the April muster included a captain, a commander and a lieutenant as well as a purser, a cook, several ships' boys, and a bosun's mate alongside the large numbers of ordinary and able seamen.[13] A substantial staff of local women and some men were on the payroll in 1812, including three porters, numerous seamstresses, washers, and labourers, and 130 nurses under a matron and a store matron.[14] This large team provided a relatively high staff-to-patient ratio, and used the resources of a dispensary and an operating theatre. In 1812 the hospital governor was busy writing testy memos to the physicians and surgeons of Haslar instructing them to refer all applications by naval officers for the early discharge of hospitalised sailors to him before any sick man was sent away too soon, asking them precisely why a number of nurses were sacked for delinquency and what exactly was the misbehaviour involved, and ordering them to supply surgeons on returned naval ships with medical equipment when urgently needed. In 1813 he was dealing with complaints that patients missing limbs were not being 'properly fitted with Artificial Legs & Arms' before discharge; his memo makes it very clear that this must stop.[15] We don't know if one of the patients who experienced problems was Waters.

Somehow Waters fought off the threat of infection and the risk of constant bleeding from badly sewn arteries. He did not develop a 'bad stump' that refused to heal, or one which grew extra spurs of bone for no apparent reason (now called heterotopic ossification). He did not succumb to pain or melancholia, though he must have had his moments as he grappled with this new version of his body. Pain matters: increasingly disability scholars have called for realistic attention to its effects on the body, and Waters' story reminds us how especially important this is when exploring the lives of Regency amputees.[16] Another amputee, Lieutenant George Spearing, who lost his left leg below the knee following an accident, described how:

> I suffered much for two or three days, not daring to take a wink of sleep; for the moment I shut my eyes, my stump (though constantly held by the nerve) would take such convulsive movements, that I really think a stab to the heart could not be attended with greater pain. My blood too was become so very poor and thin, that it absolutely drained through the wound near a fortnight after my leg was cut off. I lay for 18 days and nights in one position, not daring to move, lest the ligature

should again give way; but I could endure it no longer, and ventured to turn myself in bed contrary to the advice of my surgeon, which I happily effected, and never felt greater pleasure in my life.[17]

Waters learned how to stand on a wooden leg, and how to walk: this took Lieutenant Spearing nine months, but Waters was not given that long before Haslar closed its gates to him. Growing up in New York's slaveholding economy taught him that you could not hope for a perfect life. This was yet another loss. There would be life afterwards.

Waters left Haslar, and the British Navy, on 26 May 1812. He and Simpson were assessed by medical staff on 5 May and the verdict was brief: 'unserviceable'. The two men from HMS *Ganymede* were no more use to the British Navy. Their shipmate Cable, meanwhile, was sent off to a new vessel. Waters and Simpson remained at Haslar a bit longer until they were physically able to leave. It wasn't until twenty-one days later that Waters was recorded as 'Out of Service'.[18] He left Simpson, Haslar and the seafarer's life behind. Suddenly, Waters' identity was no longer that of an active sailor. From now on his life, his actions, and the perception of both of these by others would be conditioned by his disability and his wooden leg.

Overboard

Waters' disability created the necessity for his street performances and the physical challenges that those performances
involved. It affected the ways in which he was viewed and subsequently remembered. Exploring this reveals a new perspective on the
impact of nineteenth-century visual culture upon disabled bodies.

The gates of Haslar closed behind him; what would Waters do
now? Contemporary sources suggest that Waters received a 'trifling'
pension for his pains.[1] His pension wasn't that bad for its time, but it
did give him a problem. He was awarded £20 a year for life, or roughly
13d per day, in recognition of his wages as a quarter gunner. This was
more than a fellow-American received: Samuel Michael, a Black man
from Philadelphia who also lost a leg serving in the British Navy on
board HMS *Ethalion*, was discharged from Greenwich Hospital three
months after Waters left Haslar with a pension of £16 a year. It was
also better than the mean annual male wage of £15 in London during
1816–20, according to economic historian K. D. M. Snell, but a skilled
carpenter could earn as much as £60 a year in 1795 (£90 by 1843).
The problem was that Waters would now have to provide all the
necessities of life with that income: board, lodging, medical expenses,
and anything else he might need. To beg when receiving a military

pension was illegal, but he would need about twice his pension income to keep a family. Equating historic sums to modern-day amounts is always a bit of a fool's game, but £20 annually was roughly equivalent to a relative income of £19,000 today, or (calculated differently) the purchasing power today of a little over £5 per day. Waters only had 7–8 shillings a week (two days' wages for a skilled tradesman) on which to live during a period of post-war economic crisis. Thomas Brunt, a thirty-six-year-old tailor with a wife and child, on trial for his life for the 1820 Cato Street conspiracy, equated 'not 10 shillings a week' with being 'starved'.[2] Samuel Michael became a cook on merchant ships as many disabled sailors did, but Waters, for whatever reason, had had enough of the sea. He was a skilled and respected petty officer: what good was a cook's job to him? The trauma of his accident did not easily wash away, either. Nor did he become an in-patient at Greenwich Hospital. It must have taken all his determination and some luck to make his way to London, but with seemingly no means or inclination to pay for passage back to the United States, Waters had to make the best of it.

Moncrieff tells us that, 'Arriving in London, he betook himself to that wild mode of life, which best suited his savage origin; the trammels of civilized society, had no charms for a soul as free as his; he scorned the mechanical rules of man, and picked up his living wherever he could find it.'[3] A free soul: Moncrieff paints this picture in racist language and lends the actions of impoverished necessity the gilding of personal choice which he attributes to Waters' 'origin' (in other words, his race). Waters, like so many other disabled soldiers and sailors in the wake of the Napoleonic Wars, decided to seek a living on the London streets. Somehow he would have to do so hampered by the intersecting challenges of his society's preconceptions about sailors, Black men, and wooden legs.

Waters' lost limb ended one career, so he transformed it into the basis for another. Ex-military amputees were figures of admiration and sympathy in the late eighteenth and early nineteenth centuries, as David Turner's important work on disability shows. Older notions of amputees as comic persisted, however. Waters' song and dance performances were considered comic by many nineteenth-century commentators in terms that would rightly be condemned today. An account of Waters in a piece of nineteenth-century comic writing for the *Literary Chronicle*, published shortly after his death, makes this clear:

> I must, for a moment, crave the reader's indulgence, to offer, en passant, a tributary apostrophe to the memory of one of the merriest of mortals, that ever limped across my peripatetic path. Poor Billy Waters! How often have his frolicsome gambols roused me from some melancholy reverie to life and merriment! How often has a single glance at his eccentricities put to flight a whole legion of cares and disquietudes! Even now, he appears to my 'mind's eye', in all his accustomed light-heartedness, gaily dancing, to the tune of his faithful violin, upon the only leg of flesh and blood, which fate had left him, while he elevates its ligneous associate in a thousand fantastic attitudes, and with a vivacity, which the happiest biped around him might well envy.[4]

The journalist of the *Literary Chronicle* is charmed by Waters. 'Poor Billy Waters' is the object of light humour and gentle pity. There's more than a hint here of eighteenth-century notions of the 'Merry Cripple' and the dancing 'Stage Black' as well as jolly 'Jack Tar'. But there is also admiration and gratitude for Waters' 'enviable vivacity'. Still, the 'happiness' of his performance slips into the suggestion that Waters himself must have been happy; Waters' vulnerable body is viewed at a strictly surface level.

How did Waters dance on that painful stump? With only written accounts and images to go on, and ones that are filtered through contemporary attitudes to both race and disability at that, it's not easy to be sure. Dance is by definition an art of movement not of stasis. The images we have of Waters tie down his movement and freeze him on the page in purchasable form. We can make some surmises, however. Newspaper obituaries described the 'peculiar stumping of his wooden leg in an original kind of hornpipe'.[5] A white street performer recorded in Henry Mayhew's *London Labour and the London Poor* declares that:

> For the hornpipe I begin with walking round, or 'twisting' as the term is; then I stands up, and does a double-shuffle – or the 'straight fives' as we calls it; then I walks round again before doing another kind of double-shuffle. Then I does the Rocks of Scilly, that's where you twists your feet and bends sideways; next comes the double steps and rattles, that is, when the heels makes a rattle coming down; and I finishes with the square step. My next step is to walk round and collect the money.[6]

This interview takes place many years after Waters' death, but it gives us an insight into Waters' potential techniques. We can imagine him also performing jig steps, another popular solo dance and one which Mayhew's interviewee notes went down well with an Irish audience. Waters learned how to adapt his performance to the crowd to emphasise skills of balance unique to the performer with a prosthetic limb, as the street dancer in Figure 16 clearly did, and the physical comedy of the stage clown. Figure 17 suggests he balanced and maybe even spun round on his wooden leg, eye-wateringly challenging with an amputated stump.

Waters may also have integrated steps learned amongst the Black communities of New York. Dance historian and dancer Rodreguez King-Dorset points out that dance traditions drawn from the African diaspora during the height of the slave trade had notable differences from the European dance traditions which enslaved Africans encountered in the Caribbean, London, and the Americas. Dance techniques drawn from African traditions tended to involve bent

ONE-LEGGED DANCER.

16. A street dancer with a prosthetic leg photographed in London (c. 1900).

knees as if gravity were pulling the dancer's body towards the ground, and the dancer's limbs, head, shoulders and neck were allowed to move simultaneously to multiple contrasting rhythms. This would have looked very unusual to European eyes accustomed to the stiff upper body stance required in much European social and solo dance, although the hornpipe itself was potentially influenced by dance rhythms of more African origin transmitted via the Atlantic shipping routes.[7] If Waters did incorporate some non-European dance steps in his performances, it's unlikely that his skill would have been properly appreciated. As King-Dorset suggests, writing about Black Londoners dancing the quadrille at private parties, 'Any white people watching would probably have remained unaware of what was going on and attributed the exaggerations to black people's inability to dance properly.'[8] The ways in which white British audiences saw him were conditioned by caricatures and stage performances that 'placed the African body under intense ethnographic scrutiny and promulgated a sensationalist racial bias forging an indelible link to the savage, deviant, and non-human'.[9] They opened up Black bodies to mockery and derision. Whatever his skills, Waters was doomed to be

17. *An undated sketch of Waters. His name is incorrectly given – it's his image that's stuck in this sketcher's mind.*

found comic because he was Black: he was also doomed to be found comic because he was a disabled sailor.

Class as well as race governed comic performance and visual culture, as Waters was clearly well aware. Disabled naval officers and Tars were seen as examples of heroic masculinity even though their bodies didn't match aesthetic notions of the 'ideal' body. Nelson's amputated arm appeared in formal portraits, cheap prints, and popular memorabilia alike as a link between gentlemanly heroism and popular patriotism; anecdotes of Nelson frequently included a meeting with an amputee sailor in the cheering crowds, stories in which the enduring loyalty of the wounded veteran demonstrated an affectionate national community.[10] Disabled Tars, however, were also legitimate subjects for laughter – gentle, or otherwise. Sailor William Richardson recounts in 1793 how one Bandy (the ship's cook) had his wooden leg stolen by a shipmate 'by way of a frolic'.[11] In the 1810s and 1820s, amputation meant war: disabled and destitute soldiers and sailors missing arms, legs, and eyes were common sights. It also signalled comedy. Scholar Simon Dickie writes about eighteenth-century humour that:

> From Adam Smith to Goldsmith, James Beattie, and countless lesser authors, the man with the wooden leg becomes a master trope for testing the possibilities and limitations of sympathy. These men had been wounded in the service of their country, but there were just too many of them – and, anyway, who could possibly look at someone with a wooden leg and not burst out laughing?[12]

In 1819 the celebrated critic William Hazlitt declared that laughter is provoked by 'the ludicrous', which he defined as 'a contradiction between the object and our expectations, heightened by some deformity or inconvenience . . . contrary to what is customary or desirable'; the ludicrous contains an important physical dimension revealed in Hazlitt's choice of metaphorical language (that word 'deformity').[13] 'Comic humans are incomplete', writes Andrew Stott;[14] in Waters' lifetime this idea was taken literally and physically. Whether he liked it or not, Waters with his wooden limb was now a comic figure. He was subject to laughter that could be admiring, sociable, but sometimes cruel.

The unruly body of 'Jack Tar' was already often viewed through the comic mode. Sailors in transatlantic popular culture of the first half of the nineteenth century were frequently mined for comic potential as well as their manly heroism, depicted as all at sea when on land, forced out of their element and found by landlubbers to speak a strange language, or finding themselves baffled by a post-war peacetime world. The joke of *The Sailor and the Judge* (Figure 18) turns on the fact of the nautical vocabulary of the sailor applied to the land-based problem of being hauled in front of a judge for intoxication. Disabled Tars could be comic too. From the 1780s onwards images began to stress the pitiable state of disabled soldiers and sailors and demand public sympathy for them. Sentimental images drew on the perceived 'feminising' effects of disability: vulnerability, weakness, and dependency.[15] Prints exhorted the viewer to 'Be kind to a Veteran' with his body maimed in the nations' service (Figure 19). Some images were angrier: *The Sailor's Return, or British Valor Rewarded* (1783) allows the viewer to be under no

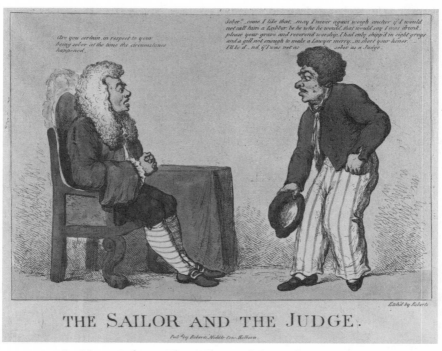

18. *Piercy Roberts,* The Sailor and the Judge (c. 1800–7).

19. Be kind to a Veteran ... (1829).

illusions about the physical and emotional cost of war (Figure 20). But the Second Treaty of Paris in 1815 marked the end of the Napoleonic Wars. As memories faded, so did sympathies, and visual codes changed. By 1840 Douglas Jerrold could write:

The Sailor Ballad-Singer has died with the long peace; he no longer attacks our sympathies with one arm and a wooden leg; maimed limbs have become scarce. Now and then, when we presume little is to be got by picking pockets – for, in all professions, there is, probably, a longer or shorter vacation – half-a-dozen fellows condescend to walk with bare, clean-washed feet, executing, as they pick their way, 'Ben Bowline', or at times plunging with one accord into the 'Bay of Biscay'.[16]

Sentimental modes of depicting disabled Tars did remain, but comic ones also spread.

More than one print – some kinder than others – contained versions of the joke that laughed at the foolish sailor mistaking a heraldic engraver's shop ('Arms Found') for a place where he could replace his wooden leg (Plate VII). Amputee sailors wheeling an amazing model ship through town, begging for alms, are treated comically in W. H. Harrison's 1831 Christmas book *The Humourist* (Figure 21); the image parodies Thomas Rowlandson's *c.* 1820 caricature *Distressed Sailors*. George Cruikshank was fascinated by physically damaged sailors, especially wooden-legged sailors, and frequently represented them as mock-heroic (humorously parodic)

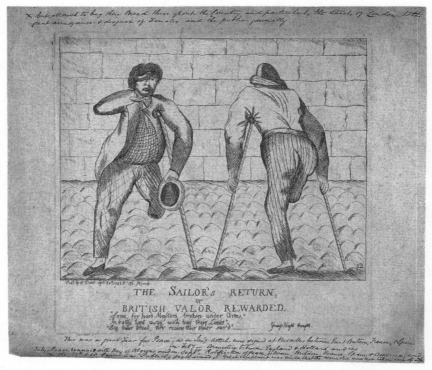

20. S. B., The Sailor's Return, or British Valor Rewarded (1783).

THE HUMOURIST AND HER CREW.

21. *'The Crew of the Humourist', from W. H. Harrison*, The Humourist (1831).

figures of fun. In *The Sailors Progress* (1819), Cruikshank suggests that there is an inevitable progression from strapping Tar to wooden-legged veteran (Figure 22). In his illustration to Matthew Barker's *Greenwich Hospital* (1826), we see a group of disabled sailors re-enacting the Battle of the Nile, wooden legs and all (Figure 23). The picture evokes sympathy and respect but also laughter as comparisons are invited between the wooden legs and the wooden chairs. As Waters would discover, the amputee soldier or sailor was both 'the smashed recipient of society's self-conscious

22. *George Cruikshank,*
The Sailors Progress
(*1819*).

benevolence' and the figure of fun who contained war's violent effects safely within stoicism and comedy.[17]

The mock-heroic mode was also used by equally well-known comic artist Robert Seymour, who included a portrait of the visibly disabled Nelson as an ironic counterpoint to his wooden-legged sailor in the third issue of his serialised book of visual jokes *New Readings of Old Authors* (1832–4, Figure 24). Beneath the image there is a quotation from Lord Byron's bestselling Orientalist romance poem *The Giaour* (1813), which emphasises the discrepancy between masculine heroic ideals and the grotesque body of Seymour's sailor.

As the nineteenth century wore on, images of the disabled Tar (including George Cruikshank's) became more good humoured and sentimental in tone, in Britain as part of the growing Victorian sentimentalism about Napoleonic-era sailors (Plate VIII) and in the US as the figure of the ordinary sailor became a symbol of the vigorous republican state.[18] By the time of the Crimean War it would be virtually unthinkable to mock disabled military men. But the disabled tar, indeed the wooden-legged man more generally, were staples of late eighteenth- and early nineteenth-century humour into the 1850s. George Cruikshank's 1819 satirical print *Landing the Treasures* spares none of the mariners it depicts, including Waters: it shows one Captain Ross and his crew bringing back some Arctic specimens after a largely unsuccessful expedition (Figure 25).[19] Near the head of the procession, Waters' feathered hat echoes the

23. *George Cruikshank,* The Battle of the Nile (1826).

"Shrine of the mighty! Can it be .
That this is all remains of thee!"

Q. 106.

24. *From Robert Seymour's* New Readings of Old Authors (1832–4). *This was a serial publication of monthly issues each comprising ten small images published in paper covers.*

hat of Captain Ross; the brave captain's folly is revealed by a comic Black street entertainer.

In image after image of Waters and of other sailors who had endured amputation, disability is used as (in the words of scholars David T. Mitchell and Sharon L. Snyder) a 'device – an artistic prosthesis' that shows Regency culture grappling with how to think about people with impairments. Mitchell and Snyder discuss films, plays and novels to show how many narratives depend upon disabled bodies as a way of expressing intangible ideas via something more tangible and graspable: the human body. They point out that stories emerge when a problem needs 'fixing' in the story's world, and that disability is often used as a form of human difference which anchors that problem in a character and makes the story happen. They call this process 'narrative prosthesis'.[20] We might call the wooden leg a 'visual prosthesis', or a visual shorthand, which enabled pictorial storytelling in Regency caricatures and was sometimes understood as heroic, and sometimes as comic. Comic images of the disabled Tar were used to depict Waters in ways that reveal how popular culture worked against him and others. But it was also something he could harness, if he could find a way.

Some days must have been very challenging: staring, pointing, and disrespectful gestures were discouraged in polite literature but a poor man in the streets with a visible disability was a target for the 'fun' of others. *Punch* magazine remembered in 1847 that, as Waters performed in the streets of Westminster, 'all the little boys in the place used to take the glorious privilege of pelting him. He thus had the freedom of the city very often presented to him in a snowball or cabbage leaf.'[21] Andrew Whiston (also known as 'Little Jemmy' because of his short stature and shown seated with his back to us amongst the 'Cadgers' of Plate XII) was subjected to bullying from 'tormentors' who found it funny to play practical jokes on him while he begged in the street simply because he was disabled; passers-by did not intervene but formed a 'laughing throng'.[22] One of the more persistent jokes associated with Waters was about the treadmill, something from which his wooden leg was said to have 'twice saved' him.[23] A ballad printed in St Giles by James Catnach mocked the

25. *George Cruikshank*, Landing the Treasures (1819).

113

treadmill's 'Revolution' with a kind of grim punning humour, but the reality of it was hard labour. Invented by William Cubitt in 1818 and installed at Brixton prison and other large jails, the treadmill involved up to twenty-four prisoners walking on a large stepped wheel that ground corn; the idea was to make prisoners 'useful' to society. Every few minutes one prisoner was allowed off and another took their place; on a twenty-four-man treadmill, prisoners got one twelve-minute break every hour. It's unlikely that Waters was sent to Brixton prison although it did happen to another man picked up twice by constables for begging in 1823: the street poor of London like Waters could 'receive an order for six days' work; the strongest Men [were sent to the] stone yard to break stones, others to the Mill, and Women and children to the Oakum Room [where they teased fibres out of old ropes by hand, which were then sold on to shipbuilders]'.[24]

The treadmill's association with the street poor of London in general, and with Waters in particular, is demonstrated in its repeated appearances as part of the *Life in London* craze. The contemporary song 'Oh! What Will Mother Say?' (which appeared in a songbook, *The Universal Songster*, illustrated by the Cruikshank brothers) declares that:

> We went to Brixton, saw the mill,
> And Billy Waters treading;
> Black Sall, with Dusty Bob and Bill,
> All merry as a wedding;
> To-morrow morn, at half-past six,
> I'll homeward bend my way,
> And when I tell my London tricks,
> Lord, what will mother say? (281)

The Adelphi Theatre advertised that its production of *Tom and Jerry; Or, Life in London* for the 1822 season included 'A Correct Model of the

Tread Mill', while over Waterloo Bridge at Surrey Theatre audiences could enjoy *The tread mill, or Tom and Jerry at Brixton* (1822). Catnach's *c.* 1822 broadside *The Tread-mill* reproduces some lines from the treadmill scene, along with a woodcut image of the Brixton Mill and a comic song about Tom, Jerry and Logic treading it (Figure 26). In the

26. The Tread-mill (*c. 1822*).

1825 caricature *The Progress of Cant* a small figure in a cocked hat with a wooden leg holds up a banner demanding 'No Treadmill'.[25] In Moncrieff's play, the treadmill is turned into a piece of 'comic' dialogue in which 'Billy Waters' declares:

> *Billy Waters.* Oh, curse a de Tread Mill, me no like a de 'here we go up, up, up,' and 'down you go down, down, down', – an' if you no work, a great big lump of wood come and knock you down so—(*Strikes beggar on head with his fiddle, who falls down*). Poor fellow, him werry sorry.

In racially caricatured dialect, which is nothing more than verbal blackface, 'Billy Waters' is made to follow his description of the treadmill with a slapstick moment of comic violence that diverts attention away from prisons and magistrates and instead lays the blame for physical suffering by white beggars on their non-white competitor.

It was also true, however, that the potent mixture of disability and comedy was, in late eighteenth- and early nineteenth-century popular culture, a basis for celebrity. 'Monsieur Timbertoe' was all the rage in mid-eighteenth-century London with his one-legged versions of the hornpipe. He was not an isolated example, though he became especially famous. So-called 'crutch dances' (where a group of hunchbacks and amputees danced to fiddle music) were established components of farces, plays and masques up till the 1790s. Scholar Simon Dickie suggests that 'no doubt appreciation was as common a reaction at these performances as derisions ... Many deformed performers were admired for their agility and skill'.[26] Like Waters, Monsieur Timbertoe was an ex-military amputee said to do 'more with one Foot, than others can with two'.[27] As biographer Ian Kelly writes about the amputee playwright and comedian of an earlier generation, Samuel Foote (1720–77), 'The loss of his leg, and the projection therefore of a despoiled masculinity, as a limping icon of pain and accident – two key ingredients in comedy – made him all the more fascinating as a star, caught, as it were, in the act of falling.'[28] Samuel Foote was known for exploiting his impairment for comic effect: one contemporary noted that, 'Where a piece has seemed to languish and flag, I have seen him, by a hobbling walk across the stage, accompanied with significant gesture and grimace, set the house in a roar.'[29] At the same time, the young Irish playwright John O'Keefe remembered seeing Foote backstage looking 'sorrowful' as 'he stood upon his one leg, leaning against the wall, while his servant was putting on his stage false leg'. At such moments, Keefe said, 'one could not help pitying him'.[30]

In the mid-nineteenth century, Henry Mayhew recorded street dancer Whistling Billy's description of a one-legged performance:

> I used to go about with a mate who had a wooden leg. He was a beautiful dancer, for all he made 'em all laugh. He's a little chap, and only does the hornpipe, and he's uncommon active, and knocks his leg against the railings, and makes the people grin. He was very successful at Brighton, because he was pitied.[31]

The hornpipe as danced by this wooden-legged dancer evokes pity and laughter, though 'Whistling Billy' can see the pathos of a 'beautiful dancer' generating this kind of audience response. The laughter at the disabled performer's expense (even if at their instigation) reveals yet again Waters' vulnerability and (quite literally) precarity as he attempted to navigate life as a disabled sailor. But Waters mastered balance through dance. With an adroitness that was characteristic of him, he turned instability into art.

To maintain a physically demanding life of performance was a constant challenge for the wealthy Foote with servants to assist him and a comfortable home in which to rest. For Waters, it was an unending struggle. Surviving amputation in the early nineteenth century, as in the late eighteenth, meant a future of near-constant exhaustion, phantom pains in the limb, and the constant potential for further accident or even attack. It took all the fortitude one had. Nevertheless, Waters' wooden leg was a symbol of survival as well as of trauma. He should not have survived the fall from the rigging. In surviving it, he could easily have lost both legs. Leonard Kriegel, in an essay called 'The Cripple in Literature', writes about his own experience of surviving polio and living with its physical after-effects in the context of late twentieth-century images of American masculinity. For Kriegel, 'what better image of survival than the cripple . . .?':

> the Survivor Cripple does what he must in order to survive. And in surviving, he cauterizes his wound, his visible stigma, into the source of his existence. Not that he is better than others – simply that he is more experienced at doing because he can't, at winning because he loses . . . Knowing that he must ultimately lose, he knows too, that his existence is his defiance. He is the self created out of necessity.[32]

Kriegel reclaims the derogatory term 'cripple' as a badge of heroic resilience long before scholars formulated a 'resistance theory' of disability.[33] As numerous scholars of disability have pointed out, the lived experience of disability involves elements of performance because when many able-bodied people see – or fail to see when they expect to see – visible disability, they have the urge to stare and to interpret.[34] Waters shaped this experience to his advantage. Waters' chances of survival as an impoverished Black man in London were made even less likely by the fact of his disability. But Waters defied such things as probability.

Finding Poll

A wooden-legged ex-sailor in the Regency period could be the butt of the joke or make the jokes himself. Waters was not a man to let circumstance defeat him easily. Like other performers before and after him, Waters' wooden leg gave him a selling point for his act. In addition, sailor humour was bawdy humour and Waters made full use of it to earn money. There were sanctimonious complaints in newspapers of his 'singing immodest songs in the hearing of ladies' and 'addressing improper observations to females' but no one thought to ask the women themselves whether they laughed.[1]

It wasn't only Waters' costume, and Waters' dance, that bore the traces of his naval life. His singing did, too. Like many a commercially minded performer, Waters had a trademark song. People's memories of that song were rather imperfect. Charles Hindley tells us that:

The burden of Billy's ditty 'from morn to dewy eve', and from
January to December, was: –
Polly will you marry me – Polly don't you cry,
Polly will you marry me – Polly don't you cry: –
Cry – cry – cry![2]

27. 'Kitty Will You Marry Kate', William Vickers' manuscript tune book (1770).

However, in another publication Hindley renders the song slightly differently as 'Kitty will you marry me'.[3] A manuscript version has survived from the 1700s (Figure 27).[4] The song was clearly an old one and had shifted and changed over time, although it's significant that Waters sang a version to 'Polly'.

Polly, and less frequently Kitty, were almost as common names for a sailor's girl as Jack was for a sailor. The songwriter and dramatist Charles Dibdin senior drew on existing vocabulary for his songs and popularised Jack and Poll even more. One of his most famous songs, 'Poll and Partner Joe' (probably first performed 1788), about a sailor who returns home to find his sweetheart with another man, was turned (in 1835) into a popular play by John Thomas Haines. In Dibdin's 'Poor Jack', the eponymous speaker articulates 'Jack Tar' with the lines 'For my heart is my Poll's, and my rhino's [money] my friend's, / And as for my life, 'tis the King's'. Poll gets her own song in 'Lovely Polly', whilst in 'Sweethearts and Wives' sailors toast their womenfolk and 'I'll give, cried little Jack, my Poll'. In 'Tom Bowling', one of his many perfections is that 'His Poll was kind and fair'. Kitty, meanwhile turns up more than once: in 'When Last from the Straits' and 'The Good Ship the Kitty'.[5] The white sailor and his lass were stock characters who were used (like the dancing couple in Figure 28) to embody the health and vigour of the nation: like Waters himself they appear in cheap prints and memorabilia.[6] Alternatively, the sailor and his lass could embody sexual threat and the unhealthiness of unbridled pleasure-seeking and debauchery. Poll was just as likely to be conceived of as a 'Portsmouth Poll', a prostitute who survived (just about) by servicing sailors despite the ever-present risks to her of disease and sexual violence (Plate IX). Unlike her more patriotic counterparts, 'Portsmouth Poll' could be Black or white, and was frequently depicted in caricatures and written descriptions as 'a thing of more than Amazonian stature' with 'brawny arms' and 'a dirty white, or tawdry flowered gown', though sailors themselves sometimes pitied the half-starved girls and women with whom (in reality) they engaged.[7] Did Waters sing of Polly to emphasise his Tar credentials?

28. Merry England (*undated*).

Sailor language offered many possibilities for bawdiness. A slightly racier version of Waters' song appears in an 1819 print of Waters (Figure 29): in this lithograph the words from Waters' song are added to the bottom. The first line ends with 'toy', making it clear that the missing word in line two that is somewhat coyly omitted must be 'boy'. This version makes it possible to see how Waters might have raised a laugh with his wooden leg: 'pick it up my boy', the verse now ends, an instruction that might apply to his fiddle playing, his wooden limb, or (in the context of 'toying' in bed with Kitty/Polly and making a baby), an equally stiff part of his anatomy. Paul A. Gilje has shown how popular song from the 1600s onwards often made use of the metaphorical possibilities of sailor language to bawdy effect, as seen to enthusiastic

29. 'Billy Waters' and his song,
as seen in an 1819 print.

salaciousness in *An Excellent New Song, Entitled a Hot Engagement between a French Privateer and an English Fire-Ship*. Ostensibly about a sea battle, the lines 'His Main Yard he hoisted and Steered / his Course, and he gave me a Broad Side' describe another kind of encounter entirely. As Gilje puts it, 'the familiarity with so many people ashore with the maritime vocabulary meant that veiling ribaldry with the maritime vocabulary would have provided only a thin disguise'; but that's, of course, what makes the song funnier.[8] At the same time, the more ribald version of Waters' song plays into contemporary stereotypes of the dangerously over-sexed and animalistic Black man.[9] The 1819 print depicts Waters with a gaping mouth and teeth, drawing on the racist eighteenth-century carica-ture tradition of depicting Black features. Although Waters' act played with multiple levels of sexual stereotyping to delight a crowd, those stereotypes were also used against him. But his popularity is clear.

Waters became linked with sailors and 'the Molls, Polls, and Sallys who bedded with and/or wedded sailors ashore' both during his lifetime and after.[10] In 1822, ten years after Waters first left the *Ganymede*, an adaptation of Egan's *Life in London* with 'real pony races!' was performed at Davis' Royal Amphitheatre in London, to great acclaim.[11] In Act II Scene 2 Billy Waters plays the fiddle while the prostitute African Sal dances a hornpipe (see Figure 2). Fifty-five years later, a review of a *Tom and Jerry; or Life in London* revival at the Surrey Theatre picks out the scene in which 'Billy Waters, the one-legged ancestor of Ethiopian minstrels, . . . discourses eloquent music to Black Sall' as she dances the hornpipe with her partner Dusty Bob the dustman.[12] All-Max is a favourite haunt of London sailors, we are told, and Egan's own description of the All-Max crowd merits quoting in full:

ALL-MAX was compared by the sailors, something after the old adage of 'any port in a storm'. It required no patronage;– a card of admission was not necessary;– no inquiries were made;– and every *cove* that put in his appearance was quite welcome: colour or country considered no obstacle; and *dress* and ADDRESS completely out of the question. *Ceremonies* were not in use, and, therefore, no struggle to place at ALL-MAX for the master of them. The parties *paired off* according to *fancy*; the eye was pleased in the choice, and nothing thought of about birth and distinction. All was *happiness*, – every body free and easy, and freedom of expression allowed to the very echo. The group motley indeed;– Lascars, blacks, jack tars, coal-heavers, dustmen, women of colour, old and young, and a sprinkling of the remnants of once fine girls, &c. were all *jigging* together, provided the *teaser of the catgut* was not *bilked* of his *duce*. *Gloves* might have been laughed at, as dirty hands produced no *squeamishness* on the heroines in the dance, and the scene changed as often as a pantomime from the continual introduction of new characters. (286)

Dance develops and reveals a community of equals, we're told, in ways which fashionable London cannot achieve. It's a vibrant scene. The reader is able to ignore the realities of life as an impoverished Londoner in this period – hunger, disease, and distress – because this dance is given the gloss of unreality by being described as a pantomime. Bob Logic pompously informs Tom, 'It is, . . . I am quite satisfied in my mind, the LOWER ORDERS of society who really ENJOY themselves' (286). The women are freely available to the main male characters:

Our heroes had kept it up so gaily dancing, drinking, &c. that the friend of the CORINTHIAN thought it was time to be *missing*; but, on mustering the TRIO, LOGIC was not to be found. A jack tar, about *three sheets to the wind, who had been keeping up the shindy* the whole of the evening with them, laughing, asked if it was the gentleman in the *green barnacles* their honours wanted, as it was very likely he had taken a voyage to *Africa*, in the *Sally*, or else he was out on a cruise with the *Flashy Nance*; but he would have him beware of *squalls*, as they were not very *sound* in their *rigging!* It was considered useless to look after LOGIC . . . (290)

Sal the Black woman is turned into a ship, the *Sally*, a vessel to be used and potentially owned by Bob Logic the white male. The racier version of Waters' song capitalised upon the bawdy possibilities of sailor language which passed around the network of popular culture and which reinforced the ways in which the poor Black population of London was understood.

The sailor's wife was another stock character of popular culture, with her own tropes and stereotypes. There were sentimental images of sailors happily reunited with wives and children, but usually the sailor's wife was either in the process of being left behind while her supposed breadwinner puts to sea, or enduring the results of injury and disability alongside her returned husband (Plate X). Pollys and Kittys needed resilience to survive the uncertainties of life as a sailor's lass: in Dibdin's song 'Each Bullet Has Its Commission', we hear that 'There was little Tom Linstock from Dover, / Got killed, and left Polly in pain: / Poll cried, but her grief was soon over, / And then she got married again'.[13] In practice many women did not wait for their husbands and lovers ashore but joined them at sea as unofficial crew members, something many a captain turned a blind eye to despite the official Navy rules forbidding women at sea. Women served practical purposes aboard far beyond keeping the men happy: John Nicol writes of their participation and courage in battle in matter-of-fact tones:

> I was much indebted to the gunner's wife who gave her husband and me a drink of wine every now and then, which lessened our fatigue much. There were some of the women wounded, and one woman belonging to Leith died of her wounds and was buried on a small island in the bay. One woman bore a son in the heat of the action. She belonged to Edinburgh.[14]

As a member of an elite unit on the *Ganymede*, Waters may well have been allowed to bring a wife with him. He may not necessarily have met her after his accident and amputation; she may have been one reason that he survived such a dreadful fall.

Next to the final entry of William Waters, 'A Black Man', in the naval pension records is a small handwritten note added by the clerk, who clearly had a tidy mind and a diligent approach to record-keeping. It's a quick reminder for a busy administrator regarding the person to whom the final instalment was handed over: 'to widow Elizabeth'. Captured at one of the most challenging moments in her life, Waters' wife steps into the national record.[15] The Navy's Tars, white or Black, may have borne much hardship in Britannia's quest to Rule the Waves, but so did the Polls who supported them at sea and ashore. The reality of that physical suffering is what Regency comic memes worked both to disguise and express. In the process they revealed the stubborn resilience of the poor.

Surviving the Storm

Waters may have been represented as a comic and ridiculous wooden-legged Black sailor but he knew how to craft a striking performance. If we return to the review by the comic writer of the *Literary Chronicle* we see that the final comment takes a different tone:

> But, he is gone; 'we ne'er shall look upon his like again.' He was truly 'one in a thousand'; for, of all my timber-legged fellow-creatures, whom it has been my lot to encounter, none bore his faculties so meekly, or knew so well how to set the rabble 'in a roar', as Billy Waters.[1]

Here we have one professional entertainer reviewing another, and noting their colleague's skill: 'none knew so well how to set the rabble "in a roar", as Billy Waters'. The write-up ends on a mock-heroic note by quoting Horace, 'Multis ille bonis flebilis occidit, Nulli flebilior quam mihi' ('He died lamented by many good men, but by none more than by me'). A 'roar' is not cruel laughter but the kind which applauds and admires. This review is a mark of respect from one comic to another. Paul Gilroy, writing about music, notes that 'the power and significance of music within the Black Atlantic have grown in inverse proportion to the limited expressive power of language . . . Examining the place of music in the Black Atlantic world means surveying the self-understanding articulated by the musicians who have made it.'[2] We need to look (or laugh) with Waters, rather than at him, to understand his creative choices.

By the 1850s 'Billy Waters' was turned into a comically misfortunate sailor by the popular singer J. G. Forde. A notice in the *Leader* in July 1858 reviews a performance at Vauxhall Pleasure Gardens of 'the "experiences of a sailor", being the sad misfortunes of "Billy Waters", a nautical burlesque, sung by Mr J. G. Ford, which, we may fairly say, may rank as one of the cleverest of its very numerous family'.[3] It's unclear here whether 'Billy Waters' signifies a representation of the precise historical person, or if Waters has morphed into a generic sailor character. The next month, the *London News* declared Forde 'the comic genius' of Lambeth's Canterbury Music Hall (one of the first purpose-built music halls in the capital), who 'causes roars of laughter by the ridiculous adventures of "Billy Waters"'.[4] But before he was ever co-opted for comedy by others, William Waters himself made choices about how he performed, and what he chose to emphasise. His extravagant costume gestured to Black Atlantic traditions of performance and leadership, but also to his time at sea. His sailor jacket presented him as a British national and his cocked hat drew on cultures of the Black Atlantic. In this context his wooden leg announced him as a survivor of wartime service. This prosthetic limb features prominently in images and descriptions of his performances. In periodicals his skill is emphasised, albeit sometimes undercut by a comic tone. In 1840 Douglas Jerrold remembered of Waters that 'They who saw thee not, cannot conceive the amount of grace co-existent with a wooden leg – the comedy budding from timber.'[5] That word 'grace' applied to Waters is striking, as if he has transcended the awkward gravity-bound movements of human beings and of disability. Not only did Moncrieff assert in 1851 that Waters was 'an adroit dancer' but Hindley reprinted this comment in 1878.[6] The fact that the wooden leg is so memorable in these reminiscences after the passage of many years points to how important it was in William Waters' act.

This raises the question: to what extent was Waters aware of the visual and theatrical codes of comic wooden legs as they emerged before and during his lifetime, and did he use them deliberately to money-making effect? On the one hand, for a Black man to dance for a (mostly) white audience was an act that carried all kinds of troubling significance. Enslaved Africans were made to jump about on deck during long and hellish slaving voyages to maintain their fitness and so their economic value, a process known as 'dancing the slaves'.[7] For a Black man to be humorous also came very close to the happy-go-lucky 'Mungo' figure. On the other hand, dance scholar King-Dorset has pointed out the satirical potential of dance. Enslaved Africans in the Caribbean copied white dances such as the quadrille and subverted them as a statement of resistance; 'mocking, satirizing, "taking-off" the way whites behaved, was particularly appropriate in dance, which obviously lends itself to just this kind of humour'. King-Dorset suggests that social dancing by Black Londoners in the 1830s would have included 'dance steps and movements that came from Africa via the Caribbean' as well as deliberate attempts 'to make fun of the way white people moved to music ... as they, an oppressed minority, asserted a reassuring sense of dance superiority over the majority'.[8] Dance can suggest power and freedom in the face of oppression, as performance scholar Noémie Ndiaye notes. The trickster of the Yoruba tradition is a limping figure who sees more than ordinary mortals, not dissimilar to Folly who is able to speak truth to kings. This kind of resistance is not always obvious to every eye: Tiffany Lethabo King suggests there is 'a kind of life that is beyond transparency, a Black life that does not willingly show or give itself away to any observer and a penetrating gaze'.[9] Laughter creates a wall around those who are the butt of the joke.[10]

Comedy can be a powerful method for small acts of everyday resistance.[11] But it can also bring people together. In Plate XI the motion of Waters' wooden leg is imitated by the small boy in the background: the boy laughs at Waters, but there is fellow feeling and admiration here too. The faces of the audience are kindly. Spectators and performers find communication and connection. Laughter is generated by what we share, not just what makes us different. Waters' performances laughed at race, class, and at the shared human condition of being broken, vulnerable, and imbalanced. His audiences laughed with him.

Frantz Fanon linked Blackness and amputation in a powerful statement of defiance in the face of his experiences of racism in twentieth-century America:

> The crippled veteran of the Pacific war says to my brother, 'Resign yourself to your color the way I got used to my stump; we're both victims.'
>
> Nevertheless with all my strength I refuse to accept that amputation. I feel in my soul as immense as the world, truly a soul as deep as the deepest of rivers, my chest has a power to expand without limit.[12]

Fanon is outraged that his Black skin is seen by a white veteran as a disability (he rejects social inequalities yet cannot align himself with a disabled man), and he refuses to equate a 'stump' as a visual prosthesis for either Blackness or victimhood. This kind of stubborn resilience against overpowering forces and overwhelming odds is demonstrated in *Billy Waters, the London Fiddler*, a popular puppet-show play from the 1850s mentioned in Henry Mayhew's *London Labour and the London Poor* in which 'Billy Waters' gets to be the star of the show instead of a minor character (Figure 30). 'Billy

Waters' describes himself as 'a poor sailor who has lost one of his limbs in defence of his queen and country'. He tells the benevolent Mrs Martin that he has been a sailor 'ever since I was twelve years old. I served eleven years in the coal trade, thirty-five years I was in the merchant service, and for forty-two years I was on board a man-o'-war,' leading her daughter Jemima to exclaim that Billy must be '106 years old'. Undaunted, Billy replies:

> Yes, miss, I've been in fifty-one general engagements besides several hundred small fights: thirteen times I've been ship-wrecked: twice I had to swim across the Atlantic ocean, and lived for three weeks at a time upon flying fish: and three times I've been blown to atoms.

The list of numbers is so extravagant that his various traumas become meaningless. His cartoon-like vulnerability becomes material for laughter. His jaunty songs clash with the repeated abandonment and disregard he suffers:

> (*Enter* BILLY *singing.*)
> I am a jolly beggar
>   And I've got a wooden leg
> Time from my cradle
>   Has forced me to beg
>   So begging I will go
>   So begging I will go.

Time and time again he is batted back by the people from whom he seeks money. However, 'Billy Waters' is '106 years old' because he has survived and endured. His character refuses to die. His very existence is a small yet notable act of defiance. He celebrates the everyday heroism of carrying on.

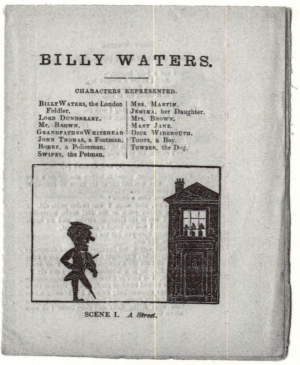

30. *Page from* Billy Waters, the London Fiddler *(c. 1850).*

As Glenda R. Carpio writes, 'Far from being *only* a coping mechanism, or a means of "redress", African American humor has been and continues to be both a bountiful source of creativity and pleasure and an energetic mode of social and political critique.'[13] Waters knew the various ways in which white observers expected him to be comic, and how to delight them. After all he had been through so far in his life, the simple fact of being alive to be amusing was a declaration of skill and of strength. But close attention to representations of his wooden leg also shows the many challenges that he was up against, and how uncertain was his balance. This became only more evident as he began to establish himself in London.

~ FIDDLE ~

In Which Waters Arrives on the Streets

St Giles, London, 1819

It's a faithful friend, this fiddle.

Solid-looking, handsome, even, it's got a slightly worn appearance and a few dents; not unlike its owner, he thinks. But it sings out surprisingly loudly over a noisy crowd, and it has proved a valiant earner.

Again, not unlike its owner.

The Rose and Crown is crowded like it often is, and stuffy with the smell of wood smoke, stale sweat, and cheap gin. Sooner or later someone will call for a tune. He will oblige. He sits in the shadows as close to the fire as he can. For warmth like this, it's worth tolerating the unpredictable company.

At the Theatre Royal Covent Garden, not far from here, the violinists emerge after performances with their violins when they have worked in the safe and dry. The famous Mr Bridgetower, whom people say is the son of an African prince, has a music degree from Cambridge and plays the violin at Hanover Square for the Prince Regent.

All he has are his fiddle and his family. For them, he will always keep dancing.

The Notorious Slum

When Elizabeth Fitzgerald realised that the famous Billy Waters was her new lodger, did she spot an opportunity to help him or to exploit him? 'Widow Fitzgerald' was one of many small-business owners in a part of town packed with cheap lodging houses. Perhaps she didn't notice or care who slept in her properties as long as the rent came in. In the parish of St Giles, home to London's most infamous slum, money was scarce and time and energy were limited.

London was a metropolis of over a million people when Waters arrived: twice the size of Paris.[1] How did Waters live, and how was that life depicted? Exploring Waters' experiences in St Giles parish shows us the significance of his representation as a St Giles beggar. Waters the man turned himself into 'Billy Waters' the street 'character' so he could make money. He performed a jovial version of poverty to reel in paying punters. Focussing on Waters' time in St Giles reveals how people looked at Waters and saw the 'King of the Beggars', but also how Waters played up to this role to create and sustain his street performances and his family's livelihood. However, Waters' performance of precarity also reveals the precariousness of the act of performance itself: the performer never quite knows how their acts will be received. Existing ideas about Regency celebrity culture don't quite fit Waters, as unlike successful white figures such as poet Lord Byron or actor-manager Samuel Foote, Waters did not have the resources to manage his own 'brand' to the same extent as they did, or to benefit properly from its use.[2] Waters and other well-known street people experienced a slightly different version of celebrity. Fame is a many-edged sword, as Waters was about to find out.

Performing in a theatre is clearly different to performing on a pavement or in a public house because they are different venues. Yet St Giles was a place that was understood by anxious policy-makers and reader-hungry journalists in essentially theatrical terms. That is to say, St Giles and its inhabitants were understood through ideas drawn from theatre as far back as Shakespeare's day. In a culture increasingly obsessed by Shakespeare, most literate Londoners would have known that 'all the world's a stage'. But Waters' depiction as Beggar King shows us how the *Life in London* craze took that idea and suggested that if all modern Londoners were somehow performers, then it was the 'beggars' of St Giles who showed them how to be so.

Neighbourhoods matter in people's lives even in large cities, and scholars should pay them serious attention.[3] Astonishingly (given large gaps in records about Waters' life), we know that Waters lived in St Giles by 1823, and we know where: the Rookery. A newspaper and a London periodical both claimed that he 'resided with his family in the house of Mrs Fitzgerald, Church Street, St Giles's'.[4] A parish document from the same year gives his 'abode' as George Street, in the parish of St Giles-in-the-Fields, Middlesex. Church Street and George Street are around the corner from each other, which may account for any confusion. These were well-known streets in the Rookery, London's most notorious slum.

St Giles' High Street, Bainbridge Street, and George Street (now the north end of Dyott Street) edged a tiny, overpopulated area, which contained some of the meanest streets and courts in the metropolis: cheap lodgings, poor tenements, rampant disease, and high crime. An able-bodied pedestrian might walk the perimeter in ten minutes. As desperate immigrants kept arriving, 'flimsy wooden buildings were erected in every available space in courtyards behind the brick-built houses'.[5] Its maze of courts and passageways – shaded out in contemporary maps (Figure 31) – added to its dangerous reputation. Here were some of the most disreputable lodging houses in London, where men, women and children were packed into multi-occupancy rooms. Collectively this slum was known as the Rookery, or the 'Holy Land': not because of a saintly reputation (far from it) but because of its predominantly Irish Catholic population. Many came over to find employment as labourers and stayed to work in the nearby building and brewing industries (in 1814 an accident at one of the St Giles breweries killed eight Rookery dwellers when thousands of gallons of beer escaped, causing a house to collapse). Historically the Rookery was at the end point of three major routes into London.[6] It was the final destination for a steady tide of human hope from around Britain and its colonies.

The Rookery has a complicated history in its descent from an investment property for its wealthy freeholders in the 1600s to the slum it was by the 1820s. Over time the original land holdings were portioned off and parcelled up, and let to various small tenants and subletters. The Fitzgeralds (if they were all related) seem to have controlled quite a bit of the Rookery from around 1810 onwards, with interests in properties in Church Street, Church Lane, Ivy Street, Buckridge Street, and George Street, including the notorious Hand and Crown pub. The parish authorities seem to have been at a loss to keep track of them, as Church Lane and Church Street kept swapping their names on parish maps. No doubt when the parish rates collectors came around, the Fitzgeralds and other landlords were ready, shifting tenants from one house to another to bamboozle the parish officers and generally cause confusion. In an

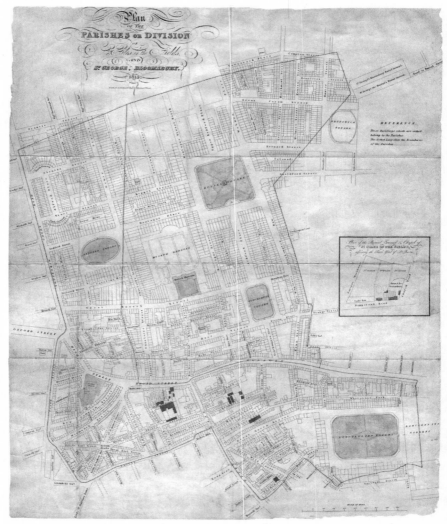

31. *Map of St Giles-in-the-Fields parish (1815).*

area brimming with Irish names (Clancy, Kelly, Kennedy, Sheehan), the Fitzgeralds were probably immigrants like Waters, or at least descended from immigrants. In 1780 there were approximately 20,000 Irish immigrants in London, and the vast majority of these lived in St Giles; more came over in the early 1800s to escape famine.[7] Impoverished Irish migrants shared the bottom of the social hierarchy with poor Black people.

This was not a safe or comfortable place in which to live. Decaying houses, their windows stuffed with rags or patched with paper, stared at each other across the Rookery's narrow streets. Strung across the streets were washing-lines drying ragged clothes. Gutters filled with filth and stagnant water, pavements were strewn with muck and cabbage stalks, house walls bulged with damp. The Fitzgeralds' houses would have been old, dark, unsanitary and freezing cold, although equally 'the sensationally grim accounts of contemporary journalists' obscured the fact that 'many Rookery inhabitants were industrious people, struggling to earn an honest crust in menial occupations'.[8] The landlords of the Rookery had a reputation for doing very nicely off the letting and subletting of their cramped rooms for extortionate rents. One of the cheapest lodging houses was known rather ironically as 'The Kip', given that residents paid to sleep sitting down leaning on a rope that was untied at dawn.[9] Some lodgings were a little more savoury, but only a little. One 1787 writer who claimed to be a lodging-house keeper in St Giles said his rooms contained 'a sump bedstead, a flock bed, a pair of sheets (frequently only one sheet), a blanket or two, a chair or two, (generally without backs) and a grate but mostly without shovel, tongs, and poker'.[10] A watercolour from 1844 suggests some inhabitants might have had a broader range of possessions, but we should distrust its mode of urban picturesque (Figure 32). A local worthy, the Reverend W. Gurney, asserted that one lodging house in the area was 'kept by a Mrs McArthy, a very respectable woman: she would not admit any who drank, and she has a great many who sleep at her house'.[11] Perhaps the Fitzgeralds' establishments were similarly well run. The chances are, however, that they were not.

It's here, in this dangerous and unsanitary slum, that William and Elizabeth Waters arrived by 1823. They had been in London since at least 1819, but where they lived and what they did between 1812 and 1819 we don't yet know. All we know of Waters' wife is that single

32. *John Wykeham Archer*, A Cellar in the Rookery, St Giles's (1844).

name, Elizabeth. We are left with what historians have managed to glean about London's Black population in the early nineteenth century. Statistically speaking, then, Elizabeth Waters was likely to be white. This is because there were far more Black men than Black women in London, because Black men had been more in demand as servants and slaves since the sixteenth century. In addition, Black men were more likely to take jobs as sailors, soldiers, and labourers that enabled migration and travel. It is also possible that Elizabeth was Black or mixed race. Without knowing more about her, Elizabeth is very difficult to track down. Two newspapers claimed in February 1822 that Waters and his wife only cohabited and weren't in fact married, though by Waters' death they must have been as widows required proof of status to collect pension payments.[12] There is another theory that suggests that Waters' wife might have been a woman called Ann Manly, who married a William Waters in St Anne's Soho in April 1822.[13] And what about Mary Waters of Philadelphia, who supported a William Waters' claim to US citizenship? Pension fraud was not impossible, and Waters' landlady Mrs Fitzgerald was called Elizabeth, though you could be hanged for impersonating a sailor's widow.[14] But given that naval records are the most reliable sources of documentation that we have on Waters, and given the Navy's carefulness over matters of money, Elizabeth seems the most plausible name that we currently have for Waters' wife.

When we catch up with Waters in London, life has transformed for him. According to Busby, by 1819 Waters had:

> a wife, and, to use his own words, 'one fine girl, five years old', and is not a little proud to perceive a resemblance in the child to himself: thus we find the same feeling of self-love from the lowest to the highest; and thus humble man, in that respect, prefers himself to the greatest in the nation.

A parent's natural love for their child seems beyond the comprehension – when found in a poor man – of the pompous Busby.[15] An 1823 broadside ballad about Waters invokes 'my little son' and the *Morning Advertiser* states he had 'a wife and two children', so we are looking for a family of about four (relatively small by contemporary standards, so they may well have lost some children in infancy).[16] With a surname as common as Waters, however, they vanish into the archives.[17] A William and Elizabeth Waters ran a butcher's shop in Oxford Street and raised three children, but then fell upon hard times and the father did a brief stint in St Giles Workhouse between 1821 and 1822. This William Waters was around five to ten years older than William 'Billy' Waters, however.[18] What this does show is how common the experience of precarity was amongst ordinary Londoners. If the Waters family of Oxford Street with their own shop fell into hard times, how much greater were the challenges facing the Waters family of the Rookery?

As a Black or mixed-race family, Waters and his wife and children were part of a significant Black London (perhaps 15,000 people out of 1 million, although estimates vary). This had been true for over two centuries: 'by 1596 there were so many Black people in England that Queen Elizabeth I issued an edict demanding that they leave', historian Gretchen Gerzina tells us.[19] As David Olusoga writes, in the Georgian and Regency periods Black Londoners were 'everywhere, scattered across London, and not limited to any district . . . numerous enough to have been a feature of city life but still unusual enough to have remained an exotic novelty, worthy of mention in the accounts of travellers and the reports of journalists' and more likely to be poor than otherwise.[20] In the Rookery Waters would have seen many non-white faces and heard many different dialects and languages spoken. One neighbour was Blind Toby, a well-known Black man from Church Lane who 'walked on two hand-crutches' and bound his head with a white handkerchief.[21] The slave trade was ended in Britain with the 1807 Slave Trade Act, and Lord Mansfield had ruled in 1772 that it was unlawful to ship an enslaved person from England against their will. In 1823 the tentatively named London Society for Mitigating and Gradually Abolishing the State of Slavery first met, in a London pub, and quickly developed into a large network of campaigners.[22] But all of this did not change the fact that Black British families had an ambiguous status in law until the 1833 Slavery Abolition Act.

Mixed-race and Black families in Britain were a matter of comment for caricaturists, dramatists and writers. The impoverished population of London was much more diverse than the wealthy classes, and interracial marriages weren't uncommon. They would still have suffered comments and stares. Some feared the 'contamination' of national bloodlines: George Cruikshank's *New Union Club* (Figure 33) is a particularly nasty example where the mixed-race baby held up by its parents is split down the middle, with one side Black and the other white.[23] In this racist parody of an Abolitionist dinner, which has descended into chaos, the drunken disorder is sped on by the sound of Waters' fiddle. Grinning and grotesque, he (along with several other known figures) is reduced to a distorted caricature, as art historian Temi Odumosu has pointed out.[24] Joseph Johnson's hat bobs in the background. In the bottom right-hand corner, a disabled white sailor is pursued by a Black man with an alarming expression; the print threatens anarchy and even potential cannibalism if slavery is abolished in the West Indies. The radical William Cobbett, convinced of the rights of English working men, in 1804 described relationships between white women and Black men as 'disregard of decency . . . defiance of the dictates of nature', a 'beastly propensity'.[25] The Waters family lived their lives against the backdrop of these kinds of attitudes.

Can we picture the Waters family as part of an organised Black community in London? The phrase 'St Giles's black-birds' appeared in a book entitled *An Essay on Colonisation* (1794) in relation to London's Black population.[26] However, Kathleen Chater argues this was probably the writer using 'a French colloquialism to characterise unscrupulous people living by their wits in St Giles'.

33. George Cruikshank, The New Union Club *(1819).*

Nevertheless, there were so-called 'Black balls', or dances, to which whites were not invited, and in 1787 Joseph Curry, accused of theft, fled into an East Smithfield pub hoping to hide amongst the forty or so Black people within. When twenty-two-year-old 'J. F.' from St Domingo was arrested in Park Lane in 1820 (for no legal cause), 'five other blacks' attempted 'a rescue'. Sometimes white and Black Londoners banded together to beat off authority: in the 1760s magistrate Sir John Fielding complained that Black runaway slaves had the sympathies of the white lower classes on their side.[27] 'It was entirely possible for a black family to exist in domestic harmony and with a sense of community with both white and black friends and neighbours,' Gretchen Gerzina's important scholarship has shown.[28]

Certainly the Waters family were not unique. Black Londoners appear regularly in the Cruikshank brothers' *Life in London* illustrations, where they are mostly low class or servants: a footman, a boxer, an orange-seller, a bandsman. There are notable exceptions; the well-dressed men in the crowds at the Royal Academy (Plate XIII) and the Royal Exchange support David Olusoga's point that 'the key to social acceptance was money'.[29] Class and economic status always determine where you live in London and if you were living by your wits like Waters was forced to do, the St Giles Rookery was one of the places in which you were very likely to find yourself. The Rookery was a world away from the broad avenues of Oxford Street and the Strand that were right on its doorstep. Instead, most nineteenth-century depictions associated St Giles with a poverty experienced and largely created by a disreputable and deliberately non-conforming population. Where he lived played a key part in forming Waters the man and 'Billy Waters' the character.

Waters' St Giles was a real place on the London map, with real streets, real taverns, and real slum housing. Ballad singers and sex workers, street sellers and labourers starved and loved and struggled in its tiny triangle of buildings. But 'St Giles' and its Rookery

I. Waters grew up in an Atlantic world shaped by migration and the slave trade. Robert and George Cruikshank depicted the diversity of an East London public house in their illustrations to Pierce Egan's popular book *Life in London* (1821). New York, Waters' home city, was even more diverse.

II. By 1819 Waters had attracted the attention of artists and caricaturists. This is by T. L. Busby, who was fascinated by the street poor of London and elsewhere. It distorts Waters' features into racist caricaturing.

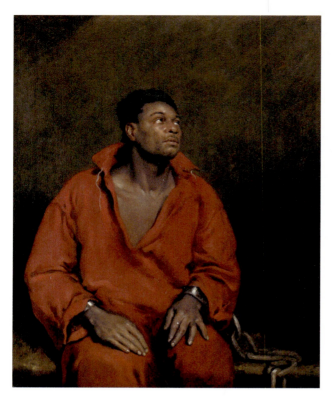

III. John Philip Simpson's 1827 painting *Ira Aldridge (The Captive Slave)* was sat for by Black actor Ira Aldridge and was designed to appeal to white abolitionists. It shows the sentimental mode of depicting Black people in the nineteenth century.

IV. By contrast Édouard Manet's 1863 painting *Portrait of Laure (La Négresse)* depicts Laure as neither caricatured nor sentimentalised, but just another citizen of a modern metropolis.

V. As a young man Waters became a sailor. His musical talents may well have helped him to secure work on board ships. William Hogarth's *c.* 1745 painting *Captain Lord George Graham, in his Cabin* includes a Black sailor-musician who plays a drum to amuse Captain Graham.

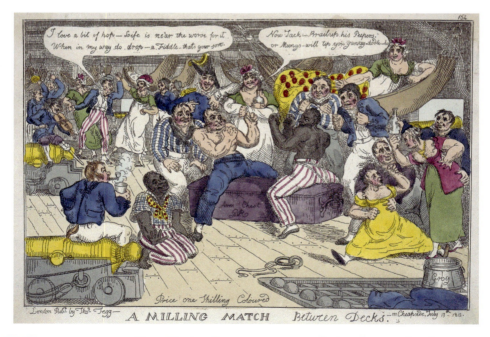

VI. Waters was a petty officer. Black sailors were common during the Napoleonic Wars, as shown in William Elmes' 1812 caricature *A Milling Match between Decks*, published the year Waters left the British Navy.

VII. Disabled soldiers and sailors were sometimes depicted as heroic objects of pity, and sometimes as comic jokes. In a visual joke aimed at disabled bodies and dating from the eighteenth century, here the ex-sailors mistake a provider of heraldic arms as the solution to their impairments.

VIII. By the 1840s veterans were depicted sentimentally in British paintings, although some comic images persisted. This is Andrew Morton's *The United Services* (1845), where children learn patriotic valour from veterans including a Black man.

IX. It wasn't just men who were impacted by the Napoleonic Wars. 'Jack Tar' the sailor had his counterpart 'Portsmouth Poll' the prostitute, celebrated in this image by Thomas Rowlandson (1807).

X. Poll was also the name used for faithful wives and sweethearts of sailors, who were popular subjects for sentimental prints like this one by William S. Leney, *The Sailor's Wife* (1793).

XI. Once he left the British Navy, Waters established himself as a well-known street performer in London: he danced, sang and played the fiddle, wearing a colourful costume as seen here in an 1823 print by S. Alken.

XII. Waters also played in public houses for money. This is an illustration by Robert and George Cruikshank for *Life in London*, which first showed him as one of a group of deceitful beggars, or 'Cadgers'.

XIII. Class and wealth could open up some social opportunities regardless of race in 1820s London, as this Robert and George Cruikshank illustration of a Royal Academy exhibition shows. But nothing like this was open to Waters.

XIV. The Cruikshanks started a trend: soon there were lots of books and pictures celebrating the life of the 'Cadgers'. This image by Robert Cruikshank is an illustration to Charles Westmacott's *The English Spy* (1826).

XV. Waters wasn't the only famous Black Londoner: this 1824 portrait by John Dempsey is of Charles McGee from Jamaica, who became a well-known crossing-sweeper.

XVI. Waters' image was used after his death as part of the fashion for the racist stereotyping of blackface minstrelsy. This is the frontispiece to W. H. Montgomery's *Negro Melody Quadrilles* (*c.* 1850–80), which is sheet music of minstrelsy classics. But Waters also left an important legacy for Black performers.

(the two became synonymous despite St Giles parish containing nicer streets and being bordered by well-off areas) was also a highly fictionalised place created through an amazing outpouring of ballads, plays, caricatures and cheap print. In following Waters into his neighbourhood we therefore have to be careful to distinguish representation from reality. Rosemarie Garland-Thomson, in her groundbreaking book on disability, *Extraordinary Bodies*, defines representation as 'a cultural interpretation' of actual people, places, and events (such as the bodies of St Giles' inhabitants, and the streets in which they lived their lives). For Garland-Thomson, an understanding of representation is vital because, she argues, the ways in which we represent people and ideas tend to create the ways in which we think about those people and ideas.[30] This has huge significance for the texts that we read and the images that we consume. Most nineteenth-century writers and artists who depicted St Giles had little or no personal experience of the world as endured by the people they represented, and so under their hands St Giles and its 'beggars' became stand-ins for a carnivalesque kind of poverty, often in tandem with physical disability. They were flattened out into a one-dimensional idea of poverty, when (like any of us) they were multifaceted people in a complex place. Ideas about St Giles relied on its difference, its 'otherness', from the lives and bodies of the imagined reader. Disability was one shorthand for this difference. St Giles became a spectacle created though pictures and descriptions. This spectacle was one of dangerous depravity or excitingly attractive outlaws, depending on your perspective. Representation created the ideas about St Giles that circulated around Regency popular culture.

This is not to say that St Giles' reputation as a 'one of the most disreputable districts in London' was undeserved.[31] But it was developed and passed from text to text by several generations of writers and artists. Critics have speculated that it was the setting (across almost exactly 100 years) for representations as diverse as

Hogarth's print *Gin Lane* (1751) and the slum 'Tom All-Alone's' in Dickens' *Bleak House* (1851–2). A Mr John Parton, Vestry Clerk, described the Rookery in 1822 in words that exemplify many of the ideas about it which filled accounts of the place:

> Dirt, and an appearance of extreme indigence, are the characteristics of the whole of this quarter. The streets are narrow; and the houses, for the most part old and ruinous, present, with the squalid looks of the inhabitants, a picture of wretchedness scarcely to be equaled in any other part of the metropolis. Much of this misery, however, it must be confessed, is rather apparent than real. The mode of living followed by the people who dwell here is such that they prefer, and arises more from choice than necessity; drink and profligacy consume what would in many instances supply the decent necessaries of life; and though the very centre of mendicity, perhaps more money is expended wastefully in it, than serves to maintain the inhabitants of far more respectable neighbourhoods.[32]

Parton conflates the 'narrow' streets and 'ruinous' houses with the 'squalid' inhabitants: all are characterised by 'Dirt'. As Mary Douglas writes in her seminal study of how society treats those it considers 'abnormal' in some way, dirt is 'matter out of place'.[33] The poor of the Rookery and their locality for Parton are also 'out of place' in modern London, an unsightly blot on the metropolis.[34] Parton reproduces another key (and very old) trope of these kinds of descriptions that we see again and again in relation to Waters: that of the 'fake' beggar.[35] Parton assumes that St Giles' residents are beggars, not workers. Their lives of mendicity (or begging) are 'more from choice than necessity', and they could live like so-called 'decent' and 'respectable' people, Parton claims, if only they chose to do so. Living in St Giles, Waters was already at risk of being labelled lazy, dirty, and disreputable in the eyes of those who ran the city.

This kind of language echoes down the decades as later writers look at, and look back at, the Rookery. In the 1830s Dickens described the people of the area in *Sketches by Boz* as 'dirty men, filthy women, squalid children'; again, the taint of poverty and the suggestion of tainted morals are interlinked in Dickens' choice of words. By the 1840s the tropes about St Giles were so well established that Douglas Jerrold could use it as a shorthand for poverty and cunning in his novel *St Giles and St James*. A broadside ballad called *St James's and St Giles's* (one of several nineteenth-century ballads structured around the contrast between rich and poor) does a similar thing, and its use of contrasts in fact minimises the deprivations of real poverty.[36] Looking back from the vantage point of the 1860s, writer John Timbs calls the Rookery 'one great mass, as if the houses had originally been one block of stone, eaten by slugs into numberless small chambers and connecting passages. The lanes were thronged with loiterers; and stagnant gutters, and piles of garbage and filth infested the air.'[37] With this language of stagnation and decay, Timbs implies that the St Giles Rookery and its inhabitants are a kind of contamination which threatens to obstruct London's development into a shiny modern metropolis.[38] The existence of the Rookery persisted in popular culture long after much of it was torn down in the 1840s to make way for New Oxford Street.[39] Charles Dickens exclaimed of St Giles: 'what wild visions of . . . want and beggary arose in my mind out of that place!'[40] St Giles remains somehow stubbornly pre-modern in these accounts, which makes it both dangerous and dangerously attractive. It provided writers, artists and audiences with an example of a supposedly freer, unregulated, pre-modern lifestyle that increasing regulation and legislation was busily sweeping away (some felt) to London's disadvantage. Ideas about St Giles as a place seeped into ideas about Waters as a person.

This makes it challenging to reconstruct Waters' life there. For instance, in 1832 the popular comic artist Robert Seymour produced

34. Robert Seymour, Beggars Beginning the Day (1832).

Beggars Beginning the Day (Figure 34), which gives us more possibilities for what Waters' Rookery lodgings might have looked like. The beggars are getting ready for 'work' in their windowless garret room, which appears to have been shared overnight by six adults, two adolescents, a baby and two cats. There is barely any furniture, and few comforts apart from the sparse provisions on the table. The beggars themselves are preparing to cheat the unwary: one exclaims (using the 'cockney' v), 'Vy Jim you've forgot to tie up your leg.' But we should be cautious, as this is also a highly theatrical image with ideas drawn from the stage. Social historian Joseph Harley has shown that even people classed as 'paupers' (receiving financial aid from their parish) owned basic furniture and sometimes even a clock, picture, or teapot.[41]

Dickens' immersion in popular culture throughout his life conditioned him to read the Rookery through the kind of melodramatic language that seeped out from the theatre and into printed texts. In melodrama, disability scholar Martha Stoddard Holmes has shown, bodies and their differences were used as shorthand for plotting and characterisation.[42] Disabled bodies in particular were used to evoke pity – or to suggest villainy. Surface appearances were understood to correspond to inner character, in a kind of stagey shortcut. St Giles Rookery was a notorious slum, there is no doubt about that. Its inhabitants were real people with documented lives. But it was also a place that was understood by anxious policy-makers and reader-hungry journalists in essentially theatrical terms. In other words, St Giles both created, and was understood through, melodramatic tropes taken from popular theatre. Its inhabitants were also understood in theatrical terms, as performers.

This affected Waters because these tropes linked economic precarity to a certain idea of character: one that (unlike the realist novel) saw individuality as one big performance. 'Characters' with a large 'C' in accounts of St Giles do not have deep interior lives but are presented as all surface, whose readable bodies define in clear terms who and what they are, and where they fit in society. Though the capitalisation of nouns was still common in the Regency period, the notion of 'Characters' draws upon a tradition in comic writing dating from Theophrastus' influential sketches of various types of individuals to be met with on the streets of ancient Athens.[43] At the same time these Characters are constantly performing and constantly adaptable to the purposes of whoever decides to describe them, depict them or act them out on stage. They are used to suggest that in the city no social identities are fixed, and that urbanites spend all day long performing. Scholars Lisa Freeman – writing about Georgian theatre – and Rachel Teukolsky – writing about Victorian caricature – see this trend as a riposte to the more rounded characters being developed in the realist novel. The 'beggars' of St Giles as they were depicted on the page and on the stage provide the missing link for this version of character in the Regency period. They were an alternative model of what it meant to be an individual from the intricately imagined creations who were beginning to populate novels. In the process they seemed to provide middle-class viewers with an alternative vision of society to the supposedly orderly modern world.[44] In some ways it did not matter to these viewers if Waters became an actual performer on London's streets. As he was a destitute inhabitant of St Giles Rookery, many middle-class observers would have already thought of him as performing poverty to win their charitable contributions.

When did Waters and Elizabeth first arrive in the Rookery? What happened to them between 1812 and 1823? The Rookery was the last desperate refuge of the destitute. Had the Waters family always lived within its miserable confines? Had things once seemed better and brighter? When Waters began his career as a street performer, he may not have thought it would lead to the Rookery.

Public Enemy No. 1

Street performing was an obvious option for a man with no theatre connections yet with performing abilities, but it was also risky. It was an exposed, and exposing, profession. You were battered by the weather and threatened by competitors, thieves, and lads out for a 'spree' at your expense. Punters might see you not as a person, but as a Character. You could easily be mistaken for, or designated as, a beggar. But it did offer the hope of intense connection with an audience, public recognition, and a steady stream of cash. Elizabeth would have contributed to the family budget when she could, using what scholars have called 'the economy of make-shifts', the getting-by in any way one found (one St Giles resident explained at his trial that 'my wife and I went out to sell some cabbage nets, and white rags'),[1] but by 1814 she was pregnant with their daughter. What they needed was more money, and as his disability changed or limited his options of labour or service, Waters' fiddle was a risky but plausible option. The first images of Waters in his costume appear in 1819, so at some point then or before then Waters joined the numerous 'pauper professionals' (as historian Tim Hitchcock calls them) who took to the streets of the metropolis daily to beg, scratch, steal, or perform for a living.[2]

Did street performing frighten Waters at first? Was it a blow to his self-esteem? John Bezer, an unemployed shoemaker in 1848 with a family to feed, took up street singing in desperation but his first attempts stuck in his throat and left him 'almost choking'.[3] Yet Bezer was no professional; he realised his singing was merely a cover for begging. Waters, by contrast, could not have played, sung, and danced (with a prosthesis) simultaneously unless he was an experienced fiddler.[4] Waters was said to call his occupation 'an honest living by the scraping of cat-gut' (so-called cat-gut, taken from cow intestines in slaughterhouses, was used to make fiddle strings).[5] We might now call Waters a busker, although the term had not then acquired its modern meaning.[6] Distinctions between beggars and the professionals who used the streets of Regency London by choice or necessity as their place of business – street sellers of food and goods, ballad singers, acrobats, and musicians – were not firmly defined, which allowed people to deny Waters his professional status. This is why so many nineteenth-century commentators obsessed about whether Waters and others had a pension or other means of support. Why shouldn't Waters decide to use his musical talents for commercial gain? This only becomes an issue if you see such activity as begging, not performing.

Where did Waters perform? Plate XI gives us a clue: this 1823 print positions us at Charing Cross by the equestrian statue of Charles I. It's a great spot: behind us is the western end of the Strand, and ahead is the start of Pall Mall, so there's a great deal of foot traffic. It's also an open space, so he has managed to build a substantial crowd around him. More significantly still, this statue is used to define and measure the central point of London (it's next to what became Trafalgar Square, eventually presided over by another amputee sailor, Admiral Nelson). To perform here is the ultimate declaration of ownership of the city. He's enticed all kinds of people to stop: well-dressed and ragged children, a fashionable couple, a man with a billboard taking advantage of Waters' crowd to publicise his own wares. Even the street traders have paused, sensing an opportunity as punters gather. Someone else has seized the moment: a pickpocket takes advantage of the congestion and distraction to filch a handkerchief from an unwary pedestrian.

Waters likely varied his pitch to not weary a crowd: he was 'Well-known throughout the Town!' He supported 'himself, and those dependent on him, by Fiddling, Dancing, and Singing, through all parts of the metropolis', said Busby, 'by which he originally amassed a considerable portion of browns (half-pence) at the West end of the town'. Charing Cross, the Strand, and Oxford Street were all very close to St Giles. *Punch* remembered him in Westminster, and he could have ventured as far as Piccadilly or some of the side streets if the pavement surface and his wooden limb did not prevent him. Newspaper reports suggest Waters performed in Orange Street (behind what is now the National Gallery) and Red Lion Street. Several booming theatres drew crowds that were potential audiences for Waters: Drury Lane Theatre, Theatre Royal Covent Garden, the Adelphi, the Lyceum, the Coburg across Waterloo Bridge on the Surrey side of the Thames, the Minor Theatre in Catherine Street, Strand, and the concerts at the Crown and Anchor Tavern on the Strand. Waters probably had a regular pitch outside the Adelphi Theatre on the Strand, between Trafalgar Square and Fleet Street: Moncrieff places him there. Then, as now, this built a reputation and a relationship with regular tippers, though he judged the balance between being a familiar face and not too over-exposed. There is some evidence that he may also have performed (or at least been imitated) at Vauxhall Pleasure Gardens, though no evidence that he performed at any of London's seasonal fairs.[7] Certainly the part of London we now call the West End (the space between Bond Street, Oxford Street, Drury Lane, and the Strand) is the place with which he was most closely associated. There was no point venturing east into the City of London: their vagrancy laws were much stricter.

Negotiating crowded streets on his prosthetic leg, Waters headed out to earn money for his family. Emerging onto the Strand or Oxford Street, Waters arrived in a world of tempting emporia, inviting print shops, busy coffee houses, and bustling theatres. The principal streets of Westminster were 'wide, and well paved in the middle, with a broad foot-way of flags, raised above the carriage-way for the safety and accommodation of passengers', and therefore offered an ideal stage for the enterprising performer.[8] But they were also noisy: cart wheels, carriage wheels, newspaper boys ('Terrible Murder at Limehouse!'), street vendors ('Buy My Lavender!', 'Watercresses!', 'Knives to Grind!'), and ballad singers who, unlike Waters, sang their songs as a way of selling the printed sheets they held and teaching the buyer how the ballad went. This is where the high pitch of the violin came into its own, as it cut across the busy hubbub. We should picture Waters choosing his spot with care: a corner of a street, maybe, so he is visible in more than one direction; against a doorway or a wall as a makeshift back-drop; raised on steps as an impromptu stage. Where could he form and hold a crowd? Was a main street the best? Or somewhere a little less congested, where passers-by dawdled rather than raced to work? He needed somewhere flat to dance, don't forget. He performed with constant companions: phantom pain from his amputated limb, and real pain from his stump. Sawn bone is not designed to be load-bearing. Any kind surface was welcome. Determination kept him going.

How did Waters play? The violin itself was a very different instrument from the one we know today, music historian Paul Roberts says, 'its neck shorter and angled differently, the bass bar lighter, the soundpost thinner, the bridge flatter', and no chin rest.[9] The bow was also shorter and did not curve like modern bows. Thanks to Roberts' work we can imagine Waters placing his fiddle low against his shoulder, and he gripped it with his left hand rather than his chin as it sloped downwards. Waters did not write music (that we know of) but played crowd favourites: not just 'Polly Will You Marry Me' but tunes like 'Sprig of Shillelagh' and maybe even 'Yankee Doodle' (an American figure who wore a feather in his hat).[10] He varied his choices depending on who stopped to listen, and who moved on. It's a repertoire of basic jigs, reels, and hornpipes, but 'with a much greater variety of rhythms and time signatures than today'. This is a fiddle technique that cuts across national boundaries: 'with his shuffle bowing, cross-tunings and preference for drones, he must have sounded very like an old-style fiddler from Kentucky or Virginia – with his use of baroque gracing and decoration he must also have sounded like the more elaborate of the western Irish players'.[11] Once again we see the influence of the wider Atlantic world on Waters' performances.

There were many reasons why a spot outside one of the theatres like the Adelphi was a prime location for a busker. For a start, theatres provided a regular foot traffic of punters who had left their homes specifically to be entertained. The Adelphi's usual bill of fare was melodramas with names like *The Red Robber* and *The Amazon Queen*, and musical farces, but also rope dancers, pantomimes, monkeys, and 'wonderful dwarfs'. In October 1819 the theatre (opened in 1806 as the SansPareil) reopened as the Adelphi after extensive refurbishment with its new name, a new company, and new owners – Messrs Jones and Rodwell. There were gloriously refurbished public areas and the astonishing innovation of gas lighting (the first theatre to try this invention). The repertoire now included adaptations of popular novels alongside the melodramas. The Adelphi was turning into a thoroughly modern theatre, but still much cheaper than the Theatres Royal at Drury Lane, Haymarket, and Covent Garden as a night out for non-elite audiences.[12] Theatricals at the Adelphi started at 6.30 p.m. and ran all evening, with half-price entry at 8.30 if you only came for the 'afterpieces' or comic additions to the main show. A box cost 4 shillings, and the Pit – which held 800 people – was 2 shillings, but the cheapest seats in the gallery (which held about 300 people) were only 1 shilling, and servants sometimes accompanied their middle-class mistresses and masters so got to enjoy performances from up in the 'gods'.[13] Waters, therefore, had three shots at attracting a paying audience: between 5.30 p.m. and 6.30 p.m. when most theatres opened, around 8.30 when half-price entry began, and at the end of the night when theatregoers emerged and wanted to prolong their entertainment. Of course, unlike the actors inside the theatres, Waters' earnings depended on how the weather governed people's behaviour. Between 1794 and 1820 was a period of bitter winters and a little ice age with deep snows, hard frosts, and 'frost fairs' on the Thames; 1816 was the year 'without summer', after the eruption of Indonesia's Mount Tambora sent an ash cloud around the globe.[14] Waters was vulnerable to sun, wind, and rain. But during the theatre

35. *The Adelphi Theatre.*

season of October to July, which followed the rhythms of wealthy and fashionable London, he was sure of an audience.

The stories associating Waters with the Adelphi link Waters to the kinds of popular entertainments found on its stage. But they also contrast his status as a lone itinerant performer with the dawning emergence of the powerhouse that would become the theatrical West End. At the start of his performance career, the developing West End was a plus for Waters. This part of town wasn't only Waters' performance space, it was a space where all Londoners and visitors could see and be seen. The poet and essayist Charles Lamb confessed that 'I often shed tears in the motley Strand, for fulness of joy at such multitude of life'.[15] As one 1820 guidebook put it, in the West End 'the pleased rambler views alternately numerous warehouses stored with valuable merchandise, and shops overflowing with the most choice and elegant, as well as useful, productions of nature and art'.[16] In print-shop windows the latest prints, illustrations, and caricatures caught the attention of passers-by (satirised in innumerable caricatures which then in turn made the activity of 'reading' shop windows more fashionable). In its theatres, productions that responded to this illustrated material and provided inspiration for it were showing nightly. In its coffee-houses and taverns, people met to dissect the latest hit play or caricature; they browsed theatrical memorabilia in the Lowther Arcade and visited the numerous bookshops. From the Royal Academy galleries at Somerset House to Wigley's Promenade Rooms near Charing Cross (displaying, among other delights, a newly invented 'Travelling Automata', capable of speeds of up to 6 miles per hour), the emerging West End was a place of visual spectacle. At the Museum of Living Animals housed at Exeter 'Change on the Strand, you could see (for half a crown) 'an ourang outang from China', 'the laughing hyena', and 'an enormous elephant'. Alternatively, Barker's Panorama promised to challenge your curiosity with 'a succession of views of scenes in nature or art, or subjects of history', all painted onto a vast canvas like an early cinema experience.[17] In short, spectacle, display, and the art of seeing and being seen were built into the very bricks of London's buildings and the stones of its carriageways. Waters made use of that.

Before long, Waters' act caught the eye of a curious artist. Thomas Busby was a painter, engraver, and illustrator who lived in what is now Fitzrovia in the heart of London's early nineteenth-century artists' quarter. Busby was a man fascinated by costume: he also produced *Civil and Military Costume of the City of London* and *The Fishing Costume and Local Scenery of Hartlepool*. These were beautifully produced books destined for the well-to-do collector; it wasn't only caricatures that shaped responses to street people. Waters features as the first image in Thomas Busby's *Costume of the Lower Orders* (Plate II), and his inclusion shows that Busby recognised the potential cross-class reach of Waters' appeal. The key elements of his act are all present: sailor's jacket, fiddle, and wooden leg raised as if dancing to his own music. Out of twenty-two images in the book, Waters is one of only three named people; he's there because he is a specific metropolitan spectacle as well as a generic example of lower-class street culture, his features distorted to fit the racist template that contemporary caricature had developed.[18] Busby reissued images from the book as prints (Figure 29), a common practice at the time, making Waters' image available to purchasers who could not afford the full volume but could manage the price of a single-sheet print. Busby's book and the illustrations within it were designed to capitalise on the fascination with so-called 'Cries of London' (or the dress and songs and habits of street sellers and street performers in the metropolis). Images that depicted these people, often animated by text which recorded their activities and their trades, are called 'Cries', and this genre circulated around many different European capital cities from the 1500s onwards, eventually being copied in North America in the 1800s. As historian Sean Shesgreen explains, 'Spelled with a capital "C" ... the metaphorical term "Cries" identifies the storied images that represent sounds silently, sounds and voices that, in life, were common, vulgar, transgressive, even threatening, socially and politically."[19] Waters' representation here is similar to that of other lower-class Black Londoners in the 'Cries' genre, such as Joseph Johnson and the crossing-sweeper Charles McGee (more of McGee later). Both of these men were depicted in John Thomas Smith's book *Vagabondiana* (1817). The 'Cries' genre turned the lower classes into a spectacle that was safe for the implied white middle-class consumer – because it was silent. Busby's pictures aestheticise street people. We're held at a distance from engaging with Waters on any deep emotional level. He's a Character, only.

But this image of Waters is not just trying to present him as a spectacle. The 'Cries' genre also claimed to offer a reading experience that was both an authentic depiction of known Londoners, and an authentication of the reader's own London experiences of street life and street people. Authenticity carried the meaning of being 'true to life', although it was also an ambiguous concept in a literary culture where popular characters could be lifted from one context into another with no legal reasons not to. It was a power move, which suggested a privileged viewer who could pronounce judgment on what was authentic and what was not. Busby's introduction claims that of all the many books about 'London Cries', his collection is 'unusually interesting', because it is unusually authentic: we're told that these coloured images are 'drawn from known individuals', while the works of Busby's competitors are 'too often sketched from memory' (iii). On one level, Busby's pictures are intended as authentic representations of London street life. At the same time, posed like theatrical prints and turned picturesque, these street poor are set apart to be looked at and to demonstrate that the metropolis is a place of spectacle where every public act is also understood as a performance. This tension between theatricality and authenticity became attached to Waters as his image began to circulate, meme-like, around visual culture.[20]

Theatricality as a concept is an aspect of performance. Used as a specific term by Thomas Carlyle in 1837 for a set of ideas that had been circulating for centuries, theatricality is defined by the reactions of the spectator, whether that spectator is a passer-by in the street or seated in a theatre.[21] When the spectator is allowed to take up a position of critical distance from the performer instead of encouraged to feel absorbed sympathy, this creates a sense of theatricality. Busby invites the reader to enjoy these images at several removes from them as people (just like descriptions of King Charles encouraged the reader to see only the 'jubilee' and not the realities of enslavement that contextualise the Pinkster festival).[22] Instead, Busby's text emphasises their theatricality, especially when he gets down to describing 'Billy Waters, the Dancing Fiddler':

> THIS eccentric man was born in America, and lost his leg [at sea] . . . being rendered incapable of serving England, he supports himself, and those dependent on him, by Fiddling, Dancing, and Singing, through all parts of the metropolis; affording a lesson to the thoughtful, and no little amusement to the thoughtless. Billy is remarkable for good humour and industry, for the feathers in his hat, the grin of his countenance, and the sudden turn and kick out of his wooden limb, and his efforts to please are well rewarded from the pockets of John Bull.[23]

The Waters described here is an 'eccentric' representative of carnivalesque fun. Like St Giles itself, he is both real and not real. Furthermore, in Busby's version of Waters, he is drawn on his own, picked out from the crowd rather than shown as part of a busy street scene.[24] Isolated and silenced, his energies are contained so as not to trouble the implied reader. Waters' most obvious counterpart in the book – the one-armed American fiddler originally from Providence, Rhode Island, who lost his limb in the 1807 naval battle at Dardanelles – is the only one shown with a street scene behind him (Figure 36), but its lack of colouring separates the fiddler from this stagey backdrop. As Marcus Wood points out, pity can become exploitative when it asks the spectator to dwell on the sufferer's body as their own 'aesthetic property'.[25] A loud and mighty klaxon should go off in our heads when we realise that it was Thomas Carlyle – author of the racist pamphlet *An Occasional Discourse upon the Negro Question*, first published in 1849 – who first defined 'theatricality'. This fact shows how troubling theatricality is as a way of representing Black bodies. Yet images of Waters largely ignored questions of personal ethical responsibility towards others.

Waters was becoming well known by 1819; but like all performers he still faced stiff competition, and not just from the 'Mechanical Fiddler'. In this post-war period of demobilisation, dislocation, urbanisation, and competition from cheaper foreign markets, hardship and destitution meant street sellers and street performers were everywhere visible. A restive population of low-skilled, politically disenfranchised, desperate people – who had seen none of the gains from industrialisation and all of the losses – flocked to London.[26] Busby noted that 'Itinerant musicians are numerous in London; particularly so, from November to June. They may be seen in groups of two, three, four, and five persons, enlivening the town, and impressing their hearers, very often, with regret that

36. *The 'Mechanical Fiddler'* (1819).

they are not better employed.'[27] To distinguish himself from the many other demands upon people's attention Waters had to rely on what Tim Hitchcock has rather poetically called 'the rhetoric of rags', or the verbal and visual strategies of self-presentation used to draw a sympathetic (and ultimately paying) audience. Charles Lamb, in an essay on defence of beggars, described it thus:

> When a poor creature (outwardly and visibly) comes before thee, do not stay to inquire whether the 'seven small children', in whose name he implores they assistance, have veritable existence. Rake not into the bowels of unwelcome truth, to save a halfpenny. It is good to believe him ... When they come with their counterfeit looks, and mumping tones, think them players. You pay your money to see a comedian feign these things, which, concerning these poor people, thou canst not certainly tell whether they are feigned or not.[28]

We might recognise this kind of language today, which suggests that all street performers must in fact be beggars, and feigning 'Characters', too. It frames the poor as entertainment. Passers-by expected disabled beggars to perform disability in obvious ways to demonstrate their claim to assistance, but that very performance could then be read as suspicious evidence of cunning fakeness, as disability scholars Tobin Siebers and Lindsey Row-Heyveld point out.[29] The tension between St Giles as a real and as an imagined space spilled out onto the real streets where Waters and others had to earn a living.

This meant that not everyone saw the distinction between a street performer and a beggar; far from it. As James Hepburn points out in his study of nineteenth-century broadside ballads, surviving ballads celebrated 'considerable numbers of both unworthy and worthy beggars', with many references to 'cadging' and descriptions of 'dodges employed by beggars to incite pity'.[30] This wasn't new: Row-Heyveld has shown that since the 1500s popular culture celebrated and fretted about potentially counterfeit beggars.[31] But the sheer numbers of the visibly destitute on the streets of the metropolis and other major towns and cities in the Regency period made the governing classes twitchy. Fears that 'the low' might take over the streets were expressed in prints and caricatures like William Heath's *Butter Cups & Daisies*, which featured Waters and his fiddle as well as Andrew Whiston (Figure 37). Still, Waters told a magistrate in 1821 that he earned 2–3 shillings a day on the streets, perhaps more as he downplayed his pension to only £14.[32] He was as good a breadwinner for Elizabeth and his daughter as any skilled tradesman. Before 1821 the family was relatively comfortable. They were far from wealthy, of course, but they didn't need to lodge in the Rookery.

But trouble was brewing for them. Four years after Waters left the Navy, a Parliamentary Select Committee published its 1816 report on 'Mendicity in the Metropolis'. This Committee had a brief to investigate the extent of begging in London, and suggest solutions to what was now perceived as a growing problem. Over several months between 1815 and 1816 the Committee listened to testimony from clergy, magistrates, police, poor law officials, employers, and philanthropists. Their final report concluded that there was indeed a much higher number of beggars than before or even during the

37. *William Heath,* Butter Cups & Daisies a sketch from Low-Life (1822).

Napoleonic Wars. Furthermore, many of these were *professional* beggars, inflicting 'gross and monstrous frauds' on the unsuspecting public, when they were in fact able to earn more from mendicity than 'the sober and most industrious artisans and labourers' could from an honest day's work. Even worse, these deceitful professionals were training their children in this criminal culture, and the existing poor law and policing officials were failing to get a grip of the situation. The evidence was considerably more nuanced than these conclusions suggested: several witnesses presented conflicting testimony. But a narrative was emerging, in which all street workers were simply beggars performing a particular kind of character for economic gain.[33]

This narrative circulated through print and visual images and was both reinforced and challenged as it went. It filled the newspapers and magazines as the press reprinted long sections from the report, complete with witness statements testifying to the deceitfulness of London beggars. The *Quarterly Review* reprinted minutes from the Committee in October 1815 which drew no distinction between those 'who subsist by begging and plunder', who 'fake blindness' and other disabilities, and those who 'hire instruments of music, and go about in parties'. Presumably the latter group performed together as a band; yet they are in the same paragraph as those described as 'imposters and blasphemers'. None of this groundswell of middle-class anxiety was good for Waters. Samuel Roberts, watch-house keeper of St Giles' and St George's, Bloomsbury, was 'quite positive that many of these beggars are in a much better situation than many of the working people', and he claimed he saw them faking disability 'with an arm and a leg tied up, and so on'. Roberts testified that 'they will cook a turkey and put sausages round it, and call it *an alderman in chains*', and he had seen 'a little black man' with silver and copper in bags who had the cheek to request help when he was robbed of his takings, and heard the man spent 50 shillings a week at public houses in St Giles.

Another local called John Furzman agreed, saying that he'd seen this man order beer and gin like there was no tomorrow, and been told stories that a pub landlord looked after £10 of his money while he was out 'begging'.[34] Moncrieff thought they described Waters.[35] Suddenly, in an authoritative parliamentary publication, were stories that those soliciting money on the streets were living very well indeed, and were even fabulously rich: Joseph Butterworth Esq. said 'that the visitors of the "Stranger's Friend Society" well know a negro beggar, . . . who has retired to the West Indies with a fortune, it is supposed, of about £1,500 obtained by begging'.[36] The confident opening of Butterworth's testimony is somewhat undermined by that significant word 'supposed', which sneaks in towards the end. The whole thing reads more like the plot of a melodrama than a piece of factual evidence (though there was a story behind it: of which, more later). Yet potential members of Waters' paying audience read this and had their opinions coloured by it.

Things were about to get a whole lot worse. This language had political significance: the 1816 report of the House of Commons Select Committee into begging in London declared that 'Out of 400 beggars in St Giles, 350 are capable of earning their living.'[37] In response to the Select Committee report, a charity called the Society for the Suppression of Mendicity (also known as the London Mendicity Society) was founded by William Bodkin in 1818 along with a group of 'gentleman volunteers' with social concerns and professional ambitions. Its declared aim was to reduce the 'evil' of begging by organising financial and practical help – but with conditions. The charity operated a system of tickets, which members of the public could give to beggars instead of money, and could be redeemed at the Mendicity Society headquarters. They kept registers of persistent 'Beggars and Imposters' (clearly considered synonymous), and prosecuted repeat 'offenders'. They established offices in Red Lion Square, right in Waters' territory.[38] A satirical 'Ode' to Bodkin in the periodical the *Mirror* noted that while Bodkin pretended to be a friend to the poor he was in fact 'paid to "run them through"' (a play on the Shakespearean meaning of bodkin as a dagger).[39]

The distinction between busking and begging was of little interest to the Mendicity Society; on 13 December 1821 Waters was arrested twice on the same day for 'begging and collecting crowds in the street' and 'singing immodest songs'.[40] They refused to recognise him as a professional performer. The Mendicity Society nabbed him first in Orange Street, but he managed to talk his way out of trouble with a promise to mend his ways. He then promptly carried on, sticking two fingers up to authority. He refused to fear them, like he'd refused to fear so much else. The outcome is unclear, but it couldn't have been good. Attitudes hardened as the century progressed: an 1843 article on 'The Music of the Streets' slid easily from a description of Waters to the now well-worn trope of the wealthy beggar:

> Billy Waters, of cocked-hat and wooden-legged memory, died, it was said, a man of substance ... Numerous instances may be adduced of beggars accumulating fortunes. Lately, the newspapers reported that James Lowell, the (to Londoners) well-known gipsy tinker, retired from the world the possessor of £700 in copper, gold, and silver, including a considerable heap of farthings.[41]

In 1850 Henry Mayhew classified street performers as 'showmen, or those who exhibit or perform something in the street' and therefore part of the class of 'those that *will* work' as opposed to 'professional beggars' or 'those that *will not* work'.[42] But during the first part of the nineteenth century this distinction was rarely maintained. Street performers were just beggars with an instrument, and all beggars were Characters with bodies waiting to be taken over by the middle-class do-gooder – or the middle-class artist and writer. This version of character provided by stage and images was beginning to have real impacts upon how people viewed Waters and other vulnerable Londoners. It created a particular kind of fictionalised celebrity for Waters. His dance was becoming even more precarious.

The Beggar's Opera

For those who never visited London but first encountered Waters in images or on the printed page, the place he was most closely associated with was not only the streets but also the public house; and it wasn't among his family but among a rowdy set of drinking companions. Sometimes he's got African Sal and her partner the Dustman there with him, sometimes he doesn't (this is despite the fact that in *Life in London* African Sal lives in East London). Waters, to these readers, was to be found amongst the roistering social scene of St Giles low life. It wasn't only on the streets that Waters began to be viewed as a fictionalised Character instead of a vulnerable individual. It happened in prose writing as well. This linked Waters to another meme-like figure in popular culture whose meanings have not been properly explored: the King of the Beggars. It shows us another way in which people looked at Waters, and the effects of this on him and his family.

According to contemporary sources, Waters was not just any beggar, but the King of the Beggars. Moncrieff declares that:

In the year 1812 Billy was solemnly inaugurated *ex cathedra* into the sovereignty of mendicityship – King of the Beggars – at the cellar of St Patrick in St Giles', a rank he supported with great satisfaction and majesty.[1]

The idea that Waters was the Beggar King circulated during Waters' lifetime, too, and several contemporary sources call the pub he supposedly frequented 'The Beggar's Opera'. The name 'Beggar's Opera' was of course a sly nod to John Gay's satirical ballad opera of the same name from 1728, which poked fun at aristocratic society and Italian opera via its cast of anti-heroes, thieves, and prostitutes (it made instant stars of its leads and spawned a memorabilia industry all of its own). The name is another example of the ways in which St Giles and its inhabitants were understood as fundamentally theatrical as well as objectively real.

Was Waters really always to be found in a public house? Like many professional entertainers and with a family to support, he played in the evenings around St Giles for money, earning 2–3 shillings a night or more on top of his daytime earnings.[2] Whether it was true or not that Waters was a late-night roisterer was not really what Regency and early Victorian popular culture concerned itself with. Instead, images and descriptions of Waters in public houses turned them into another performance space, like the street or the theatre, which writers wrote about, worried about, and fantasised about. The 'Beggar's Opera' was a stage onto which writers projected a theatrical understanding of what a Character might be.

To call Waters the 'King of the Beggars' evoked as many associations for Regency and Victorian readers as calling him 'Robin Hood' might now. The Beggar King was probably most well known in this period from the hugely popular bestseller *The Life and Adventures of Bampfylde Moore Carew, Commonly Called the King of the Beggars*, which was first published in 1745 and was in print for the next hundred years (including an edition published in 1812, the year Waters left the Navy). This outlandish 'autobiography' claimed that Carew ran away from his Devonshire school at fifteen to join a group of medicants and lived on his wits and his theatrical abilities from that point until he settled back in Devon and died there in 1759. The description Carew gives of his election as Beggar King owes a lot to Thomas Harman's 1566 book about so-called vagabond society, *A Caveat or Warning for Common Cursitors*, via the popular seventeenth-century play *Beggars' Bush* by John Fletcher and his collaborators. According to Carew, medicants are summoned to London 'from all parts of the kingdom' where they choose their new leader from several experienced candidates using white and black balls to signal agreement or dissent. Then they sing a lively song, reproduced in Carew's book in full, which celebrates the beggar's lifestyle:

> At the crowning of our king,
> Thus we ever dance and sing;
> Where's the nation lives so free,
> And so merrily as we![3]

Carew's narrative rode the popularity of so-called 'gallows literature' and the demand for books of 'cant', or street slang. Also in this genre was *The History of Andrew Whiston, King of the Beggars* (1826), which recounted the adventures of Whiston ('Little Jemmy'). Later in the century a Sherborne man called George Atkins Brine laid claim to the title. Some reports claimed that Waters was chosen as the Beggar King before Whiston because of Whiston's drink problem (which suggests that Waters himself was no drunkard).[4] The 'King of the Beggars', then, was associated with carnivalesque pleasures and a storytelling tradition from page and stage which dated from the 1500s.

With Waters and his successor Andrew Whiston, the 'Beggar King' was also associated with what Rosemarie Garland-Thomson calls the 'extraordinary body' of the disabled beggar. There was a strong link between mendicity and disability in the period, and beggars' bodies were seen as extraordinary in the multiple ways in which Garland-Thomson uses the word. Disabled people were more likely to be impoverished, to be considered incapable of waged work, or to be held somehow separate from what Garland-Thomson calls 'normate' bodies and 'normate' society (the people who, by virtue of their particular types of bodies, dominate a society and decide how it runs).[5] Images and descriptions of extraordinary bodies turned disabled beggars into a spectacle to be consumed by the imagined 'normate' reader or viewer. Beggars existed outside the rules and conduct of so-called 'respectable' society and their 'irreverent individuality' made them 'extraordinary' in this different sense, and extraordinarily attractive.[6] Popular culture celebrated them and stereotyped them. Fictionalised beggars danced their way across caricatures, broadsides and stories, and with his costume and fiddle Waters was one of the most recognisable. Waters may in real life have performed in the West End streets for money, but what popular culture was really obsessed by was the idea that afterwards Waters played his fiddle all night for fun with his fellow Cadgers inside their boozy dens. Popular culture was not interested in Waters' wife and family; his companions in these texts are his fellow 'beggars'. His economic precarity was associated in these narratives with being a Character with a capital 'C'. Unlike in a realist novel, this kind of Character did not have fully imagined family ties.

The 'Beggar's Opera', otherwise known as the 'Rose and Crown', was both a fictionalised and a real public house in the Rookery. It was here that Waters was said to come and relax, and sing and dance after hard hours busking outside the Adelphi. Reportedly kept by a man named Sheen (or perhaps Shehan, judging by the tax records), the 'Rose and Crown', James Pearl's 'Robin Hood' and John Fitzgerald's 'Hand and Crown' were only a few doors away from Fitzgerald properties.[7] Collectively these and other nearby pubs were known as the Back Slums of the Holy Land, part of the St Giles Rookery. It was claimed that a public house in Whitechapel had once been known as the Beggars' Opera, but in 1816 one Joseph Butterworth told the Mendicity Committee, of which he was a member, that 'there are two public houses in Church-lane, St Giles's, whose chief support depends upon beggars': the 'Beggar's Opera' (the Rose and Crown) and the Robin Hood.[8] The worthies of the Mendicity Committee were obsessed by the idea that, beneath the noses of those who sought to bring order to the burgeoning metropolis, another kind of London entirely was flourishing beyond their control.

On any given evening at the 'Beggar's Opera', Waters could push through the door into the smoky atmosphere and find sex workers, chimney-sweeps, labourers, and street sellers, from Ireland, Devon, St Giles, and the West Indies. Drumming and thumping on the ceiling of the room above signalled dancing in full swing. There could be a hundred or more people crammed into the space (so Butterworth told the Mendicity Select Committee excitedly). Perhaps he saw Pierce Egan there: Egan spoke fluent 'St Giles Greek', the area's impenetrable slang, useful when sneaking the Cruikshanks in to see for themselves. In the corner might be one of the two chief printers of nearby Seven Dials, James Catnach, with his colleague the notorious Bat Corcoran, who used the place to flog Catnach's ballads to the ballad singers.[9] Catnach played a vital role in spreading the stories about these public houses. One of the stories was that the Prince of Wales and friends (before he was George IV) went in disguise to the 'Beggar's Opera' and enjoyed a riotous evening there amongst all the Cadgers (Plate XIV). Catnach printed a biography of Mother Cummins, who in some accounts was said to own the 'Beggar's Opera' and run it with panache as part-brothel, part-rogues' den.[10] Charles Hindley, in his *History of the Catnach Press*, fully bought into this story and explained that:

at that time 'Beggar's Opera' where the Prince and nobles resorted was at the Rose and Crown, Church Lane, St Giles . . . In the Beggar's Opera, were assembled matchmakers, beggars, prigs and all the lowest of the low. There was old black Billy Waters, with his wooden leg, dancing and playing his fiddle, and singing:–

> Polly will you marry me – Polly don't you cry,
>
> Polly come to bed with me; and get a little boy.

Some were dipping matches, some boiling potatoes and salt herrings, some swearing, some dancing – all manners of fun, &c.[11]

Hindley's account of the 'Beggar's Opera' sounds suspiciously like a description of the *Life in London* scene, as illustrated by the Cruikshanks (Plate XII). The 'Beggar's Opera', then, existed somewhere in that attractively slippery hinterland between fiction and reality.

All of this is overlaid with heavy doses of melodrama. The Minutes of the Mendicity Committee contain numerous local worthies who testify to the riotous living and energetic carousing that took place at the public houses in the Rookery. The Rev. Wm Gurney testified that he had 'seen tables set; one very long table, covered with a coarse cloth, but a clean one, and there was something roasting'. Mr Sampson Simpson, overseer of the Parish of St Giles, was certain that the beggars 'were the worst of characters, get violently drunk, quarrel and fight, calling for gin, rum, beer, and whatever they like; ham and beef and so on; broken victuals none of them will touch'. The idea that these people could afford to eat 'whatever they like' seems to have particularly offended him.[12] In sharing this testimony with the Mendicity Committee, the witnesses were participating in the communal development of the fictionalised St Giles in ways that turned Waters from a person into a kind of nineteenth-century meme.

It is the 'Beggar's Opera' into which the reader is led in *Life in London* – which first appeared in 1820 – and it is in the 'Beggar's Opera' that we encounter Waters. *Life in London* was a picaresque tale with elements of London travel and conduct guides. Published in affordable weekly parts, it entertained readers with scenes of metropolitan partying at society events and pubs alike as friends Corinthian Tom and Bob Logic take Tom's inexperienced country cousin Jerry Hawthorn on sprees around London. It says something for the importance of visual images in the development of the *Life in London* craze that a figure who is referred to only as 'the black one-legged fiddler' in the text (347) came to be associated so much with the *Life in London* phenomenon as a whole. At first glance, the picture *Tom and Jerry 'Masquerading it' among the Cadgers in the 'Back Slums' of the Holy Land* (Plate XII) claims to be an authentic glimpse into Waters' life in St Giles, his fiddle the soundtrack to merriment. Yet this personal life is also framed, by the presence of Tom and Jerry the white well-to-do observers, as a spectacle to be enjoyed by the white middle-class reader. The 'scene' Jerry witnesses amongst the Cadgers in the Holy Land, and so by extension the picture which the reader sees, is described by Jerry as 'the climax' of everything he has 'witnessed' in London so far (346). The position of the picture and its accompanying description – it's the last of the big set-piece scenes – adds weight to this statement. The tension between St Giles as a real geographical location and St Giles as an idea in popular culture appears very strongly here. What also emerges is a tension between two competing claims: we're asked to believe that this is an authentic scene with real people, but also that these people are Characters whose lives are one jolly performance.

In *Life in London*, Waters and the Cadgers reinforce lots of things important to the whole book's interest in what visual authenticity might be and mean. The visit by Tom, Jerry and Bob to the Holy Land comes after their trips to the theatre and the masquerade, but

Tom assures Jerry beforehand that even 'the *Grand Carnival*' is 'nothing to it, by comparison' (342). On one level, there is nothing authentic about the beggars whom the three friends intend to visit: Tom promises such sights as women who hire children so they can pose as distressed mothers and cripples who abandon their crutches to 'join in a *reel*' (343–4). According to Tom, 'a volume would not contain one-half of the impositions that are daily practised upon the public by the beggars of the Metropolis' and they are about to enter an 'assemblage of *rascality*, *wickedness*, and *deceit*' (345). As teaser-trailers go, it's a pretty good one. These beggars, we are assured, earn 'much better living than thousands of hard-working journeymen in the Metropolis' (345). They create elaborate performances of poverty when they beg in the streets and get great enjoyment from fooling the gullible. This insulates the reader from any worries about social responsibility for the poor. Yet it is these very performances that make them one of the sights of London that Tom feels Jerry absolutely must see, in order to return to Hawthorn Hall having experienced authentic London life. Like the Green Room at Drury Lane theatre, the Rookery is where the costumes come off and the performance is revealed, proving how canny the Cadgers are. The Cadgers recognise Tom and his companions as fellow performers, as they soon see through their 'outward appearance of *Beggars*' (342). The Cadgers represent 'a portraiture of the versatility of human nature' (347): in other words, *everyone's* willingness to pretend and to lie. The 'extraordinary scene' (342) is 'a *rich* view of Human Nature' (343); indeed, the word 'scene' is repeated again and again as if the illustrations are theatre scenes, and Egan is supplying the sound to the Cruikshanks' visuals. As Jerry puts it, 'I have heard *talk* of the *varieties* of "LIFE IN LONDON", but what I have already seen beggars description,' with one of Egan's characteristic puns on the word 'beggar' (227). Waters was firmly positioned by this hugely popular narrative as a Character.

The tension between St Giles as a real place and St Giles as an imagined place enabled a parallel tension between real and imagined versions of Waters to emerge. Egan's depiction of Waters relaxing with his friends at the 'Beggar's Opera' started a trend (later increased by Moncrieff's play *Tom and Jerry*). James Catnach brought out a series of broadsides with eye-catching cheap woodcut versions of the Cruikshanks' illustrations, and with verse summaries of Egan's plot. Catnach's *Life in London . . . Attempted in Cuts and Verse* features a quieter version of the Holy Land illustration (Figure 38). Waters and his fiddle are clearly visible, particularly as the background of the tavern has been emptied out. Just as the original serial was abridged into a series of short comic verses by the enterprising Catnach, so the scene was simplified for the cruder woodcut image. Below the woodcut is printed 'The Song of the Cadgers in the Holy Land', which declares:

> Now he that would merry be
> Let him drink and sing as we
> In palaces you shall not see
>   Such happiness as here.

'Black Billy' has arrived 'as brisk as a bee' and the Cadgers (we're told) have gathered round him as 'He struck up his fiddle'. Waters is turned into a focal point for fun. The broadside allows the reader to view him theatrically.

Any account of London low life now needed its scene at a beggars' feast. Imitations of Egan's prose were in print almost immediately, and one of the earliest and most successful was *Real Life in London* (1821–2). In this narrative, illustrated by Henry Thomas Alken, Richard Dighton, and Charles Heath, friends Tom, Bob, and Sparkle visit a gin shop on Shoe Lane (between Fleet Street and Holborn) and it is here, rather than in St Giles, that they encounter Waters:

CUT VI.   *Beggars Opera---Tom, Jerry, & Logick, among the Cadgers in the Holy Land.*

38. *Illustration from a James Catnach broadside edition of* Life in London (*1822*).

in one corner of the tap-room sat Billy Waters, a well-known character about town, a Black Man with a wooden leg was fiddling to a Slaughterman from Fleet-market, in wooden shoes, who, deck'd with all the paraphernalia of his occupation, a greasy jacket and night-cap, an apron besmeared with mud, blood, and grease, ... was dancing in the centre to the infinite amusement of the company, which consisted of an old woman with periwinkles and crabs for sale in a basket – a porter with his knot upon the table – a dustman with his broad-flapped hat, and his bell by his side – an Irish hodman – and two poor girls, who appeared to be greatly taken with the black fiddler, whose head was decorated with an oilskinned cock'd hat, and a profusion of many coloured feathers: on the other side of the room sat a young man of shabby-genteel appearance, reading the newspaper with close attention, and puffing forth volumes of smoke.[13]

This Waters is a ladies' man, not a family man, whose appearance seems to attract the 'two poor girls'. The rather wandering style and complex punctuation of this passage matches the wandering narrative. The scene in the gin shop opens with 'Billy Waters' as its focal point and keeps meandering back to him as the scene develops, as if Waters' presence and his fiddle playing is a musical refrain that tries to hold the composition together. The gin shop's mixed community of the poor (but employed), the very poor, and the 'shabby-genteel' adds to the sense of barely contained chaos. Waters is introduced to the reader as 'a well-known character' because he is an individual who is famous for being extraordinary and whose external appearance (race, disability, costume) reveals all there is to know about him. This is also used to suggest his whole life is one jolly performance. He is a Character because he is all surface.

The carnivalesque language of this scene also reinforces this roistering version of Waters:

'. . . let's have the Sprig of Shelalah, ould Blacky moor come, tune up.'

The old woman being supplied with a pipe, and the fiddler having rosined his nerves with a glass of *blue ruin* to it they went, some singing, some whistling, and others drumming with their hands upon the table; while TOM, BOB, and Sparkle, taking a seat at the other side of the room, ordered a glass of brandy and water each, and enjoyed the merriment of the scene before them, perhaps more than those actually engaged in it . . . in a few minutes Limping Billy and Mother Mapps joined the Slaughterman in the dance, when nothing could be more grotesque and amusing. Their pipes in their mouths – clapping of hands and snapping of fingers, formed a curious accompaniment to the squeaking of the fiddle – the broad grin of the Dustman, and the preposterous laugh of the Irishman at the reelers in the centre, heightened the picture. (183–4)

Stereotypes about Black people and the Irish were pretty similar (lazy, drunken, with incomprehensible English). 'Grotesque and amusing', Waters and his fellow roisterers are a 'picture' and a 'scene'; the description can't quite decide if what it's trying to convey is a visual or a theatrical image. It's certainly a very noisy one, as theorist Mikhail Bakhtin tells us that all good carnivalesque festivals should be. Unlike in performance, the 'singing', 'drumming' and 'whistling' is something a text or a picture might struggle to convey, although these repetitive present participles help to give some sense of the music's beat and the general hubbub. Waters' fiddle playing is emphasised even more subversively in the procession with which the scene ends:

> Sparkle called to TOM and BOB, and putting them tip to his scheme, Hookey was quickly mounted [on the donkey] . . . Then giving the Irishman and the Dustman some silver, to act as Supporters or Esquires, one on each side, they proceeded along Shoe-lane, preceded by Billy Waters flourishing his wooden-leg and feathers, and fiddling as he went . . . (189)

With the Irishman 'roaring out a song' and the Dustman ringing his bell (two other visual and stage stereotypes), they are 'accompanied with an immense assemblage of boys, girls, men, women, and children, collected from all the courts and alleys in the neighbourhood, joining in a chorus of shouts that rent the air' (190). In defiance of worthies like the Mendicity Society, they lay noisy claim to the streets and to their right to public space and public notice. Nevertheless, the idea for this procession of rough music originates with Bob, Tom, and Sparkle, the middle-class observers who implicitly frame and sanction it as 'their spree' (190) and so carefully limit its subversive potential.

Only four years after *Life in London* and *Real Life in London* were published, according to *The English Spy* (1826), whatever had been true about the existence of the Beggar's Feast had already passed into history:

> Formerly, the Beggars' ordinary [gathering], held in a cellar, was a scene worthy of the pencil of a Hogarth or a Cruikshank; notorious impostors, professional paupers, ballad-singers, and blind fiddlers might here be witnessed carousing on the profits of mistaken charity, and laughing in their cups at the credulity of mankind; but the police have now disturbed their nightly orgies, and the Mendicant Society ruined their lucrative calling ... scarce a vestige remains of the disgusting depravity of former times.[14]

Despite calling such scenes 'disgusting depravity', there is a strong note of regret in this elegy for a lost world. Yet even if you could no longer head to Church Street to listen to Waters' play nightly, you could still 'set out on [a] voyage of discovery to that most delectable region, well known as the Holy Land' via printed texts and images well into the late 1830s.[15] Nostalgia drove a thriving interest in the genre.

Waters turns up in George Smeeton's *Doings in London* (1828) relaxing with his friends at the 'Beggar's Opera' once again. *Doings in London* was slammed by the highbrow *Literary Gazette* as describing 'many things we could have wished never to have seen in print'; they immediately reprint them as an exciting extract. This version of Waters is a strange mixture of fact and fiction, where the tension between theatricality and authenticity is not so much explored as completely ignored. Yet again we have a scene where a more knowledgeable guide (here straightforwardly called Mentor) leads an inexperienced young middle-class man around 'town'. In a set-up straight out of *Life in London*, the pair must disguise themselves to play at being Cadgers, whilst in fact cadging themselves entry into a party to which they have no invitation:

'In order', said Mentor, 'that we may obtain an admission to the meeting of beggars, or cadgers, as they are called, we must disguise ourselves, and be dressed in rags; and I will speak to the landlord of the Beggar's Opera, in Church Lane, and, I have no doubt, he will gain us an interview.' (113)

So far, so familiar. But alongside these fictional techniques, *Doings in London* purports to offer an approach to the Cadgers full of objective fact. Waters, for example, is introduced in language taken directly from newspaper reports of him:

'That beggar you see fiddling, is the equally notorious *Billy Waters*, the king of the beggars elect: he is a most facetious fellow, full of fun and whim, and levies great contributions from John Bull, from the singularity of his appearance.' (114)

This comment is lifted almost verbatim from a magazine, while descriptions of other well-known Characters (such as a woman supposedly known as 'the *barker*', who 'gets her living by pretending to be in fits, and barking like a dog', and her partner Granne Manoo, who 'scratches his legs about the ankles, to make them bleed') come directly from the Mendicity Committee minutes and the 'biography' of Andrew Whiston (113–15). This scene and its accompanying illustration recirculated in the periodical *The Casket* in 1832, when the words of the landlord are reprinted this time as 'History' (Figure 39).[16]

In a period when 'illustration' was understood much more broadly as a category than it tends to be today, it wasn't just in printed materials where the visual representation of 'Billy Waters' took off. Prints of Waters influenced illustrations, which inspired memorabilia, which led back to illustrations; the reuse of Waters' image did not stop there. Like many Characters and celebrities, he made the shift into everyday knick-knacks. As Egan himself noted,

The Merry Doings of the Jobial Beggars.

39. Billy Waters in the pub, from Doings in London (1828) *and reproduced in* The Casket – *an 1830s penny periodical.*

characters from *Life in London* adorned handkerchiefs, mantel-pieces, and tea-tables:

> The *Lady* . . . was able to amuse her visitors with the adventures of TOM and JERRY on her highly-finished TEA-TRAY . . . The *Country Folks* were delighted with the HANDKERCHIEF which displayed TOM getting the best of a Charley; and DUSTY BOB and BLACK SAL 'all happiness!' . . . and the *Connoisseur*, with a smile of satisfaction on his countenance, contemplated his SCREEN, on which were displayed the motley groups of high and low characters continually on the move in the Metropolis.[17]

Images of Waters circulated in exactly the same way. As Tom Mole writes, 'being a celebrity in the Romantic period meant seeing one's images proliferate, evolving or deforming' as they went, and though it did not only happen to Waters he did not have the resources to protest at this treatment, should he have wanted to.[18] From 1821 onwards, manufacturers brought out ceramic figurines of him based on different illustrations, as others continued to profit from Waters' image.[19] They were still being made into the 1860s, and possibly beyond, so there was clearly still demand. Brighton Museum has several different versions with varying degrees of quality but all perpetuating Waters' fame. The dynamism of Waters' act was frozen into a silent caricature, a post-abolition Black body still available for purchase. Again, though, it's his performance that is emphasised, not his struggles; these mantelpiece ornaments were purchased to be enjoyed, not as reminders of the daily grind of poverty. 'Billy Waters' was moving freely around the network of popular culture. To use modern parlance, by 1821 'Billy Waters' was going viral.

Becoming 'Billy Waters'

How did becoming 'Billy Waters' affect William Waters himself? Waters responded to the culture of Character and caricature in which he lived in ways that tell us a lot about him. Unlike some better-known Black violinists of the period, he had no high connections on which to draw. The Chevalier de Saint-Georges, mixed-race son of a wealthy French planter, was a celebrated concert violinist, composer, and fencer whose paternal wealth ensured he mixed in the highest circles, despite the frequent racial prejudice to which he was subjected: 'adored by audiences, hailed by composers, celebrated by critics, writers, and poets, Saint-Georges had succeeded in bringing about a startling reversal: the black man as Enlightenment hero'.[1] In Waters' own lifetime, the violinist George Bridgetower – whose Black father worked for a Polish prince and whose white mother was described as 'a lady of quality' – was befriended (briefly) by Beethoven and sponsored by the Prince Regent. Bridgetower's brother Frederic was less famous but still dedicated *Six Pathetic Canzonets* to Italian diva Madame Catalini 'by permission'.[2] Waters' material was very different from these musicians because of his training and his audience, but he didn't necessarily play that differently. Performers of all kinds used the so-called

Baroque stance, where the instrument was held 'against the chest or shoulder or under either side of the chin, sloping downwards and gripping with the left hand, and using various bow grips' (Waters uses this stance in Figure 29), and there were far more similarities between orchestral and vernacular techniques.[3] Waters, however, was up against even greater economic and social challenges than established violinists. But he'd fought the odds before and won.

Waters was a creative survivor: in a crisis he saw possibilities in the materials to hand. Waters' choices suggest deliberate tactics: he provided the age of spectacle with the stuff it loved. Waters turned himself into a 'Character' with 'hat and feathers' and 'peculiar antics', which is evidence of a canny commercial strategy.[4] Scholar Julia Fawcett calls this tactic 'over-expression': the deliberate use of extravagant costume and gestures by eighteenth- and nineteenth-century celebrities anxious to create a public persona that attracted notice yet could also be interpreted in multiple ways.[5] Waters' strategy worked: in 1823 songwriter William Reeves could write:

His life was one continu'd round
Of pleasure and of glee;
His fiddle caus'd the hearts to bound
Of children as big as me.[6]

No fool, Waters knew the stereotypes that would be applied to him and played up to them. Tim Hitchcock calls this the 'mask' of the beggar: the poor of Regency and early Victorian London were in dialogue with print and visual culture the whole time and they knew it.[7] Waters wasn't alone in this: for example, Thomas McConwick made sly use of the stereotype of the 'Stage Irish' when he sang 'Spring of Shillelagh' and other Irish tunes, all the while brandishing an actual shillelagh and sporting shamrocks on his hat.

McConwick, like Waters, was a canny professional: 'the English populace were taken with the novelty', as he joked with his crowd and played up to the comic Character they expected. In 1845 William Read, an itinerant crossing-sweeper, told another Mendicity Committee that 'the most successful garb for a man to assume was that of the country labourer', as people assumed he had only recently arrived in London and so needed support more than others.[8] 'Black people', writes Smith in *Vagabondiana* in 1815, 'as well as those destitute of sight, seldom fail to excite compassion' (34). As Jensen puts it, 'a street performer who played up to what made them distinctive could do very well'. But Waters did even more: he drew on multiple cultural traditions. Enslaved Africans in 1820s Montevideo, scholar Simon Gikandi tells us, elected kings and queens at holiday time in an echo of remembered rites. These 'monarchs-for-the-day' then 'dressed in the most striking manner, with the most brilliant outfits that one can imagine, [and] paraded through the city'.[9] By embracing the Character of the Beggar King as part of his performance, Waters turned a white English Character into a Black Atlantic one, and became more than monarch-for-the-day. He became king of the streets. Before long Waters was written about as one of the 'public and distinguished characters' any visitor to London should see.[10]

Waters knew how to harness the public appetite for spectacle and novelty for his own ends. *Life in London* was an example of a new understanding of popular culture itself as a performance in which readers could take part when they imitated their favourite characters and collected memorabilia. At the same time, critic Jon Mee tells us, 'the audience of culture in the 1820s . . . were aware of the precarity of performance', which included their own precarity as they tried to navigate and make sense of their own place in their society. Indeed, uncertainty was part of the very structures of Regency publishing: print historian Brian Maidment comments upon the exhausting amount of work jobbing engravers like Robert

Seymour and others took on as they toiled to feed families in what was 'a volatile and unforgiving environment' for publishers too.[11] If we look again at Plate XI from 1823, the boy imitating Waters' dancing in the background shows that Waters is not the only person on stage here: every Londoner in the scene forms part of the urban spectacle, to be gazed at by the viewer. Waters knew how to capitalise on this to survive. Paradoxically, Waters represented 'real life in London' precisely because he was a performer.

Praise for Waters was not always respectful, as that cheeky dancing boy makes clear. Waters and other members of the street economy of Regency London made economic precarity visible day after day; their presence claimed their right to public space and to making money. Writers and artists took this to make their own kinds of products. Waters' presence on the streets opened him up to the threat of being depicted as a 'freak'; the undated print *30 Extraordinary Characters* (Figure 40) includes Waters along with

40. 30 Extraordinary Characters (*undated*).

other spectacular and entertaining 'novelties' past and present, including the Colossus of Rhodes (a giant human-shaped statue destroyed in antiquity) and Anne Siggs (a well-known beggar displayed as a wax figure at Mrs Salmon's Waxworks in Fleet Street in 1812). Emerging ideas about commercialised celebrity were not so far removed from the much older concept of 'wonder' at the fascinating 'freak', as Julia H. Fawcett argues, and Waters was navigating between the two models.[12] Waters was playing a dangerous game. He probably knew it.

As the Regency era began to anticipate the Victorian age, ideas about manners and morals changed. A new middle-class and upper-class generation was horrified at what it perceived as the lax morals and rowdy habits of its parents and grandparents. The kind of language that was acceptable in company or in public also changed: Lady Sarah Lennox (1745–1826) was told off by her fastidious grandchildren for using the word 'belly'.[13] Public morality was all. Yet in 1826 *The English Spy* looked back with nostalgia at an imagined period before the 1822 and 1824 Vagrancy Acts when aristocratic and ragged patrons alike crowded into the public houses of St Giles for cross-class drinking sessions. The 1835 *Dens of London Exposed* is careful to draw a distinction between known facts about St Giles and 'that fraternity called "Cadgers"', and what it calls the 'hearsay' that had grown up around it. Indeed:

> The story, too, in that by-gone piece of notoriety, 'Pierce Egan's Life in London', about the beggar's opera, where the lame and the blind, and other disordered individuals, were said to meet nightly, in a place called the 'back slums,' to throw off their infirmities, and laugh at the credulity of the public, was, not a great many weeks ago, trumped up into a paragraph in one of our weekly journals as a fact just discovered, and the curious were referred to a certain house in St Giles's, in corroboration thereof. Indeed, we think it would be easy to prove that what

little is known of the Common Lodging House, and those people the Cadgers, is neither more nor less than mere reports, and which, like the generality of reports, contain not always the truth. (4–5)

Yet for all its promised objectivity, worthy of what it calls the dawning 'Age of Inquiry' (9), *Dens of London* still relies for its account of Cadger life on such well-worn tropes as the disabled Jack Tar, the beggars' meal, and the evening carouse.

In none of the stories about the Rookery does Waters have a wife beside him, just his fiddle. Did he really spend all his free time in public houses and neglect Elizabeth and the children? All of William Waters' concerns in newspaper reports of his arrests by the Mendicity Society are for his family. After a day of pain and performance he worked again for them at night. His family gave him a stake in his adopted country, kinship ties that the system of enslavement tried to sever. To pretend otherwise was just another slander levelled at him. The Character of 'Billy Waters' was only possible if it was imagined without any domestic life, family ties, or trappings of the everyday.

Edward Albert from Kingston, Jamaica, interviewed by Henry Mayhew for his famous book on the London poor, tells Mayhew that his wife is a mixed-race Englishwoman: 'I couldn't get on to anything without her,' says Albert, with powerful simplicity. Their home is one 'scantily furnished' room in a 'dirty and rather disreputable alley' but 'a kettle was singing over a cheerful bit of fire' and their baby son James smiled and crowed.[14] Waters and Elizabeth built a life and a family together. If we look with him, rather than at him, we see the fierce drive of a father to provide a better future for his children.

For the Character of 'Billy Waters', domestic life was erased. Linked to 'Jolly Jack Tar' and 'King of the Beggars', 'Billy Waters' has no domestic ties. He's too theatrical. An 1840 serial text from

Bentley's Miscellany extracted as 'The Beggarman's Craft' in *The Mirror* noted with something like regret that because of parliamentary legislation (and changing times) 'the tatterdemalions of the Beggar's Opera no longer enjoy the privileges that belonged to their ancestors . . . as in more recent times, the happy, but bygone days of Dusty Bob and Billy Waters . . . Well might Epicurus say, "Poverty, when cheerful, ceases to be poverty." '[15] For those who longed for what they saw as a freer, more joyful era, 'Billy Waters' stood for life and vitality, and an alternative vision of what society might look like, what it might value and how it might be run. But in 1821 Waters' strategy began to backfire spectacularly. It had almost worked *too* well. What he hadn't counted on was that writers and playwrights could now more easily treat him as public property and a portable idea. He started to lose control of his fame. In 1821 the success of Egan's *Life in London*, which popularised the idea of the deceitful Cadgers, was a blow for Waters and his family. And then Moncrieff wrote his play.

❧ WIG ❧

In Which Waters Appears on Stage

Charing Cross, London, October 1822

He takes a break from dancing, lowers his fiddle, rests his leg. The chill wind tugs at his hat. A discarded playbill from a nearby theatre skitters along the pavement. It's not been a good day for earnings yet, despite all the passers-by. Nor was yesterday. It's been like that for a while now. This thought gnaws at him.

He worries about his family, his health, and his strength.

He worries that their income is dwindling while their spending keeps going up.

He worries how his wife would feed and house two children if she was left on her own.

The weary man in the tattered blue jacket shelters from the fretful wind, and thinks, and plans, and worries.

Tom and Jerry

So now we are back where we began: the opening night of Moncrieff's play *Tom and Jerry*, 26 November 1821. A white actor known as Signor Paulo is assembling his 'Billy Waters' costume. Before he puts on his feathered hat, he reaches for a white powdered wig.

Waters' wig was a provocative piece of costuming. 'A judge's full-bottomed cauliflower wig', Moncrieff calls it, and it certainly caught people's eye. One children's picture book of London street Characters (which teaches middle-class children that the people of the street are separate, different, not real people at all) features a picture of Waters and declares, 'Here's Billy Black, Who's forced to beg, With fiddle, wig, And wooden leg.'[1] This wig was the ultimate piece of irreverence, which cocked a snook at judges, the Mendicity Society, the courts, and all the forces ranged against him as street performer and poor man who had the audacity to become a celebrity. It was a carnivalesque headpiece that claimed the power of the judiciary but mocked that power at the same time. For a man who was subject to all the efforts of the Mendicity Society to contain him and his fellow 'pauper professionals', it was an audacious touch. It was all the more daring after 1821 when the Mendicity

Society was gunning for him. This was partly Moncrieff's fault, as we shall see.

It was also a politicised gesture. Judges in Britain and the colonies were white; in donning the wig Waters wore a form of whiteface. Why is this significant? For starters, Lord Mansfield wore a white wig when he pronounced his most famous judgment. Furthermore, the idea of Waters as a Beggar King spread even more widely from 1821 onwards because of Moncrieff's depiction of him in *Tom and Jerry*. In some ways the fact that Moncrieff took an unnamed figure in Egan's *Life in London* and gave him a speaking part was an act of appreciation and a great publicity moment for Waters. There were two huge (and related) problems with the play for Waters, however: he was depicted as a fraud, and he was depicted in blackface. By the 1820s there was already a 300-year-old theatrical tradition of white actors depicting Black characters on stage using blackface. *Tom and Jerry* gives a new perspective on the unpleasant history of blackface, a milestone on the way to the horrors of blackface minstrelsy, which hasn't yet been properly explored. Waters' wig, headgear of footmen as well as judges, skated along the line of whiteface mockery in a longstanding Black performance tradition, which scholar Marvin McAllister calls 'whiting up'.[2] When Paulo donned the same costume, the mockery was all in the other direction. The consequences for the Waters family were cataclysmic.

The *Tom and Jerry* 'Billy Waters' was a comic blackface role. When the Adelphi looked about for their 'Billy Waters' they hit upon Signor Paulo, the stage name of Paulo Redigé the Younger. Redigé was the son of well-known Sadler's Wells rope-dancers Paulo Redigé Senior (stage name 'The Little Devil') and his wife, who was known as 'La Belle Espagnole'. Young Paulo 'might be almost said to have been born within the walls of that theatre'. Signor Paulo, to give him his stage name, got his big break when he replaced the famous clown Grimaldi in the 1817 season, although he took a while to win over the pro-Grimaldi Sadler's Wells crowds.[3] Before long he was celebrated for his clowning and seemed the obvious choice to play the comic part of 'Billy Waters'.[4] A surviving undated image of Paulo in his costume as the pantomime character of 'Clown' gives some kind of indication of why, as the outline of 'Clown' is not dissimilar from Paulo's costume as 'Billy Waters' (Figures 41 and 42). 'Clown' has exaggerated clothing, extravagant headgear, and a painted face.

What distinguished blackface clowning, though, was often an emphasis on childish fun, which implicitly infantilised Black people. In some images, Waters is depicted as a childlike figure of fun (Figure 43). Signor Paulo copied Waters' hat, jacket, wig, and fiddle, and mimicked his disability. He also blacked up his face. Since the

41. Signor Paulo as Clown (*undated*).

BILLY WATERS.

42. *Signor Paulo as 'Billy Waters'* (1880).

nineteenth century, people have speculated whether Waters was asked to perform as himself on stage, and refused. If he did turn down any such offer, who could blame him? The part was offensive and he had good reason to be suspicious of authorities. As an independent Black performer, Waters stood out in white-dominated popular culture, though there had been Black actors on the English stage before and would be throughout the nineteenth century.[5] The end result was that his creative idea was stolen from him when Signor Paulo turned Waters' act into a blackface performance of a bullying, cheating Character by a white actor.

Recent scholars of blackface practices have emphasised the ways in which they were all about power and control. Noémi Ndiaye's research shows that blackface performance was thriving across

Europe four centuries before the appearance of blackface minstrelsy on the American stage. Already, white performers were busy creating fanciful versions of 'African' dance, stereotyped 'African' dialect, and blacking up their faces with burnt cork or soot. It wasn't just productions of *Othello*: Charles Dibdin's comic turn in 1768 (shortly before Waters was born) as the enslaved servant 'Mungo' in Bickerstaff's perennially popular *The Padlock*, and Edmund Kean's performance as the tragic avenger 'Zanga' in the 1815 revival of Edward Young's *The Revenge*, helped to make them stars. They were both white actors. Perhaps Signor Paulo harboured similar hopes for himself. In Signor Paulo's representation of 'Billy Waters' these racialised techniques came together in a blackface performance.

Blackface supported transatlantic enslavement, where particular sections of people were seen as commodities: 'fungible', that is, interchangeable, replaceable, like agricultural crops.[6] Theatre scholar Miles Grier argues that in Shakespeare's era, Black characters – and frighteningly the bodies of Black people – were seen as surfaces 'to *be read* by a white expert', rather than individuals with the right be to active readers and makers of meaning themselves.[7] Blackface marked

43. Life in the Holy Land, *possibly a magic lantern slide for children.*

out 'Billy Waters' as a Character to be read, as well as performed, by the white interpreter. As scholar Ayanna Thompson points out, from the 1500s onwards Black bodies were valued more as objects to exhibit than as skilled performers in their own right with their own multitudinous experiences and ideas of what being Black meant to them.[8] To risk stating the obvious, there is no such thing as one experience of being Black, and any attempt to define authentic representations of 'race' implies a more powerful observer who is allowed to decide what is authentic and what is not. But blackface performance techniques suggested that there might be a typical 'Blackness', which white society could define, categorise, and spread across texts, bodies, and media.

Signor Paulo must have been thrilled: *Tom and Jerry* was an instant hit. 'Nothing like it had ever been known in theatrical annals': seats were booked ages in advance and people flocked from around the country to see it. The fact that 'the serious press inveighed against it, ministers denounced it from the pulpits' and religious groups stood at theatre doors warning people away was fantastic free publicity; 'respectability . . . flocked to catch a glimpse of that naughty world they dared not visit in any other way'.[9] Writing from the vantage point of 1898, a correspondent for the *Era* newspaper noted that '*Tom and Jerry* attracted all London', despite (or because of) the fact that 'it had no pretension whatever to literary merit'.[10] This was no idle comment: Moncrieff bragged that it shut down the Strand at 3 in the afternoon due to the sheer number of eager playgoers, and a playbill for the return of *Tom and Jerry* to the Adelphi for the 1822 season declared that the production had been 'Honored by overflowing Houses for 93 successive Nights last Season', so of course it was returning.[11] *Tom and Jerry* 'made the fortune of the Adelphi', though not the fortune of either its playwright or William Waters.[12] It was performed 'in every minor theatre in London', but 'that of the Adelphi, owing most probably to the excellence of its cast, was *the* one'.[13] Moncrieff's version became the standard production, which is worth remembering, as it was this script that played a key role in depicting Waters as a fictionalised Character rather than a real, talented individual.[14] What would this mean for Waters? To find out we need to explore the play and its performances with new scrutiny.

Moncrieff's adaptation was entirely unauthorised. It turned Egan's idea into something else. But rather than describing it as a plagiarism or derivative in some way, we should instead see it as part of the network of popular culture. It still did terrible harm to Waters. Not only did the Adelphi playbill claim for Moncrieff the title of 'Author', in place of Egan, but it cheekily announced that it would improve upon Egan's serialised version:

> Tom and Jerry, it will be seen, have a moral Purpose and an Aim, and are not left on the Town, but conducted to a final Home. Sue and Kate are proved to be very different Characters from those they have been represented; and the Public will be glad to learn how their old Friend Logic was extricated from the disagreeable Situation, in which his original Godfathers left him.[15]

The Adelphi production was overseen by Robert Cruikshank, and the sets drew upon the Cruikshank brothers' illustrations.[16] Indeed, Moncrieff's famous (although probably apocryphal) defence against a plagiarism charge levelled at him by an angry Egan was that '[I] wrote my piece from the inimitable plates [pictures] – Cruikshank's plates – and boiled my kettle with your letterpress [printed words] – that's the plain fact.'[17] Moncrieff's production specifically linked illustration to the scenes on stage, as playbills proclaimed the production to be 'An animated Picture of every Species of Life in London'.[18] Egan's own adaptation for Sadler's Wells made great play of the fact that it used the original creative team by having Egan's text and George Cruikshank's sets. For all adaptations, high value was placed on bringing the pictures to life and using original actors across productions in costumes that were the exact replicas of the pictures.[19] This emphasis gave Waters much more prominence in the play than in the book, with a key scene and a listing on the playbill. This in turn prompted the production of new images, which placed 'Billy Waters' centre stage to reflect the character's importance in the play (Figure 44). In this play, Waters' role as a performer is used in celebration of his fellow 'beggars'. Moncrieff may have thought he was celebrating a particular London lifestyle. But the effect was that the play turned the idea of Waters as a performer into a weapon against the people of the Rookery.

'*Enter* BILLY WATERS, *dancing*': with this stage direction, Signor Paulo burst onto the Adelphi stage in blackface. Waters' image

44. A View in the Holyland'!!! (c. 1821).

signified both authenticity and theatricality in Moncrieff's play. The promise of 'Billy Waters' on stage offered by the playbill was a guarantee to the audience that this was an authentic adaptation of Egan's narrative and a genuine product of the *Life in London* craze.[20] But it also added weight to the play's claim that it showed real London life, laid before the audience as a shared experience. The Cumberland edition of Moncrieff's *Tom and Jerry* takes great pains to list the costumes, with the costume for 'Billy Waters' specified as that found in the Cruikshanks' illustration, but also on the real man outside the theatre doors.[21] 'Billy' appears in Act 2 scene 3, set in the 'Back Slums in the Holy Land' (47). As the scene opens, the stage directions tell us that the audience sees 'several well-known Characters discovered', with the capital 'C' alerting us to the fact that these are not just characters in a play, or from a serial tale, but also 'types' of urban poor from the London streets (47). After a song by these self-proclaimed 'Cadgers' on the joys of begging, 'Billy's' first appearance is designed to reproduce the audience's other encounters with his act or his image, as 'Billy' dances his distinctive jig (in a typically infantilising move, the stage directions use only the first name). This was so successful that audiences (and some critics) remained unsure if they were watching Waters playing himself on stage, or an actor.[22]

At the same time as being a figure of 'real life' in the play, Signor Paulo's dancing entrance introduces 'Billy' as a performer. It closely follows the Cadgers' opening song, a song that proclaims all begging to be one sustained performance for financial gain, '[f]or who but a slave would work, / When he like a prince might live?' (47). The reference to slavery here only hints at the growing political storm over whether to abolish slavery in the West Indies, but the script attempts to skate over such realities (although the appearance on stage of an ambivalently attractive Black Character played by a white actor must inevitably have reminded everyone). In *Tom and Jerry*, the figure of the deceitful St Giles beggar becomes emblematic of the play and of London as a whole, something Moncrieff takes from *Life in London*. In Moncrieff's play, however, it's 'Billy Waters' who becomes its embodiment. After a comic discussion about how successful they are at deceiving citizens into giving them money, the Cadgers break into another song:

> Then let us cadgers be, and take in all the flats we can,
> Experience we know full well, my boys, it is that makes the man;
> And for experience all should pay, that Billy will allow. (49)

The 'experience' of being cheated by 'Billy' and his Cadgers is presented as a humorous and inevitable part of city life, and a worthwhile experience for the young and unwary. Deciphering the authentically needy from the practised actor, it is suggested, is something the modern citizen must learn.

The play's male protagonists enter in the second half of the scene, observed by the female leads 'Sue' and 'Kate' (two other roles greatly expanded from Egan's original book). All are *'disguised as Beggars'* to fit into the tavern crowd:

> *Enter* TOM, JERRY, *and* LOGIC – *disguised as Beggars, with Placards on their backs* – TOM'S '*Burnt Out – lost my little all.*' – JERRY'S '*Deaf and Dumb.*' – LOGIC'S '*Thirteen Children.*' &c.
> *Sue.* Here they are – I know them in spite of their rags.
> *Tom.* This, my dear Jerry, is a rich page in the book of life, which will save you many a pound, by exposing the imposition of street mendicity. – It almost staggers belief that hypocrisy is so successful, and that the fine feeling of the heart should become so blunted, as to laugh at the humanity of those who step forward to relieve them. (50)

Of course, echoing Egan's *Life in London*, Moncrieff's tongue is firmly in his cheek here; 'Tom' and 'Jerry's' disguises expose them as just as mendacious as the Cadgers. Indeed, it is only by acting the part of beggars that they can get the necessary experience for urban survival. Virtue will only triumph if it understands the essential theatricality of the city – and has a little help from those more knowing (for all the men's supposed worldliness, the women see through their disguises instantly, although the men never recognise the women). Just as in Egan's narrative, the audience is sheltered from any need to worry about the Cadgers because it is assured that the poverty of all beggars is just one big act. The big difference was that Moncrieff's play linked all of these ideas specifically to 'Billy'.

While allowing the poor agency, pleasure, and power on stage, then, the scene also undermined William Waters. 'Billy' enjoys significant status in the scene: promoted from the background (though eye-catching) of the original illustration, Moncrieff's 'Billy' directs the action, is violent and aggressive, interacts with 'Sue', and bullies the landlord of the tavern in the verbal version of blackface that Noémie Ndiaye has usefully called 'blackspeak':[23]

Jemmy. Gemman, have you ordered the peck and booze for the evening?
Sold. Suke. Aye, aye, I've taken care of that – shoulder of veal and garnish – Turkey and appendleges – Parmesan – Filberds – Port and Madery.
Billy. Dat dam goot, me like a de Madery – Landlord, here you give this bag of broken wittals, vot I had give me to-day, to some genteel dog vot pass your door: and make haste wid de supper, you curse devil you!
Billy. . . . (*takes candle, and looks at supper*). Vy, what him call dis?
Land. Why, the turkey and the pie, to be sure.
Billy. De turkey and de pie! I tink you said de turkey and de pie, – what! de turkey without de sassinger! him shock – him wouldn't

give pin for turkey without dem – me like a de Alderman in chain.

Land. I'm very sorry, Mr Waters, but—

Billy. You sorry! I'm sorry for my supper, you damn dog. (49–50)

'Billy' scorns the 'broken wittals' given to him by a well-meaning member of the public and orders 'Alderman in chains', the slang for turkey and sausages used by the Mendicity Committee as an example of beggars living well. 'Billy' is full of vitality and agency, eventually ordering his companions to carry him off when the scene closes just as constables are threatening to break down the door. But he is also reduced to an aggressive racial and comic stereotype. His accent – marking him as an unmistakable 'other' – and his dancing connect him with the other popular working-class characters in another scene 'Dusty Bob' and 'African Sal', who were known for their comic pas-de-deux (these were not real individuals but cultural stereotypes of 'the Dustman' and 'the Black Prostitute').[24] 'African Sal' was performed in drag and in blackface. Her femininity was doubly compromised.

Surely some in the audience must have realised that this depiction of 'Billy' was a horrible thing? There must have been a few Black Londoners in the audience, so how did they feel? Did anyone who had passed Waters on their way to the theatre squirm in their seat? Or did everyone in the audience laugh along at Paulo's antics? Paul Redigé was the child of immigrant parents, and stereotyped himself because of his southern-European heritage. The flexibility and agility required to tie his leg up so he could wear and then perform with a wooden limb is astonishing. By acting 'Black' and 'disabled', Paulo emphasised his physicality and asked the audience to admire how well he could mimic William Waters himself, whom many of the audience would have just seen on their way to the Adelphi. But he also felt able to make Waters' act his own. He added the performance of disability to blackface a decade before this was explicitly done in the United States with famous American black-face performer T. D. Rice's impersonation of a Black, disabled plantation-slave 'Jim Crow' (although arguably Early Modern blackface traditions of stilted speech and movement already linked Blackness and disability to denigrate Africans as debased and defective).[25] Paulo showed that it was possible to perform disability, allowing audiences to wonder if Waters was a 'fake' amputee too; Tobin Siebers calls this 'disability drag' and likens it to blackface because of how it keeps disability off-stage whilst also transforming it into something altogether different.[26] James Grant's book *Sketches in London* (1838) has a scene in which three St Giles beggars arrange 'a sort of rehearsal, such as takes place in a theatre when a new piece is about to be produced', during which one tries and fails to convince his friends that he can successfully pass as an amputee with a wooden leg.[27] 'Comic' plays and books sought to entertain but cast doubt upon street people with a disability. Paulo's 'Billy' protected consumers of popular culture from the uncomfortable realities of the urban poor, both Black and white.

Waters had a sailor's courage, and Moncrieff wrote in 1851 of an incident which, although unverified anywhere else, may hold a grain of truth. Music journalist Tony Montague uncovered the account. Moncrieff claimed he saw Waters 'hovering' outside the Adelphi and Waters expressed a desire to see Paulo's performance. Moncrieff smuggled him into the theatre for free before the punters arrived and seated him at 'the front of the gallery'. At Paulo's entrance, 'Poor Billy's astonishment and consternation knew no bounds' and when Paulo began to play (badly), Waters roared out: 'Dat am not me! Him play better den dat: Dat von damned great poster! Him play de fiddle wid him for de hundred pound!' Paulo, thinking this a joke or a heckle, took up the challenge and played the jig 'Moll in the Wad' to audience delight. But when Waters returned fire and played 'his real fiddle' the audience turned on him – perhaps thinking this *another* imitation 'Billy Waters' – and threw him out. Waters barely made it down the stairs.[28]

This is Moncrieff's very melodramatic account, written for money in ageing poverty. It even got reprinted in Australia. Did it happen? Maybe. Or maybe it was a figment of Moncrieff's guilty conscience. Imagine the horror, though, of witnessing this aggressive theft of your act.

Moncrieff deserved to feel guilty: he gave 'Billy Waters' a speaking role that denied him individuality even as it seemed to celebrate him. It's a complete distraction from social realities. On the one hand, the Cadgers are given identities, personalities, and the freedom to have fun. On the other, they are depicted as cheats and frauds. Poverty and social exclusion are turned into an enjoyable romp. It was real Londoners such as Waters who suffered the consequences. Moncrieff's exuberant Cadgers scene displays no unease about this. Instead, it furthers an idea of Waters as all surface and no depths.

Versions of the play carried this character with them across London. In summer 1822 the Royalty Theatre's production of Moncrieff's play achieved a real coup: not only did they put on Moncrieff's play but they persuaded Signor Paulo to repeat his role as 'Billy Waters'. 'Billy' also appeared in other stage versions of *Life in London*. Frustrated by Moncrieff's success, Egan brought out his own production at Sadler's Wells, complete with pony races and a Mr Hartland playing 'Billy Waters'. Davis's Royal Amphitheatre rather cheekily advertised its own 1821 production as 'an Entirely New, Whimsical, Local, Melo-Dramatic, Pantomimical, Equestrian Drama in Three Acts, With New and Splendid Scenery, Machinery, Dresses and Decorations, founded on a Popular Production, which has lately engrossed the whole of London, called Life in London'. This version had pony races and a substantial speaking part for 'Billy Waters' played by a Mr Collingbourne, a comic actor. The Olympic Theatre's first adaptation in November 1821 had no 'Billy Waters', 'Dusty Bob', or 'African Sal' listed on the playbill or the published cast list, but by 1823 their new production starred Mr Hartland as

'Billy Waters'.[29] Productions in London involved all kinds of other entertainments: boxing matches, horse races and songs were included within and between the acts. A street puppet show of 'Billy Waters' drew a crowd of women and children in Pentonville on a fine day in August 1825 and you could still buy a 'Billy Waters' puppet in 1867.[30]

It was a short step from Signor Paulo in blackface as 'Billy Waters' to 'Billy Waters' as a masquerade costume for white party-goers. The Cruikshanks drew a Grand Masquerade Ball for Egan's *Life in London*, though there's no obvious 'Billy Waters' costume in the illustration. But at the first Masquerade Ball of the 1823 London Season, held at the King's Theatre, revellers partied late into the night wearing costumes drawn from 'every notorious part that ever was represented on stage, from the deepest tragedy to the buffoonery of Billy Waters'. A Fancy Dress Ball at Westminster Hall in 1841 was much talked about because professional actors joined the throng and a Mr Eliason played 'Billy Waters'.[31] 'Billy Waters' party costumes weren't only seen in London. We know this thanks to a man named Benson Earle Hill, who left the army for acting in 1822 after being wounded and later wrote his rollicking memoirs of a theatrical life. He was well aware of Waters, 'the black, well known about town', and tells the story of when he spotted two men at a Grand Masquerade Ball in Bath in 1840, who suffered the socially awkward misfortune to arrive in the same costume: 'The Waters' ... dressed precisely alike', faced off 'in hostile parlance':

'Go, you wuss dan de dam n—er as 'tend to be me, at Delfi play-ous. Me go see seberal times. Him 'bleege to ab seen how me walk, hear how me talk, but you! Berry like nebbaw in Lunnon!'

'Yes, often; I have seen him, you, me! Pray don't be so loud!'

'Loud as me like sar! No, you see only my pictuss! gran gentleman come, on dere knees, ax me to sit, sar! You hold a fiddle? You man o' colour you! Me no rest till me play you out, me wash you white; you may be Bath Waters . . . but, by Gor A-mightee, you no Billy Waters!'[32]

This noisy stand-off over who is the most authentic 'Billy Waters' is won by the gentleman who *speaks* like the stage version of Waters at the Adelphi as well as *looking* like him. The masquerader who can only manage 'fashionable English' is unmasked as an imposter and retires in disorder. This story might be a source for Moncrieff's 1851 Adelphi anecdote. Sometimes it was Waters himself who was a shorthand for imposters: the King's Theatre dancing teacher wrote a humorous book on dancing and fancy-dress balls in 1824, which uses Waters and 'Dusty Bob' as metaphors for the imposter dancing instructor who only knows how to 'hop about'.[33] But on the whole these costumes were something that white partygoers could put on and off with no ill effects. Of course, things were different for Black performers.

The 'Billy Waters' Character had a lasting impact, as fiction was reprinted as fact. Sometimes these references look harmless at first glance. For example, in George Daniels' *Merrie England in the Olden Time; Or, Peregrinations with Uncle Tim and Mr Bosky* (serialised in *Bentley's Miscellany* in 1840 then republished with Robert Cruikshank as one of the illustrators), the benign Uncle Timothy explains about the liveliness of the 'olden times'.[34] A footnote includes a 'comic' song about the Mendicity Society's threat to Waters' livelihood:

Mendicity Bill,
Who for prowess and skill
Was dubb'd the bold Ajax of Drury,
With a whistle and stride
Flung his fiddle aside,
And his sky-scraper cock'd in a fury!

Waters is 'Mendicity Bill' in this song: a jolly trickster and 'the bold Ajax' of Drury Lane. It's another crossover between the man and the picturesque hero. The street poor of Regency and early Victorian London were in dialogue with texts like this: they knew they would be compared with how the middle classes thought 'beggars' *should* act, and how actors played beggars.

For Waters, the success of *Tom and Jerry* had some potential to be good news. Now a much more famous figure, represented on stage nightly in London and in the provinces, Waters was in a position to make lots of money from happy theatregoers – tourists and Londoners alike – who wanted to see the real Waters perform. Or was he? Things did not work out that way at all. Moncrieff blames the terrifying appearance of an arch-nemesis with a similar name, in the shape of the Mendicity Society's William Bodkin:

> ... when a rival *Billy* (BODKIN), by being placed at the head of the mendicity society, virtually became King of the Beggars in his own right. This (as he conceived it) cruel usurpation by Bodkin, pierced Billy to the heart. From that moment he drooped – like another black hero he exclaimed – 'Othello's occupation's gone.[35]

The Mendicity Society had it in for Waters now he was famous, those two arrests on the same day in 1821 suggest. Really, however, it was popular culture, in the shape of the fictionalised 'Billy Waters', that was William Waters' nemesis. It brought him to the Mendicity Society's attention, for one thing. For another, money made by theatre managers of the Adelphi and elsewhere, profiting from the use of Waters' distinctive image and act within their productions, did not get shared with Waters the original creator. There were no intellectual property laws there to protect him. Worst of all, the representation on stage of Waters as a well-fed, demanding, and successful beggar seems only to have turned the public against him. Why should they give him money when they had just watched him abuse the tavern Landlord on stage and laugh at the well-meant gifts of 'broken vittals' given by a public denounced as gullible? It seems that this was the question theatregoers began to ask themselves. Waters reportedly thought so, at least:

> BILLY latterly became unfortunate, which he attributed to the production of *Tom and Jerry*, with who he was made to take *madeary* (Madeira), and treat 'bags of victuals' with contempt.[36]

Elsewhere, Moncrieff admitted it: he wrote that Waters was only outside the Adelphi because 'he often wandered to, and hovered round, the spot to which he owed his ruin'.[37] Smuggling him in to see *Tom and Jerry* for free hardly compensated for what Moncrieff (and others) had done. Moncrieff himself saw no riches from the play, but died in poverty.

As William Reeves summed up in 1823, 'Folks they went t'see Tom and Jerry, / And on Billy turn'd their back' (*Lines on Billy Waters*). Being a Character enabled others to turn William Waters the man into 'Billy Waters' the meme. Attention to the viral nature of popular culture reveals the complex ways it impacted upon vulnerable people off whom (in many cases) it fed. In a brutal economic irony, Waters was in danger of losing the very livelihood that he had fought so hard to develop. What on earth was he to do now?

Ludgate Hill

W hat must it have felt like, to know that audiences were laughing at you, or rather a white actor pretending to be you, on stages across London? It was a recognition of your achievements, of sorts. But as the passers-by became less friendly, as they muttered 'we know YOU don't want charity' or yelled out 'Alderman and chains!', and as the coins that jangled into your bowl or hat dwindled to a trickle and then threatened to dry up altogether, how did *that* feel? By 1823, Waters found himself in a perilous situation. The King of the Beggars? If he was, he was also a man with mouths to feed and, thanks to *Tom and Jerry*, his family was going hungry.

How did a man as resourceful as Waters try to boost his falling income? The theatre historian Hazel Waters (no relation), in her book *Racism on the Victorian Stage*, invites us to pay attention to 'the black crossing-sweeper (who haunts theatrical criticism wherever black characters or storyline are involved, and who deserves his own footnote in history)'. Hazel Waters doesn't have the space to say much more apart from the following: '[o]ne such crossing-sweeper achieved it. Billy Waters, who played the fiddle on the streets as well as keeping a crossing, was made into a character in W. T. Moncrieff's 1821 play *Tom and Jerry*.' Moncrieff also claimed

Waters was a crossing-sweeper outside the Adelphi on top of everything else, but that after *Tom and Jerry*, people 'crossed the road without contributing'.[1] So we should ask: did Waters work as a crossing-sweeper as well as a street performer, especially once his income began to plummet?

Answering this question involves a discussion of the unpleasant associations between skin colour and dirty faces, race and class, in Regency and early Victorian Britain.[2] The crossing-sweeper braved traffic and filth in British and American cities to clear a path through horse dung, human waste, rubbish and accumulated dirt ready for the well-dressed customer to cross the street. He (it was usually but not always a he) was a figure who combined connotations of lower-class life with racial identity because of his dirty face, a dirt associated in many representations with Black skin. The figure of the Black crossing-sweeper shifted and spread 'Billy Waters' across new texts and different audiences; this is another instance of Waters' fame spreading because his image resonated with other figures (like 'Jack Tar' and 'Beggar King'). Ideas associated with 'Billy Waters' then influenced the representation of Black crossing-sweepers on page and stage, as well as the depiction of real-life crossing-sweepers. Connections between Waters and crossing-sweepers hint at otherwise invisible aspects of his life experience. They also reveal the impact of the relationship between race and class on people like Waters and his family in Regency and early Victorian London.

If Waters used that 'economy of makeshifts' we encountered earlier to diversify his income, an important motivation must surely have been his family. Did the Waters children try to help? By 1823 the children could have been at most nine and one years old, still old enough to contribute to the household income. A small ragged child or infant could be a useful prop, their frail body making the case for public support without the need for words; a contemporary lithograph treats this fact with both humour and pathos (Figure 45).

45. A disabled soldier plays the violin while he and his wife sing the ballads they are selling and their elder child holds out a hat for coins (c. 1820).

Family relationships in impoverished households were necessarily conditioned by the constant fight to find food for empty bellies and lousy bodies, but there is no reason to suppose that parents felt any less affection for their children or were not grieved by the conditions under which their children lived. Parents who were crushed under the load of poverty simply did not have the luxury of being able to protect their children from working when time was short and winters were cold.[3]

46. *Ludgate Hill, approximately 1746. Detail from Rocque's*
Plan of London.

Did Waters become a crossing-sweeper in the attempt to support
this family? He was sometimes remembered as a crossing-sweeper
in the press. For instance, in March 1843 Waters appeared in a piece
of verse in the newspaper *The Age* about the two obelisks that stood
at a spot known as Waithman's crossing. This was at the foot of
Ludgate Hill at the junction with Fleet Street (heading east–west)
and what is now Farringdon and New Bridge Street (heading north–
south), just above Blackfriars Bridge (Figure 46):

> All remember Billy Waters
>   Who, on Ludgate Hill,
> Out of sweeping Waitman's crossing,
>   Make him private bill;
> And as the nickname once is given,
>   We are sure to keep,
> All ven dey do BILLY mention,
>   Allway call him 'sweep!'[4]

'Sweep!' is the cry for the crossing-sweeper, as the hurried pedestrian didn't bother to distinguish them from a chimney-sweep. Sweeping crossings, like sweeping chimneys, was an occupation taken up by the low class, the unskilled, and the very desperate, who had no other option but to tolerate downright dangerous working conditions. These were dirty occupations, symbolised by the visual shorthand of dirty faces. In a coffee shop not far from the Adelphi in *Life in London*, we meet a sooty-faced chimney-sweep. The hand-coloured plates vary in skin-tones from copy to copy, with the effect that dirt and Blackness are made casually indistinguishable (Figure 47). At the same time, many of the Londoners who turned to crossing-sweeping were, for reasons of long-term inequalities, Black and also Asian.[5]

In Regency London, Waithman's crossing was between the prisons of Fleet and Bridewell, now long gone. The first obelisk to be erected at this junction was popularly thought to be a memorial to the eighteenth-century radical journalist and later politician John Wilkes (1727–1797), and it was followed in 1833 by the obelisk

47. *Robert and George Cruikshank,* MIDNIGHT. Tom & Jerry
at a Coffee Shop.

with a plaque to Robert Waithman, a local trader who rose to become lord mayor, sheriff and MP (1764–1833). The verse about 'Billy Waters' takes the arrival of the new obelisk to imagine, in mock-heroic style, what the ghosts of Wilkes and Waithman would have made of each other. The imagined rivalry between the two obelisks and their attendant spirits is, by the sixth stanza, represented by the actions of a familiar figure:

> And Billy Waters, who so often swept
> Thy patriot pedestal, O odd-eyed Wilks!
> Would now have also brush'd, and begg'd, and kept
> *His* name from dirt who dealt in shawls and silks.[6]

Wilkes, founder of the Hellfire Club who inspired the rallying cry 'Wilkes and Liberty!', has to accept the new proximity of a memorial to a linen draper. And the fact that Waters the crossing-sweeper would (had he still been alive) have kept *both* monuments clean is something of a final straw. In some ways crossing-sweepers were a point of connection between different kinds of Londoners as they served myriad customers with the sweeping of their brooms. The most famous example of this in literature is probably Little Jo from Charles Dickens' *Bleak House* (1852–3). Sweeping a crossing was judged a more 'respectable' option than performing or begging, because the crossing-sweepers performed a useful function within the urban economy. But they were still perceived as low class.

A picture of the crossing published in 1830 shows the first obelisk, and also the small figure of a crossing-sweeper standing beside it (Figure 48). Was this really Waters? Crossing-sweepers appear relatively frequently in Regency and early Victorian visual culture, often in picturesque attitudes like in Figure 49, and this continues into the mid-nineteenth century. In an 1842 sketch by George Cruikshank (Figure 50), the Black crossing-sweeper watches ruefully as a white

48. Ludgate Hill, from Fleet Street.

lady's long skirts do his work for him. Black skin could be an advantage in what was a competitive marketplace (Figure 51 shows crossing-sweepers literally fighting over a crossing, a common Regency visual joke). The London *Daily News* declared as late as 1884 that:

> There is no doubt that, other things being equal, a black crossing-sweeper would take a great deal more than a white man. A negro is a stranger in a strange land; he is presumably friendless, and, being pretty certainly a native of a hot country, he may be supposed to suffer more from the wet and cold of our climate than an English-man. All these considerations would enable a steady blackman to make a good thing of a well-located crossing.[7]

There is a strong degree of sympathy expressed here, although the assumption that a Black man cannot be a 'native' of Britain like the

The smallest donation thankfully received!

49. The Smallest Donation Thankfully Received! (c. 1830).

'English-man' goes unquestioned. This is not a random thought-experiment by the *Daily News*: the association between Blackness and crossing-sweepers goes back to the 1820s. Waters himself left no reported words about crossing-sweeping. The lives of crossing-sweepers are difficult to trace and we seldom hear their experiences recounted in their own voices. Many had some form of disability. If the accidents of life left you unable to secure other work, sweeping a crossing was one way to survive on the streets (Figures 52 and 53). It's not impossible that this was also true for Waters.

The man in the picture of Waithman's crossing in Figure 48, however, appears to have all limbs intact. This particular crossing-sweeper was not Waters but Charles McGee. Born in Jamaica,

McGee was another man originally from elsewhere in the Atlantic world who found his way onto the London streets:[8]

> The following plate presents the portrait of another black man of great notoriety, Charles M'Gee, a native of Ribon, in Jamaica, born in 1744, and whose father died at the great age of 108. This singular man usually stands at the Obelisk, at the foot of Ludgate-Hill. He has lost an eye, and his woolly hair, which is almost white, is tied up behind in a tail, with a large tuft at the end, horizontally resting upon the cape of his coat. Charles is supposed to be worth money. His stand is certainly above all others the most popular, many thousands of persons crossing it in the course of a day. He has of late on the working-days sported a smart coat, presented to him by a city pastry-cook. On a Sunday he is a constant attendant at Rowland Hill's meeting-house, and on that occasion his apparel is appropriately varied.[9]

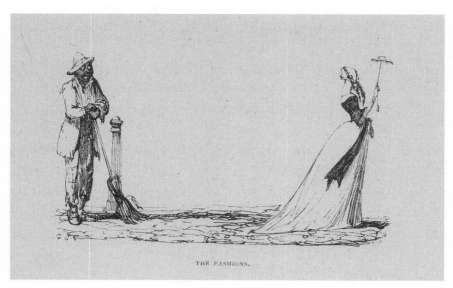

THE FASHIONS.

50. A caricatured Black crossing-sweeper leans on his broom grinning at a lady with a long train, whose dress has cleaned the road (1842).

51. *Crossing-sweepers fighting at what looks like Ludgate Circus* (1838).

Images of Charles McGee quite clearly place him with a broom next to the railings of the obelisk (Figure 54 and Plate XV). Why then is it Waters, and not McGee, who is sometimes remembered at Waithman's crossing? One reason must be that popular culture assumed a certain degree of interchangeability between lower-class Black Londoners. McGee fascinated George Cruikshank almost as much as Waters did: Cruikshank was a regular visitor to the nearby office of his satirical collaborator William Hone, and McGee turns up in their jointly produced satirical news sheet *A Slap at Slop* in 1821, at the height of Waters' own fame (Figure 54).[10] Waters and McGee appear together in both the Cruikshank brothers' illustration for *Life in London*, and George Cruikshank's earlier 'New Union Club' (also in Figure 2). In both images it's easy to tell them apart, you would think, especially with the exaggerations of caricature: Waters with his wooden leg and fiddle and hat; McGee with his broom. In J. Bysh's *Cries of London* for children, Waters and McGee appear on separate pages and with different pictures.[11] Yet clearly on some level they were considered not distinct, but part of the steady flow of barely differentiated Black poor in London. Waters' white wig and McGee's white hair looked the same to some nineteenth-century eyes. An 1881 writer even suggests that McGee 'was the original

52. *Thomas Shotter Boys,* View from Lombard Street, *looking towards Cheapside and Princes Street, with the Mansion House on the left; near the lamp post is a wooden-legged crossing-sweeper (1842).*

THE ONE-LEGGED SWEEPER AT CHANCERY-LANE.

[From a Photograph.]

53. *'The One-Legged Sweeper at Chancery Lane'* (1851).

"study" for the famous Billy Waters in *Tom and Jerry*.[12] This tells us that although in some ways Waters was seen as a very distinctive Character, in other ways he was treated as not very distinct at all.

Commentators get Black crossing-sweepers mixed up and then use them for different purposes: sometimes as markers of 'real life in London', and sometimes as part of an urban theatricality where London Characters switch roles with ease and play many parts. For Irene Tucker, 'the racism of race' partly lies in how 'raced subjects are deprived of the recognition of salient qualities of individualism and instead understood to be 'just like' those exhibiting the same racial marks'.[13] The figure of the Black crossing-sweeper is a powerful indication that Waters and his family were not thought of always as unique individuals. Black bodies especially were somehow interchangeable. In Figure 55 even Charles' surname is different and his detailed face is added to a fairly generic body. All the more reason, then, that white actors like Signor Paulo felt able to play Black characters on stage in blackface. And all the more evidence that blackface had nothing whatsoever to do with authenticity, but everything to do with power. It's these attitudes with which Waters had to contend.

Not only did blackface performance undermine Waters once *Tom and Jerry* appeared on stage, but the figure of the Black crossing-sweeper also diminished his memory when it was performed in blackface. Crossing-sweeper plays were hugely popular in the so-called 'minor' London theatres during the 1820s and 1830s, but aren't much studied.[14] C. M. Westmacott's *Othello, the Moor of Fleet Street* (Adelphi, 1833) – in which McGee is turned into 'Othello' the

54. George Cruikshank, 'Charles McGee' (1821).

CHARLES MACKEY.

55. *William Roberts,* Charles Mackey (c. *1820s*).

crossing-sweeper – is about a marriage between a white and a Black Londoner and it plays around with two fashionable 1830s topics: Shakespeare and the *Life in London* craze. First performed at the Adelphi where *Life in London* was staged, scene 4 is set in '*The Beggar's Club in the Holy Land*', just like Moncrieff's *Tom and Jerry*, specified as '*Interior of a public house in St Giles where the London beggars hold their festive meetings*' (a clear reference to both the Cruikshanks' illustration and *Tom and Jerry*). We get drinking songs taken directly from Egan's *Life in London*, well-known street Characters, and elements of the wedding feast from Act 2 scene 3 of Shakespeare' *Othello*. Westmacott freely borrows from Shakespeare and from Egan, the national poet and the Cadgers' feast, which complicates distinctions between so-called 'elite' and 'popular' culture. Dirt, class, race and blackface all collide in racial mockery. Audiences were asked to laugh at the racial stereotyping, the colloquial re-writing of Shakespeare in which all ends happily, and mixed-race marriages (clearly a source of anxiety). Diversity is a fact of London life in this play, but like in *Tom and Jerry*, Black parts performed by white actors interlink skin and dirt and blackface. Blacked-up faces express unease about the possibility that the generic boundaries between street people and Shakespeare, 'Billy Waters' and 'Othello', 'low' and 'high', might break down.

In the carnivalesque European traditions of mumming, chari-vari, and May Day, and in the American reimagining of noisy ritual celebrations such as Pinkster and the Callithumpians, some scholars have pointed to a longer blackface tradition than the kinds of caricatured performances of nineteenth-century minstrelsy. Eric Lott has argued that blackface involves 'love and theft', as it plays with the possibility of racial mixing and explores the idea of racial equality. Stephen Johnson agrees to an extent, suggesting 'It's complicated'. But is it? Writing more recently, Ayanna Thompson has pointed out that blackface hands over the performance of race to white actors only. This means that there is no such defence as 'white innocence', nor can blackface be defended as a desire to admire and to emulate Black cultures in an authentic way on the part of the white actor. Blackface is all about power and control, even when – especially when – the performer and the audience doesn't realise that it is. For Matthew D. Morrison (who adds an acoustic element to blackface, 'Blacksound', or the mimicry and appropriation of Black music) it's worse than this: blackface is a form of terror, he argues. It's a cause, symptom, result, and legacy of slavery which generates real effects upon real bodies and real lives. There's desire, but no love in it: it's the expression of white assumptions about Black bodies. Sean Murray shows blackface connects disability to Blackness to frame both identities as inferior to white, able-bodied movements and speech.[15] E. Patrick Johnson and Homi Bhabha suggest optimistically that there were instances where the coloniser learned from the colonised, or where the colo-nised borrowed the cultural tropes of the coloniser as a strategic form of resistance – and that human culture was eventually the richer for these encounters. The human cost, they emphasise however, was high.[16]

For Waters, blackface performance by white actors of any class was yet another dangerous problem to negotiate. Blackface enabled white performers and audiences to define Black cultures, and left performers like Waters forced to conform to the stereotypes of the 'stage Black' on those rare occasions when they could grab some attention for themselves. Frederick Douglass was in no doubt: blackface imitators were 'the filthy scum of white society, who have stolen from us a complexion denied to them by nature, in which to make money, and pander to the corrupt taste of their white fellow citizens'.[17] Blackface Cadgers and crossing-sweepers show us the network of popular culture gone toxic. Scholars are starting to say that the period during which Waters was alive saw particular kinds of racism, which coincided with anxieties many white people had about what a post-slavery world might hold.[18] Blackface not only allowed dominant white culture special rights to say what being Black meant, it also allowed some whites to deploy those rights to terrorise people like Waters. Paulo's blackface 'Billy Waters' at the Adelphi showed Waters the horrific side of a meme culture writ large.

Dirty Faces?

Waters faced a world in which the figure of the Black crossing-sweeper was used to attack Black performers and bring them down a peg or two. Another reason for the confusion (deliberate or mistaken) between Waters and Charles McGee was the ways in which Black performers were likened to crossing-sweepers in order to deliberately undermine them both.

These cultural ideas surrounded the daily lives of the Waters family and the memory of 'Billy Waters'. As its title suggests, 'Negro Melody – "Song of a Sweep"', a 'comic' song published in the newspaper *The Age*, deliberately linked race to a lowly status through the implicit connection of dirt. It is *'Chaunted by* Mr DYCE SOMBRE, *in the character of* BILLY WATERS'.[1] In other words, this is not a song by Waters himself, but a performance (albeit one that's printed not actually sung) that uses 'Billy Waters' as a Character.[2] By stanza two, the song quickly takes on the character not of Waters, but of the imagined performer, the memorably named Mr Dyce Sombre, who is made to declare that 'I den follow Billy's business'. Sombre's sweeping-up is also all to do with money, but with having lots of it, not with begging for spare change:

But as I've rupees in plenty
   Scraped into a heap,
Dat is von plain reason verefore
   I am called a 'sweep'.

Black and Asian sweeps are conflated: the implicit connections between lowly status, skin colour, and blackface get especially significant, because Dyce Sombre was another real historical person (Figure 56). He was the first dual-heritage Anglo-Indian to be elected to the British parliament. With a biography that reads remarkably like the plot of a Wilkie Collins novel, and an inherited fortune, the 'half-caste Croesus' (as the *London Daily News* called

56. *Charles Brocky,* David Ochterlony Dyce Sombre.

him nastily) came to England in 1836 when he lost his lands in India after they were seized by the East India Company on dubious grounds. Despite an aristocratic marriage and a brief stint as an MP (before his election was annulled for corruption), Sombre struggled to fit into Victorian high society. This situation worsened in dramatic fashion in June 1843 when his estranged wife's family had him imprisoned as a lunatic and made a bid for his money.[3] Sombre, for all his wealth, is depicted in *The Age* as nothing more than a crossing-sweeper: someone who speaks the pidgin dialect of the non-white, low-class comic act. The trope of the 'nabob' beggar, wealthy despite his appearance, is used against this dual-heritage figure. The song ends with the lines:

> So though priest and layman also
> > In my harvest reap,
> Dey get all my cash, and *I* get
> > Only called 'a sweep'.

Sombre suffers the inverse fate of Waters: locked up because of his fortune rather than suffering because of poverty. Nevertheless, the image of the dirty-faced crossing-sweeper, beyond the pale of society precisely because of his indeterminate skin colour, is used against both men in this song. Their countenances mean that they cannot be countenanced as part of respectable society.

Faces and their skin colour, or colouring, were of great interest in the nineteenth century. Skin was thought of as something to be read and interpreted, a frontispiece which told you something about the story within. Faces revealed class as well as race; the experience of race in Britain was always classed. Jennifer DeVere Brody critiques exactly this kind of 'arbitrary, culturally determined desire to limit and delimit, to name and order, to distinguish and create identities'.[4] Aviva Briefel has shown the ways in which hands and their skin colour in Victorian culture 'might betray the fact that race was *not* actually inscribed on the body'.[5] Waters and his family were trying desperately to survive in a city where to be Black in a competitive marketplace for charity might give you an edge. It marked you out as 'foreign' or 'exotic', and people assumed you were far from home, so gave money accordingly. But an 1864 George Cruikshank print presented dark skin as a warning sign of dangerously subversive potential within (Figure 57). The print uses a visual vocabulary drawn from crossing-sweeper images, 'Billy Waters' images, and the Cadgers scene, to threaten a world where a Black one-legged crossing-sweeper is in charge. The wooden leg and sailor costume of Waters has been adapted into the crossing-sweeper context and several of *these* Cadgers brandish brooms. 'Billy Waters-ness' is replicated and adapted by Cruikshank for a new satirical target, but he expects the viewer to be sufficiently visually literate to spot the connections. People who saw it displayed in print-shop windows, or

57. *George Cruikshank,* Report of a Meeting Held at the Cadger's Hall
(c. 1824).

even bought a copy for themselves, may well have been familiar with Black abolitionist campaigners such as Equiano (whom we last met as a young powder-monkey) who together with Ottobah Cugoano in the late 1700s formed the Sons of Africa, a group of educated Africans in London dedicated to ending the Atlantic slave trade. They would have heard of ex-sailor Robert Wedderburn's abolitionary activities, and perhaps shuddered at the execution of William Davidson for being one of the 1820 anti-government Cato Street conspirators. Cruikshank's image makes Black Londoners out to be a ridiculous but also a threatening presence.[6]

'Billy Waters' became associated with that perceived threat. One comic periodical especially vicious about crossing-sweepers was *Figaro in London* (1831–8), an illustrated forerunner of *Punch*. Henry Brougham, then lord chancellor, was prominent in the passing of the 1833 Abolition Act, which banned enslavement in most UK-held territories, and *Figaro in London* noticed his endeavours in the following fashion:

It is true that the descendants of Billy Waters, in this country, including the dirty little black who sweeps the crossing at Charing Cross, will hail and cheer the illustrious Brougham whenever he passes by; but we very much question the utility of the emancipation project of the Ex-Chancellor. We might as well insist on emancipating the footman, and striking the last rim of gold lace from the hat of the livery servant, as to make such a terrible fuss about altering the condition of the negroes, who it has been proved over and over again, are much happier in their dependent condition. We should be glad to see Lord Brougham devoting his time to the improvement of the condi-tion of the starving millions at home, rather than giving up his mind to the upsetting of all the arrangements of the n—rs, and thus induce them to resort to all sorts of tomfoolery to show their *intellectual equality*.[7]

The targets here of *Figaro*'s biting pen are numerous, but we might notice that Waters' direct 'descendant', part of the 'family' of Black poor, is imagined as a crossing-sweeper who is not just Black, but 'dirty'. All Black people are imagined here as lower class; they are equated with the 'footmen' and 'livery servant' and others in a 'dependent position'. *Figaro* gives more importance to the *white* poor, described as 'the starving millions at home' (because of course no one could be Black and British) who are more worthy of Brougham's attention. Here a dark face is the mark of the outsider who is not part of respectable middle-class society, and who relies on that society for financial support. No doubt *Figaro* saw Waters' skilled act as 'tomfoolery'. *Figaro*'s bitter language denies any kind of equality to people like the Waters family, and it uses the meme-like 'Black crossing-sweeper' to do so.

The troubling associations linked to the Black crossing-sweeper were not exclusive to Waters as a performer or as a Character. It was used to contain 'uppity negroes', to borrow Ayanna Thompson's highly ironic phrase.[8] Ira Aldridge – 'The African Roscius', as he was popularly known after a Roman actor who used to be enslaved – another African American from New York, was also linked to this figure in reviews by one particular magazine. These reviews give us further insight into the kinds of attitudes Waters encountered, and why he might have been thought of as a crossing-sweeper. Throughout 1833, *Figaro in London* used the figure of the crossing-sweeper in a rhetorical move to link Black skin with dirt.[9] Aldridge was not the first Black actor to grace the English stage, but for the *Figaro* reviewer he is immediately associated with the dirty face of the crossing-sweeper (*The Times* also used similar language against Aldridge):

Is it because the man has a black skin that he is a ready made Othello? . . . If a sooty face, we mean, of a naturally black complexion [o]f necessity implies an aptitude for parts such as

Othello, Zanga, &c. why has not the old Commodore been long ago dragged from his crossing in Tottenham Court Road, and thrust upon the boards of Drury Lane Theatre as Oronoka or some other of the numerous Moorish parts in the Drama. Upon the same principle would not every humpbacked man be a fit representative of Richard the third.[10]

What seems to really horrify the *Figaro* reviewer was that Aldridge had the temerity to perform at the National Theatre in Drury Lane in a leading role written by the National Poet.[11] A Black actor on stage rather than a blackfaced one? *Figaro* wants none of that, and implies that Aldridge cannot possibly impress. Blackness is equated either with being low class or with a disability here; Aldridge has a physical difference and deficiency written into his skin. Footman or crossing-sweeper: these are the only occupations (not Shakespeare at a Patent Theatre) for which the Black performer is suitable. And if he doesn't take the hint, Figaro will 'inflict on him such a chastisement as must drive him from the stage'. The words of the reviewer imply physical as well as verbal rebuke.[12] That Aldridge, applauded on his 1850s London debut as Othello and as Hamlet, attracted such nastiness in the 1830s shows us the kinds of forces that Waters was up against.

Aldridge's status as an actor of Shakespeare who happened to be Black challenged *Figaro*'s assumptions of innate class and intellectual distinctions between white and Black citizens. Aldridge the Shakespearean actor laid claim to a more gentlemanly status than that which the *Figaro* reviewer felt he should be allowed (ironically this same charge of overstepping bounds is levelled at Othello in Shakespeare's play). It's a threat which Figaro attempts to counter by deploying the crossing-sweeper:

The Old Commodore from the crossing in Tottenham Court Road occupied a private box, and every species of black whether

the N—er darkened by nature, or the sweep dyed by his professional pursuits, was in attendance to do honour to his respectable associate.[13]

The wooden-legged crossing-sweeper and war veteran known as
Old Commodore (Figures 19 and 58) was also someone for whom
Waters was mistaken in popular memory. Such misidentifications
would likely have mattered very much to Waters; they don't seem
to matter to *Figaro*. Whether these lower-class faces are dark or
darkened, chimney-sweeps or crossing-sweepers, to *Figaro* none of
them are remotely 'respectable' or worth differentiating.

Low-class status and dirty faces are also linked to comic
Black crossing-sweepers in the unfinished 1838 tale *The Posthumous*

58. *George Scharf, pencil drawing
of a Black man, probably 'The Old
Commodore' (c. 1824–33).*

Papers of the Cadger's Club (abandoned after four monthly parts). One of its protagonists, Black-Berry the one-legged, one-eyed crossing-sweeper, has echoes of *Tom and Jerry*'s 'Billy Waters' and Charles McGee. It's a *Pickwick Papers* parody, but it also imitates *Life in London*.[14] We are promised 'life, fun, frolic' from 'an old one upon the town' (2) and bombarded with Egan-esque hyperbole and puns, and the same insistence on the importance of the visual: 'The scene which followed could never be surpassed; the procession which was immediately formed, beggars all description!' (11). This is the same pun made by Egan in the chapter that introduces Waters. Black-Berry is a combination of both Waters and McGee, just as the text that contains him combines *Life in London* and *Pickwick Papers*. It turns into a parodic version of the Shakespeare jealousy plot when the (white) leader of the Cadger's Club, one Jeremiah Jumper, is revealed to have designs upon Black-Berry's (white) wife so Black-Berry wants 'vengeance!' (19). This sophisticated mixture of 'respectable' literature and cheap fiction asks the reader to find it both clever and funny. *Cadger's Club* insists on the openness and porousness of popular culture and in the process draws comic energy from the mixing-up of bodies: Shakespeare's, Egan's, and Dickens' bodies of work, and the bodies of the Cadgers. The illustration to part two, which shows Black-Berry surprising Jeremiah with Mrs Black-Berry, draws attention to the fact that both men have two wooden legs (Figure 59). Black-Berry's wife is 'a lady of the same delicate and fashionable calling, with a white countenance, when it was suffered to be visible from beneath the dirt which generally covered it, and who figured at a "cross" in the aristocratic neighbourhood of Portland place' (10); the association between blackness, class and dirt is made clear. It's almost as if she has to be in blackface to be a crossing-sweeper.

The porousness of popular culture meant that Regency and early Victorian ideas linked to 'Billy Waters' spread beyond cheap

59. 'Black-Berry surprises his wife with Jeremiah Jumper' (1838).

fiction. In *Vanity Fair* (1848), William Thackeray's characters, in tackling the thorny issue of interracial marriages, cannot help themselves: the image they turn to is that of the Black crossing-sweeper. Thackeray wrote with nostalgia about how formative the illustrations to *Life in London* were for him as part of his boyhood reading. Key among his childhood memories are the 'pictures – oh such funny pictures!' Returning to it as an adult he finds 'Tom and Jerry is not so brilliant as I had supposed it to be'; the text is much less compelling, but 'the pictures! – oh! the pictures are noble still!' So much do the colour plates continue to fire his imagination, even in adulthood, that he copies one out for his readers 'to the best of my humble ability'. This nostalgic endorsement of a reading experience which has the power to drive creative imitation even across a distance of forty years was considered powerful enough for the bookseller James Camden Hotten to include it in his introduction to the 1869 edition of *Life in London*.[15] The Cruikshanks' plates led to the wider fame of Waters; they also stick in Thackeray's mind as a formative influence on his visual imagination.

In *Vanity Fair* the Black crossing-sweeper reappears to belittle the character Miss Swartz as it was used against Waters. The only other named Black character in the novel is the Sedley family's footman Mr Sambo (named for a racialised stereotype). It's not quite clear where Miss Swartz, 'the rich woolly-haired mulatto from St Kitt's' (42), fits in the class system.[16] Thackeray's illustration of her, dressed in the expensive fashions of the day, conforms to the

60. *Miss Swartz from W. M. Thackeray's* Vanity Fair (1848).

visual language of racialised caricature shared by the *Life in London* pictures and images of the Black crossing-sweeper (Figure 60). George Osborne refers angrily to 'the black that sweeps opposite Fleet Market' at the end of chapter 21:

> 'Marry that mulatto woman?' George said, pulling up his shirt-collars. 'I don't like the colour, sir. Ask the black that sweeps opposite Fleet Market, sir. I'm not going to marry a Hottentot Venus.' (256)

This ugly outburst references Sarah Baartman as well to express Osborne's horror at the thought of marriage to wealthy Miss Swartz. The additional layer of irony here is that the crossing-sweeper Charles McGee was (as we have seen) supposed to have died with a small fortune. George's remark is picked up later by his father when it becomes clear that instead of marrying the heiress, his son still intends to marry the impoverished Amelia Sedley. Angrily the father exclaims: 'Marry HER, that IS a good one. My son and heir marry a beggar's girl out of a gutter. D— him, if he does, let him buy a broom and sweep a crossing' (276). The danger, in Mr Osborne's eyes, is that George will become a crossing-sweeper by marrying Amelia because she is poor, despite George thinking that marriage to Miss Swartz will have the same result. Miss Swartz's true value is never really recognised. George comes close to it, but only so he can make a rebellious point about the virtues of Amelia to his disapproving family:

> 'Are you a friend of Amelia's?' George said, bouncing up. 'God bless you for it, Miss Swartz ... Anybody who speaks kindly of her is my friend; anybody who speaks against her is my enemy. Thank you, Miss Swartz'; and he went up and wrung her hand. (253)

But the fact that the crossing-sweeper can be used to damn both Miss Swartz *and* Amelia shows that skin is a very unstable visual marker. Crossing-sweepers keep defying attempts to define them by their countenances. Perhaps Waters and his family get the last laugh after all.

The Triumph of Joseph Jenkins

The 'Black crossing-sweeper' was used to attack Black Londoners and diminish them. But Waters' costume choices suggest that he refused to be bowed. His white wig suggested subservience then delivered judgment. This shows us how Waters and his family were looked at, but also how Waters laughed back.

Waters' options for resistance were limited. Ira Aldridge was subject to the same forces as Waters, but Aldridge had more resources: he and his supporters decided to play *Figaro* at its own game, and instigated a poster campaign. *Figaro* responded with the anger of a magazine publicly caught out. How utterly unacceptable it was, *Figaro* thundered, for Aldridge or his friends 'to deface the walls of the metropolis with a slanderous placard attributing to the editor of Figaro a desire to drive the black gentleman from the stage without a fair trial'.[1] The magazine then attacked Aldridge for playing 'white' roles. According to *Figaro*, Aldridge 'imagines that though nature has made him an Othello, he has only to resort to the paint-pot to become a Romeo. Talent is, however, not to be thrown in, in distemper colours, and not twenty coats of paint would make an actor of the black whom we have so wholesomely flagellated'; the language of racial violence is used once more.[2] *Figaro* is backed into a corner of its own making, forced to try to justify the position that a Black actor cannot use whiteface but a white actor is entitled to use blackface. For *Figaro* a Black performer cannot 'play' Billy Waters on stage, they are supposed to 'be' Billy Waters at the street crossing. The striking viciousness of *Figaro*'s reviews compared to other reviews in the British press raises the question, however, whether *Figaro* doth protest too much. What really threatened *Figaro* was the realisation that faces and skin colour are completely arbitrary ways to differentiate between people and cannot signify class or intellectual difference after all. 'It is said that the *black Roscius*', claimed Moncrieff, 'took lessons' from Waters.[3] Perhaps they were lessons in defiance.

Other Black Londoners found ways to assert themselves that Waters did not manage to use. Charles McGee, as Oskar Jensen points out, did in fact carefully save up his money. McGee knew better than to keep it with him: he gave his weekly earnings to his friend Mr Waithman and once it had built to a substantial sum he deposited it in the nearby Bank to grow 'like a young plantan [plantain]'.[4] And Edward Albert, interviewed by Henry Mayhew, found a more direct way to seize control of the narrative by writing and publishing his own account of his life. Albert, an ex-naval and merchant marine sailor from Jamaica who – like Waters – was injured at sea (losing both legs), settled with his English wife in London and scraped a living as a crossing-sweeper.[5] Scholar Natalie Prizel has located a copy of Albert's book, *Brief Sketch of the Life of Edward Albert, Or the Dead Man Come to Life Again*, and as Jensen says it's a remarkable piece of writing. Albert's book contains his prose autobiography as well as a ballad of his life, and was published in more than one town. The edition Prizel found has a striking woodcut on the cover of a ship in full sail.[6]

Abolitionist campaigner William Wells Brown also used his writing to defy racist narratives. Brown includes an account of a charismatic London preacher, actor and crossing-sweeper, Joseph

Jenkins, in one of his many successful books, *The American Fugitive in Europe* (1855).[7] Brown's account reclaims the figure of the Black crossing-sweeper for the Black performer instead of against them. Jenkins is 'a good-looking man, neither black nor white' (268) and 'a native of Africa ... the victim of a slave-trader' (274) whom Brown describes bumping into again and again (like the plot of a Dickens novel) as he wanders about London. Brown sees him perform Shakespeare's Othello with 'great dramatic power and skill' in a cheap London venue called the Eagle Saloon (270). Jenkins' skills are appreciated by his audience of ordinary Londoners; in Brown's account, working-class culture is open to a more diverse understanding of Victorian society. Jenkins is advertised on the playbills by Aldridge's moniker of the 'African Roscius', and is 'greeted with thunders of applause' (269). At his curtain-call Jenkins is 'received with deafening shouts of approbation, and a number of bouquets thrown at his feet' (270). They finally speak after Brown encounters Jenkins preaching in a London church, where he proves to be 'a most eloquent and accomplished orator' (272). And the best bit? Jenkins reassures Brown that he is now financially able to give away his crossing as a wedding portion for his daughter, and it is 'worth thirty shillings a week'. Jenkins can retire to focus on leading his band, which plays at 'balls and parties, and three times a week at the Holborn casino' (275). Harnessing the power of his abilities, Jenkins has set up himself and his family in his own way, and used crossing-sweeping to do it. Brown reclaims the narrative of the wealthy crossing-sweeper for this entrepreneurial Londoner – and states that an immigrant is 'the greatest genius that I had met in Europe' for good measure (275). If only Waters had met Joseph Jenkins.

Cultural critic Irene Tucker is interested in how the use of skin as a way of organising knowledge leads to the threat (or enabling possibility) of similarity just as much as the threat of difference. Tucker points out that if a society decides membership of a 'race' is determined by visual cues, then 'perceiving race involves, for better or for worse, experiencing individuals' likeness to one another rather than their difference'.[8] This extends, for example, to the act of conflating Black individuals into all being crossing-sweepers. But the close reader of bodies must register the points of likeness between themselves and the body they are reading if they are to select specific points of difference. Reading for difference is impossible without also reading for likeness, whether the text you are trying to interpret is a 'real' historical body, the description of a fictional character, a stage performer's body, or a book illustration. Bodies in popular culture register both difference and similarity. Jeremy Goheen argues that what he calls the 'transitory blackness' of white chimney-sweeps' sooty bodies worried Regency commentators anxious that whiteness could be contaminated.[9] But there is also a small space for registering the subversive potential of bodily similarities in nineteenth-century popular culture.

61. *Waters in a wig?*

Waters' white wig was a piece of costuming which stuck two fingers up at any ideas that Black people could not be important in Regency society. White wigs were worn by footmen as they ran errands or followed behind their white employers (or owners, pre-1807 Abolition) through the London streets. Wigs were also worn by Waters' adversaries the magistrates. Waters' wig gestures to white ideas of Black servitude whilst also gloriously undermining them. A picture in Hindley's book on the *Life in London* craze – beneath a sentence from Moncrieff that describes Waters as possessing talents 'that as an actor would have rendered him a *shining* ornament to the stage' – shows a man in a white wig and evening wear doing a dramatic reading from a book on what is clearly meant to be some kind of stage. His glasses are on his nose and he has water ready at his elbow, just in case (Figure 61). This man (intended to be Waters?) is performing Shakespeare, judging by the slightly adapted quote from *Hamlet* that precedes the picture. Perhaps Hindley meant to be satirical or simply amusing when he included this picture. Perhaps he intended the reader to laugh at an incongruous image: a caricatured Black man performing Shakespeare in public. But we might instead see an admission of everything Waters could have been – should have been – allowed to achieve, if he so chose, and was systematically denied.

In a radical thought experiment, an article in the *Englishman's Magazine* in 1831 imagines a London where the positions of Black and white people have been reversed. At first the fictional white protagonist is horrified by the changes:

I found that dreadful havoc had been made with our literature. Our amatory poetry, in particular, had suffered, – its violet-coloured eyes, rosy cheeks, and coral lips, had been exchanged for more suitable similitudes. Shakespeare's Othello and Aaron were white men. As it may well be supposed, I was quite bewildered. I could not endure the scorn of the multitude; and one day, my rage surmounting my discretion, I knocked down a respectable stockbroker, when in an instant I was seized by a couple of his white footmen, hurried away before a justice, and packed off to gaol, where I had sufficient time to ponder on the haplessness of my lot, and the miserable condition of the world.[10]

Locked up for attacking the stockbroker, the narrator is visited by an 'imp' who is both Black and white, and who explains that a new world order has arrived where Black people rule over white people:

'And can the world be duly governed by the blacks?'

The motley imp stretched forth his hand, and instantly two skulls rolled to my feet. I took them up.

'Which,' said he, 'of these skulls possesses the greater state-apartment for wisdom, true nobility, freedom, accomplishment? Examine them: look at these empty halls and see if you can discover ... Nay, man, cannot you say? There must be some private mark – some stamp – some scratch to judge by. No? You see none? Well, then, I will tell you. These are the skulls of two men, born in a rude uncivilised land: education never filled these empty cavities with golden precepts; they passed from the breast to the tomb, creatures of nature. These skulls belonged to a negro and a white man – you see no difference in their struc-ture – which is fitter to govern?' and casting them from him, they again crumbled into dust. (192)

The narrator sees that, stripped of their covering of skin, both skulls look the same. He wakes up to hear a pro-slavery activist droning on about 'Divine Providence' and the natural order of things. With his new-found perspective, this speech no longer rings true. This thought experiment is very different to the practice of blackface, which turned Blackness into something whites performed. Instead, the article places its implied white reader in the place of the Black citizen, and forces them to confront daily injustices from another's point of view. Maybe – just maybe – the skills of people like Waters opened up small pockets of space which enabled this kind of abolitionist thinking.

Waters made his own use of 'Jack Tar', 'Comic Black', and 'King of the Beggars', knowing that they would otherwise be used for him – or even against him. He made canny professional choices. But he had no opportunity to do what Jenkins did. Hampered by poverty and likely illiteracy, Waters could not provide social mobility for his family. A white-written part performed in blackface destroyed their tenuous hold on a stable family life. The journalist E. L. Blanchard judged that *Tom and Jerry* 'let out the secret of beggar luxury', while the play, Blanchard notes, 'was exceedingly profitable'.[11] 'Justice, at length, seiz'd on poor Bill': in February 1822 Waters was arrested again and brought before the Sheriff's Court of Inquiry in Hatton Garden. Told by the magistrate that he should retire to the Royal Navy's Greenwich Hospital for ex-sailors while some sort of provision was made for his wife, Waters was having none of it: knowing this arrangement would come with no guarantees of his family's safety, he declared that 'he would live and die constant to Poll'.[12] This is a quote from Dibdin's hit nautical song 'Jack's Fidelity'. In a crisis Waters performed 'Jack Tar' the faithful and patriotic sailor as the best weapon he had against power. The Mendicity Society remained unconvinced: in their Minute-Book for 1822, case number 15001 is 'W.W. An Idle & dissolute Character'.

His charm and humour got him released by the magistrate yet again. But with his reputation and his occupation ruined, before long Waters was ill and unable to work:

His day was o'er, he soon found out
Poverty with rapid stride
Follow'd him, and clamor's shout
Meant poor Billy to deride. (Reeve, 'Lines on Billy Waters')

In desperation the family pawned his precious fiddle. His wooden leg, we are told, 'would have shared the same fate, but its extensive service had rendered it worthless'; to a limb-amputee of course this wooden leg had immense value, but not, apparently, in the commercial economy of Regency London.[13] As the situation worsened, desperate measures were called for. A doctor was too expensive, and the only hospitals available required either payment of fees or a reference from the hospital governor. Waters and his friends had neither of these things. There was only one last option: the parish workhouse.

~ PERFORMANCE ~

In Which Waters Leaves a Legacy

St Giles workhouse, London, March 1823

The workhouse bell strikes 5 o'clock. It is still dark.

The bell is there to wake the Family, as the Governor likes the inmates to be known; but families are kept separate for most of the day, and certainly not allowed to mingle in the Wards.

The rest of the workhouse awakes for the first shift of the day. There is no activity in this Infirmary, however. Here, the human flotsam of the city washes up on a very stony shore.

Yesterday this Ward was cleaned and swept, and fumigated with wormwood. The smell lingers.

He lies in a plain bed, restless. He must be up, up! He must dance! Today there will be Beef-broth for breakfast. His children will be so pleased. But only if he earns some money.

One of the Nurses is up and dressed. She glances at the patients. She's a workhouse inmate herself, earning some useful pence a week for her efforts. The writing on the Apothecary's medicine bottles mystifies her. She's not going to go near the infectious ones if she can help it. Right now she thinks only of breakfast-time, still one hour away.

We'll get Milk-porridge again today, she thinks.

She avoids the man in the furthest bed as he tosses and mutters.

Workhouse

Workhouse: a word of fear which conjures up images of high walls, locked gates, forbidding buildings and institutionalised cruelty. Dickens writes so movingly in *Oliver Twist* (1837–9) about the horrors of the early Victorian workhouse. The late Georgian workhouse was slightly less systematically punishing of the non-working poor, or 'paupers' – but only slightly. In following Waters into the workhouse we can see the gap that opened up between his life and his afterlife, his ending and his survival, which continues to this day. Unlike so many marginalised people from history, Waters was not condemned to obscurity, because his Character went on to have a 'life' and a legacy all of its own. But this was all without his consent. This is a paradox of a meme culture: it trails both fame and destruction in its wake. Performance created Waters' fame, and performance created his destruction. It also offered grounds for hope, as an exploration of his legacy will reveal.

The workhouse shared by the parishes of St Giles and St George was on Shorts Gardens, near the corner with what is now Endell Street (Figure 31).[1] This was probably where Waters died, as all but one account of his last days agree: his parish burial record lists his George Street address but also the letters Wk.H. With surviving records incomplete, current best guess is that he was not a full workhouse inmate but in the infirmary. Waters' friends only had to carry him across Broad Street from the Rookery to get him there. The workhouse wasn't the only option for the distressed poor of St Giles; if you had no income, either temporarily (due to accident or illness) or chronically (due to misfortune or inability to work), you could claim 'outdoor relief' from your parish, essentially a form of benefit payment provided while you continued to live at home. In St Giles such payments were distributed at the workhouse on Mondays, Wednesdays, and Thursdays; it's possible Waters and his family made use of this assistance in the struggle to stay afloat.[2] There were also parish almshouses and a charity school.[3] Very short-term issues could be aided with so-called 'casual' relief like a one-off payment or one-night workhouse stay. Most paupers got financial assistance without entering the workhouse, or without remaining very long.[4] In 1823 the country was eleven years away from the introduction of the so-called 'New' Poor Law, which aimed to eliminate the mounting costs of outdoor relief by offering only (as a deterrent to 'sturdy rogues') admittance into large work-houses where the disciplinary regime was even tougher and the separation of families enforced even more rigorously.[5] Even so, the St Giles workhouse was built with the express intention of removing 'the nuisance of beggars' by terrifying the so-called 'lazy-grown poor' with the threat of the oppression and rigours of workhouse life. Only the 'truly indigent and necessitous', in their most desperate need, would ever dream of going near the place or troubling the parish for help.[6] Two broadsides printed in St Giles, both entitled *The Workhouse Cruelty*, detailed the appalling ill-treatment of individuals that stemmed from such aims.[7] Many Londoners preferred to die in an alley.

Despite this, in the Regency period sickness was one common reason to seek workhouse help.[8] Life in St Giles was hard, impover-ished, and didn't tend to last long. Mortality rates were high in

London in the 1810s and 1820s; this was true of the whole city, from the richest to the poorest, but was especially true of the Rookery. According to one guidebook, *The Picture of London for 1820*, Londoners succumbed to everything from Asthma to Apoplexy, Bile to Bleeding, Cancer to Chickenpox, Grief, Horse Shoe Head, Water on the Chest, Miscarriage, Lethargy, Measles, Quinzies, Small Pox, Worms, and 'Fevers of all kinds'. This was before you factored in the casualties of various accidents and violent deaths. Of the approximately 20,000 Londoners buried in 1816, a fifth were aged between thirty and fifty years; Waters was around forty-five years old.[9] Sickness was exacerbated by hunger and malnutrition. Waters' friends and family would have hoped that his stay in the workhouse infirmary would only be temporary, but feared the worst.

The St Giles workhouse was built on land purchased from a Mr Gregory in 1723, and was 'a building of considerable extent' which, according to the parish vestry clerk in 1822, 'enclose[d] within its walls all the usual conveniences of similar establishments'.[10] The buildings filled almost three sides of a square with one frontage north onto Vinegar-Yard, and one south onto Shorts Gardens, with a gate ten feet wide. The east side was a large connecting wing; the west side was formed by a wall enclosing the yard (used for exercise). The infirmary stood on the north side of Vinegar-Yard, separated from the main workhouse building to reduce the risk of infections.[11]

The workhouse master and matron (a married couple, William and Ann Reed) wanted to know two things when Waters arrived at their door: was he legally 'settled' in the parish and was he infectious? They either decided that they were legally obliged to offer him assistance because he had achieved 'settled' status, or, more likely given his American birth, that he was too unwell to survive removal from the parish and had nowhere else to go.[12] Besides, the parish officers knew that they were supposed to consider the workhouse 'an asylum for the aged, for orphans in an infant state, for idiots, lunatics and the lame, blind, sick, or otherwise infirm and diseased persons [and] such casual paupers as have not settlement in these parishes, whom it may be necessary to relieve for a time, on account of sudden illness or other calamity'.[13] In any case, a full settlement examination to be signed off by a Justice of the Peace might take a week to arrange. Migrants came from all over the British Isles and beyond to London; Waters would not have been an unusual inmate in that regard and he was unlikely to have been the only Black inmate.[14] Plenty of paupers were turned away from workhouse doors for having no settled status, or for being too infectious, or they died on the way. For all the horrors that the image of a workhouse conjures up, Waters was at least able to get a bed and medical care. The workhouse infirmary was in effect the local hospital.

At the infirmary Waters was checked over by the surgeon Mr Ogle, the apothecary Mr Burgess (who dispensed medicines) and his assistant Mr Ward. He was inspected for lice, fever, small-pox, Foul (venereal) disease, or the Itch (infectious skin complaints).[15] The commonest cause of dangerous sickness in the workhouse was fever, a high-risk illness: so if delirious, Waters would have been swept off to the isolation ward within the infirmary, kept for those 'who might not be proper to lie in the common hospital rooms, on account of their distempers and condition'.[16] He was put in a bed softened only with flock and straw.[17] Most deaths from fever occurred within one month of entering the workhouse; Waters' family and friends would have been very worried indeed by his condition.[18] What was worse, they were not allowed to visit him. Waters was now separated from everyone he held dear. But a hospital had served him well before, and this was his best chance of survival. The infirmary was stocked with drugs from the Company of Apothecaries, sherry and port 'for the infirm', as well as leeches, linseed meal, and other natural remedies. This wasn't unusual: for example, we know Birmingham's workhouse had a fully fledged operating theatre by 1823 as well as stocks of mortars, pestles, syringes, plasters, wooden limbs, and herbs and oils for making medicines.[19] His distinctive costume, however, was something he would no longer be wearing. As previously, in the Navy, he was put into institutional clothing.

Later, 'Billy Waters' became associated with the dangers and cruelties of the workhouse, and the ability of people in authority to turn a blind eye to the conditions inside them. For instance the magazine *The Satirist* printed the following verse in April 1837 as the effects of the harsher 1834 New Poor Law became apparent:

Thus this Poor-Law makes grumblers of all rogues;
    And thus the tatters rags of poverty
  Are now not see in every lane and street;
And beggars of great note, like Billy Waters,
From fear of punishment, amend their ways,
    And lose the name of paupers.[20]

Satires on the New Poor Law were common in the 1830s: these words are a parody of Hamlet's 'To be, or not to be' speech. They are put into the mouth of the Bishop of Exeter, who stands up in the House of Lords to support the New Poor Law even though he has previously been visited by the ghost of a workhouse inmate who was starved into a pauper's grave. The bishop name-checks Waters as an example of 'rogues' who could work their way out of poverty if only they tried. Yet Waters' time in the workhouse was reportedly only due to the dire necessity of illness brought on by destitution. He had resisted the authorities' attempts to contain him for so long that he must only have entered when all other options seemed exhausted.

For several days Waters lay 'in a lingering condition', unable to see his children of whom he was so proud, and separated from his wife and his friends.[21] He did not linger long. Somewhere between 17 and 21 March 1823, and more than 3,000 miles from his birthplace, William Waters died.

In George Street, his wife and family learned that their lives had changed irrevocably. In the Rose and Crown, another fiddler led the dancing. The Navy clerk who kept the pension records wrote 'D. D.' – Discharged, Dead – next to Waters' name. In the Strand, regular pedestrians looked for a cocked hat and fiddle, were disappointed, and walked on.

Accounts of Waters' death began to apportion blame. William Reeves wrote in June 1823:

> In vain he fiddl'd, danc'd and sung,
> Until he was out of breath;
> Starving he was, his bow unstrung,
> Till he danc'd – The Dance of Death. ('Lines on Billy Waters')

Writing some fifty years later, the antiquarian Charles Hindley knew exactly where the blame for Waters' death lay:

> One notable effect of 'Life in London', particularly in its dramatised form, must be recorded. It broke the heart of poor Billy Waters, the one-legged musical negro, who died in St Giles's workhouse, on Friday, March 21, 1823, whispering with his ebbing breath, a mild anathema, which sounded very much like: 'Cuss him, dam Tom – meē – Tom – meē Jerry!'[22]

Ironically the Adelphi production had recently closed, the actors worn out by their own success. Presenting Waters' supposed last words in the broken English of the 'Comic Black' of stage and minstrelsy, Hindley's account (uncredited, but repeated almost word-for-word from E. L. Blanchard's article in the *Era Almanack* of January 1877) reveals the horrible ironies of Waters' story. The play

Waters curses with his 'ebbing breath' as the enemy of his mortal body was the very play that ensured the survival of his fictionalised one. Writing in 1878, Hindley took his place in a five-decades-long fascination with Waters, which kept that 'ebbing breath' from ever quite fading away. Almost as soon as William Waters died, the creation of 'Billy Waters' the immortal street Character began in earnest.

Will and Testament

It started with his burial, his obituaries, and accounts of his fiction-alised Last Will and Testament. Waters' death was reported in twenty newspapers all carrying the same obituary, noting his costume, his street act, his popularity, and his workhouse death. Almost exactly a year later, a reprint of the obituary appeared in a collection of death notices of actors, theatre managers and ex-performers of all kinds, high and low, entitled 'Dramatic Necrology'.[1] This is astonishing for a man who died in a workhouse: as medical historian Kevin Siena writes, 'workhouses dealt with death almost daily'; the comparably large sums they spent on coffins makes this all too clear. With a high percentage of sick, frail, newborn, and elderly inmates, workhouses, though not necessarily more deadly places for the poor than the streets or their lodgings, still had a high death rate.[2] We should remember this when we realise that Waters' death was read about at breakfast tables across Britain.

Waters' family and friends were the most affected. Workhouses were responsible for the laying-out and burial fees for a deceased inmate, but would only provide the dreaded 'pauper funeral': a basic shroud, a simple coffin, an unmarked or even mass grave, and no wake. In the workhouse infirmary it was the nurse who sent for a coffin and a shroud, and saw that the body was washed, laid in the plain wooden coffin, and brought down to a room set aside for this purpose. Waters' clothes and belongings were collected by the nurse and delivered to the matron, who put anything worth keeping in store and tore up the rest for rags.[3] Moncrieff claimed almost thirty years later that Waters died in his 'miserable lodging' in the pile of straw covered by a rug which served as his bed.[4] Perhaps Wk.H. just meant he had a parish burial. If Waters died in his lodgings the scene would have been a lively one: *Life in London*-style text *The English Spy* (1826) describes a wake in St Giles where 'the solemn gloom which generally pervades the chamber of a lifeless corpse is partially removed by the appearance of the friends of the deceased arranged around, drinking, singing, and smoking tobacco in profusion'.[5] There was no chance of this in the workhouse, though hopefully one last carouse took place in the Rookery in his honour.

What kind of funeral did Waters have? The kinds of additional embellishments required to lift a 'pauper funeral' into a public demonstration of memorial, community attachment, and social standing were costly. Many poor families joined burial societies to save for the cost of polished handles, coloured beading, decorative name plates, headstones, drapes, and a wake. It's possible that St Giles parish provided a 'parish pall' (a black cloth to be draped over the coffin during transportation to the burial ground) but that practice may have already ended.[6] The indignity of a pauper funeral remained: 'Nothing', the essayist Charles Lamb declared in 1811, kept 'in the imaginations of the poorer sort or people, a generous horror of the workhouse more than the manner in which pauper funerals are conducted in this metropolis'.[7] Waters was buried swiftly in an unmarked grave in the St Giles parish New Burial Ground, most likely in the section reserved for paupers and Catholics that was furthest from both the chapel and St Pancras Old Church, unprotected from the attentions of the body-snatchers who operated in the area.[8] Now the quiet north end of St Pancras Gardens, then it was already developing into the stinking over-crowded horror of a place that was closed for burials in 1854. One W. B. Champneys performed what ceremony there was; four other people were buried on the same day as Waters, possibly in the same grave, as they all were registered as Wk.H. Funerals for London's street people could be more elaborate than we might think. Jack Stuart, 'celebrated and scurrilous ballad-singer', died in August 1815 aged thirty-five. His funeral procession wended its way from Somers Town to Old St Pancras, made up of his widow and three blind mourners all in black, his dog, and two street-fiddlers who played the 104th psalm. His wake passed into legend, more myth than truth.[9] Waters too had his family and friends, who would have stood around the grave.

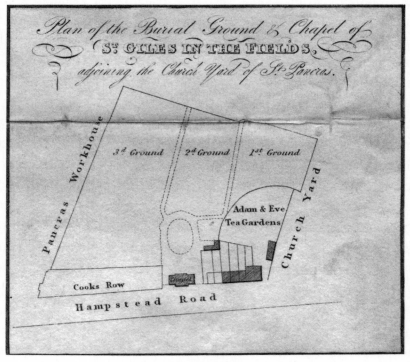

62. *St Giles Burial Ground.*

63. Detail from The Death, Last Will, and Funeral of 'Black Billy' (1823).

'William alias Billy Waters': Waters' burial record leaps out from the others on the same page. He was already acquiring an official double life as a man with a stage name. Almost immediately, James Catnach, the prolific Seven Dials publisher of broadsides, spotted a commercial opportunity. He put out a sheet called *The Death, Last Will, and Funeral of 'Black Billy'*, which ran to more than ten editions. A large and richly illustrated sheet, it contains an obituary of Waters that seems to have been written by Catnach himself, a ballad entitled 'The Merry Will and Testament of Master Black Billy', and an illustration captioned 'Funeral Procession of Poor "BLACK BILLY" (Figure 63). Catnach's obituary echoes details that we find in others, from the next day's newspapers to Hindley writing in the 1870s. Catnach already describes him as 'the famous Billy Waters', known by 'every child in London' and the 'King of the Beggars', no ordinary street performer. And what does Catnach point to as the source of this fame? Rather than solely his fiddle playing, it is 'his hat and feathers with his peculiar antics', which 'excited mirth and attention'. Costume and performance turned Waters into a famous Londoner. Costume and performance sealed his place in the collective memory after his death. They also reduced him to a set of abstract objects. His hat and feathers danced onto the pages and stages of posterity as 'Billy Waters' the fictionalised set of ideas.[10]

Fiction-making is there in the image on Catnach's broadside (Figure 63). 'Funeral Procession of Poor "BLACK BILLY"' depicts no skimpy pauper funeral. Instead, several mourners proceed and follow the hearse, including the distinctive figure of Andrew Whiston ('Little Jemmy') and someone who might be Charles McGee with his crossing-sweeper broom behind him. At the front are several street sellers and beggars and a dustman. It's a kind of street performance, which claims space in the public eye and the public memory for 'Black Billy'. If we look in the woodcut for possible depictions of Waters' wife and two children, explicitly mentioned in Catnach's obituary above the image, we might wonder if the bare-breasted Black woman with a feather in her cap is supposed to be a representation of Waters' wife. If so it's a racist one. The ballad singer behind her is another possible candidate, especially as she looks rather like Peg the ballad singer from *Life in London*. Is the small boy wiping his eyes with a handkerchief meant to be Waters' son? Perhaps we should not read this woodcut too literally. All of the procession wear black mourning ribbons hanging from their hats, and Whiston raises a glass as it passes the 'Beggar's Opera'. The suggestion is that a magnificently rowdy wake has just taken place inside. A bearer-party of six tall men carries what is clearly a solid-wood coffin, which is covered in a sumptuous black pall embroidered with the name of Billy Waters and his fate: 'down' on his luck for one last time. Waters may be 'poor' but this slow procession has all the dignity of a heraldic funeral. Nor does it go unnoticed: a figure in the upstairs window of Waters' favourite haunt, perhaps Waters' wife in a widow's cap, has thrown up the sash to weep as the cortège passes.

There is a great deal of satire in this image: it's mock-heroic. The fact that Waters is accorded such ceremonials is being laughed at as well as celebrated. Yet if we contrast Charles Lamb's description of a London pauper funeral, we can see that this is no such thing:

> The coffin nothing but a few naked planks, coarsely put together, – the want of a pall (that decent and well-imagined

veil, which, hiding the coffin that hides the body, keeps that which would shock us at two removes from us), the coloured coats of the men that are hired, at cheap rates, to carry the body, – altogether, give the notion of the deceased having been some person of an ill-life and conversation, some one who may not claim the entire rites of Christian burial, – one by whom some parts of the sacred ceremony would be desecrated if they should be bestowed upon him. I meet these meagre processions sometimes in the street. They are sure to make me out of humour and melancholy all the day after. They have a harsh and ominous aspect.[11]

Cheap, meagre, and harsh: these are not words one would use to describe the way Catnach's broadside depicts Waters' procession. For there on top of the coffin, instead of heraldic emblems or knightly equipment, are Waters' fiddle, his wooden leg, and, of course, his feathered hat. Waters, this image tells us, is not destined for an obscure pauper's grave. His costume provides him with his own particular power, which somehow transcends death, and means that 'Poor BILLY WATERS' gets a broadside of his own. The proceeds of the sale, though, went to Catnach, not Waters' family.

Catnach's broadside had already started to assess Waters' legacy, in the form of a song about his supposed Will and Testament. Partly the song is a gesture of admiration and respect; partly it laughs at the idea that someone like Waters could leave a legacy of any real note:[12]

I Master William Waters, O,
    A *Minstrel* of the *Holy Land*
Well known among my betters, O.
    And at the Adelphi, on the Strand.
Convinc'd that death will me soon call,
    This day for my old *Palls* I've sent,

And in the presence of them all,
  Thus make my Will and Testament.

I do declare with my last breath,
  And sign it in plain black and white,
That Tom and Jerry's sudden death,
  Has poor Black Billy kill'd outright.
And when that Billy's dead and gone,
  I hope his friends will not be slack,
About his death to make a song,
  And hang St Giles's church in black.

Now, I do advise my little son,
  If he should live to be a man,
To do just as his daddy's done,
  And drink good gin whene'r he can.
To the British Museum I bequeath,
  My smart cock'd hat and feathers three,
And hope the fame they will receive.
  As poor Black Billy's legacy.

Next, to the Adelphi I bequeath
  My Fiddle, which is worth a groat;
And unto Dusty Bob I leave
  My jacket for to mend his coat.
Unto Bob Logic, that run swell
  I do present my timber toe,
In hopes that he will hand it well,
  In flooring of the charlies, O.

I do bequeath unto Black Sall,
  One Penny for to buy a bun;
Likewise my Shirt so full of holes,
  A flea theron he could not run.
My Trowsers (tho' not worth a pin)

By Public Auction shall be Sold
All for to buy a drop of gin,
    To warm her heart when it is cold.

Thus poor Black Billy's made his Will,
    His property was small good-lack,
For 'till the day death did him kill
    His house he carried on his back.
The Adelphi now may say alas!
    And to his memory raise a stone:
Their gold will be exchang'd for brass,
    Since poor Black Billy's gone.

This parodic Will is envisaged as Waters' last performance; the beneficiaries are both high and low, Black and white. The Will is both a catalogue of his body and a bodily disintegration, as the various pieces of costume are bequeathed to their new owners. Like King Charles in the 'Pinkster Ode', the 'Will' suggests that all there is to know about Waters, really, is his costume. It ends on a pleasing irony, though: the Adelphi's success killed him, but now his death 'will exchange their gold for brass' and kill their success. It's not specified how.

Nineteenth-century commentators, whether Catnach in the 1820s or Hindley in the 1870s, were fascinated by his costume. Like Catnach, Hindley speculated about how Waters might have passed the items on; like Catnach, Hindley's tongue is firmly in his cheek:

At length, in the full belief that his spirit was about to flee to meet his coloured ancestors in the realms of bliss and a free hunting ground, he duly made his will, in which he bequeathed to W. Bodkin, Esq, – *Billy Bodkin*, the Hon. Sec. to the Mendicity Society: a bodkin that had so often pierced Billy to the heart – his wooden leg, earnestly desiring he might receive it in his *latter end*.

In life he had been accustomed to wear a military cocked hat, a judge's full-bottomed cauliflower wig, and a naval officer's jacket and trousers, symbolical of his being the head and arbiter of the naval, military, and judicial departments in his eleemosynary kingdom, these he bequeathed in the following manner: His *wig* he left to the COURT OF CHANCERY, in the vague hope that they might obtain with it a little of his decision in equity, and promptness in justice. His *military hat* he left to the HEADS of the HORSE GUARDS, and his *naval jacket* and *trousers* to the *old washerwomen* that manage the GREENWICH HOSPITAL. The DEAL FIDDLE, on which he had been used to scrape his *native* WOOD *notes wild*, we are happy to state, was taken out of lavender, and is now in the possession of the TYBURN *Ketch* and Glee Club – the duplicate having been bequeathed to them for that purpose.[13]

Hindley (adapting Moncrieff here) catalogues a disintegration of Waters into the respective parts of his costume: the fascination is not with his mortal remains, but the items which turned William Waters the man into 'Billy Waters' the famous performer. It's like the obsession with Tommy Cooper's fez, Marilyn Monroe's dress, or Jimi Hendrix's guitar.

Waters' costume played an important role in how he was initially memorialised in the press. In an 1824 comic article in the *London Magazine* entitled 'Raising the Dead', the author speculates how one might 'raise from the dead some celebrated character long defunct, such as the Emperor Napoleon or Billy Waters'; the effect of the comic conjunction between these two notables is created by their difference in power and status when alive, but their similarity in hat-wearing fame.[14] A similar effect is aimed for in the *Monthly Magazine* when it declares in 1836 that 'from Lord Liverpool's velvet great-coat and loose pantaloons (with the Order of the Garter occasionally fastened round one leg), to the cocked hat and ribbons of the late Billy Waters, every man has a fashion of his own'.[15]

Another comic piece, this time about the celebrated autograph hunter William Upcott in the magazine *Mirror of Literature* in 1839, claims that amongst his numerous and impressive collection Upcott had the signature of 'Billy Waters' (whether that of Waters himself or of Signor Paulo is not clarified).[16] Catnach imagined that because of his poverty Waters had little more than his costume to leave in his 'Will and Testament'. What irony, then, that it was these items which secured Waters' fame in life and his remembrance in death.

'Billy Waters' on Tour

William Waters was no more; but 'Billy Waters' the Character was still very much alive. Yet it was a survival created by acts of appropriation, and found in blackface performances by 'Billy Waters' actors. The role may also have given opportunities to actors with a disability.

Already in February 1823 Thomas Greenwood, who collaborated with Egan over the Sadler's Wells version of *Life in London*, satirised the closure of Moncrieff's play at the Adelphi with a broadside in 'immortal praise' of the 'ONE THOUSAND NIGHTS' of the Adelphi play's run, called *The Tears of Pierce Egan, Esq., for the Death of 'Life in London'; or, the Funeral of Tom and Jerry*. George Cruikshank drew a picture for it of a funeral procession for Tom and Jerry in which 'Kate', 'Sue', 'Dusty Bob', 'African Sal', 'Billy Waters', 'Little Jemmy', and various other assorted characters and Characters followed the coffins of the protagonists.[1] Within twelve hours, the ever-savvy Catnach published a version of the broadside that cost only two pence, and also depicted the funeral procession going past the shuttered doors of the Adelphi (Figure 64).

Not to be outdone, Thomas Greenwood turned his idea into a one-act play also entitled *The Death of Life in London: Or, The Funeral of Tom and Jerry*, which was performed for the first time at the Royal

Solemn Funeral Procession of Tom and Jerry.

64. *Detail from* The Death, Last Will, and Funeral of 'Black Billy' (1823).

Coburg Theatre on 2 June 1823 and licensed for the Adelphi itself in 1824. This play, which cheekily claimed to be 'Not taken from any thing, but taking off many things', was really about how performance and the circulation of popular culture ensured the survival (not the death) of popular Characters. Once again we find ourselves among 'The Cadgers at a Benefit Club Supper'; this time, 'Billy Waters' (played by a Mr Harland), 'Little Jemmy', 'African Sal' and 'Dusty Bob' are all in the same scene together, and all celebrate mixed-race lower-class life to the tune of 'Billy Waters' fiddle.[2] The Landlord bursts in with the news that Tom and Jerry are dead. 'Billy' wails that there will be 'no more maggs [half-pence] for Billy' because Death has killed 'poor Massa'. The Cadgers join in a funeral procession, which sounds suspiciously like the one in Catnach's broadside. To everyone's shocked delight, though, the dead men rise from their funeral biers: they are alive and were simply on a tour in France (a reference to the Royal Coburg's production *Tom and Jerry in France*). Happiness is widespread; marriages are planned including between Dusty Bob and Sal, and 'Billy Waters' declares himself 'so happy, me could dance for joy'. Jerry then turns to the audience and declares:

Then for *your* favor, let us nightly strive,
And let *your sanction* keep us
ALL ALIVE!!!

Death of Life in London was performed at the Bridgnorth Theatre, Shropshire, on Saturday 7 February 1824, with 'Billy Waters' in the cast list 'with his Fiddle in Mourning'.[3] Performance keeps popular characters alive. Whatever William Waters may have wanted, 'Billy Waters' did not die.

'Billy Waters' endured as a stage character around the UK long after William Waters was dead. Birmingham 1823: Mr Stump (surely a stage name) plays 'Billy Waters' at the Birmingham Theatre Royal. Was Mr Stump himself an amputee? Birmingham 1841: it's the turn of a Mr De Hayes. The playbill specifies that the Holy Land scene includes jokes about the Mendicity Society and the reference to Alderman in chains, which suggests 'Billy Waters' was increasingly considered an integral part of the attractions of the play.[4] Indeed, in the Midlands it seems that 'Billy Waters' had enough name recognition to stand on his own: an undated playbill for a 'Grand Fete' to be held during the Derby Races includes (in addition to fireworks and an instrumental concert) a puppet theatre with 'A striking representation of the well-known Billy Waters, the Black Fiddler, Represented in all the Theatres, in Tom and Jerry, or, Life in London' alongside The Grand Turk, The East Indian Juggler, Billy Button and his Wife, The Animated Skeleton, Ben the Sailor, The Polander, a Tight Rope Dancer, and The Italian Scaramouch.[5]

Hull, 1822 and 1823: Mr Stumpy (another actor with a disability? The same one?) is on stage as 'Billy Waters' and the Holy Land scene makes a big splash. 1827, and this time it's Mr J. Waites.[6] The play's metropolitan reputation is all in Hull: 'The success of this piece', a playbill declares, 'is unprecedented in the Dramatic World, it having been played in one of the London Theatres every night for Twelve Months'. In 1844 the Adelphi Theatre Company itself went on tour and took with them to Hull a 'revival' of *Tom and Jerry* with a Mr Seymour as 'Billy Waters'. You could see a version of 'Billy Waters' on stage in several northern cities throughout the 1820s, when Waters himself was already dead, in a macabre exhibit of enduring popularity.[7] Down south, 'Billy Waters' appeared at Brighton, Windsor, and Bristol Theatres Royal.[8] In Windsor, as elsewhere, 'Billy Waters' was played by an actor who specialised in comedy (a Mr Atwood). The playbills are fragile, crumbling: there will have been others that have not survived.

'Billy Waters', then, found a new lease of life around the English provincial towns and cities in the 1820s and into the 1830s. When he reached Scotland, some changes were made to his character. The Caledonian Theatre's published playscript from its 1823 production survives in the Harvard Theatre collection, with a Mr Chippendale in the cast list as 'Billy Waters'.[9] The opening 'remarks' to the published text suggest its success in London ensures its success in Edinburgh, but notes that the play 'has come through so many hands, that every theatre has a different piece', and the version at the Edinburgh Theatre Royal has been 'mutilated . . . into a mere shadow'. Indeed, the Theatre Royal's 1823 and 1824 productions of *Life in London, or, The Adventures of Tom, Jerry and Logic* don't contain Waters, suggesting either that he hasn't translated to Scotland or that this is not the Adelphi version. There is, however, a character called Dick Stump.[10] So when the publishers of the Edinburgh playscript emphasise their choice of the version 'from the manuscript of the Caledonian Theatre', they mean that they have chosen in favour of Moncrieff's script. The Caledonian's production was greeted with 'applause' by 'the unprecedentedly numerous assemblage on Saturday evening, January 25, 1823, which crowded the Caledonian Theatre'. But if anyone was hoping for salacious scenes they were doomed to disappointment: 'There is neither one word, action, or situation, in the whole course of the piece, that can possibly raise a blush, or offend the most fastidious moralist!'[11]

Something very important happened to 'Billy Waters' on its journey north. The 'Billy Waters' presented in Edinburgh at the Caledonian is different to the Adelphi one. 'Billy' is less prominent in the scene. He enters Act 2 scene 6 'shaking hands', not playing or dancing. The dialogue is slightly different, as if someone has jotted down notes from a London production but remembered the scenes imperfectly. There are no jokes about the Mendicity Society or the Treadmill, so these were presumably too London-specific. The dialogue about the Alderman in chains is kept, as is the violence towards the landlord, but the emphasis is slightly less placed on 'Billy Waters' and more on the Cadgers' general condemnation of the food and the landlord. This tells us that something significant started to happen: the meanings of 'Billy Waters' shifted when it shifted out of a London context.

Back in London, meanwhile, Moncrieff's vision of 'Billy Waters' refused to die: Mr Paulo reprised his role for an 1834 benefit performance on behalf of the Adelphi's 'Corinthian Tom', Mr Yates, alongside other erstwhile cast members Mr Walbourn ('Dusty Bob') and Mr Saunders ('African Sal').[12] One month later the play was used for another benefit performance at the Surrey Theatre, 'with Pierce Egan as *Bob Logic*; and Dusty Bob, African Sal, and Billy Waters, by the first representatives of these *unique* characters – Mr Walbourn, Mr Sanders [*sic*], and Signor Paulo, who have kindly volunteered their services'.[13] The original Adelphi cast revived the production again in 1835.[14] Mr Hartland played 'Billy Waters' opposite Walbourn's 'Dusty Bob' in *Tom and Jerry* at White Conduit House in September 1841 and again in 'the celebrated scene from *Tom and Jerry*' at Vauxhall Gardens in October that same year.[15] This activity meant that 'Billy Waters' did not stay on one side of the Atlantic for long. It was about to go transatlantically viral. The consequences for Black American performers were about to be felt.

'Billy Waters' Returns

'Billy Waters' finally made it home to New York in 1823, but he did so six months after his death, carried across the Atlantic by *Tom and Jerry*. As theatre historian Peter Reed puts it, *Tom and Jerry* was 'a transatlantic performance event'.[1] The constant interaction between British and American drama in this moment so soon after the Revolution complicated any simple timeline of London 'original' and US 'adaptation'. Indeed, the American actor Joe Cowell – who played title character Jerry Hawthorne in the first New York production – claimed to have influenced Moncrieff's scriptwriting.[2] Africans in America were first created for the stage by British playwrights, long before American-born authors wrote plays, and playwrights and audiences on both sides of the Atlantic shared the assumption that actors could 'play' Irish, English, Spanish, Algerian, or African characters – as long as they were white. 'Billy Waters, the wooden-legged ancestor of all Ethiopian minstrels', the magazine *The London Reader* declared in 1877: in other words, the originator of both Black and blackface minstrelsy.[3] This is a claim too far, as minstrelsy has a history dating back to medieval European festivals. But did *The London Reader* mean Billy Waters the man or 'Billy Waters' the meme-like Character? *Tom and*

Jerry proved hugely popular in the new Republic, so Waters became known in America as well as around Britain.[4] This transatlantic legacy came at a price, however, both for Waters' memory and for Black Americans. 'Billy Waters' had even more significance in the slave-holding society of the fledgling United States. Waters' skilful body represented a threat to the white establishment. Keeping Waters as a blackface role was one way of containing that threat.

It was in New York that the process of taking over Waters' legacy began. The first performance in New York, at the prestigious Park Theatre, was on 3 March 1823, when Waters himself had less than three weeks to live.[5] The new United States was not really what we might call a theatregoing nation in the immediate aftermath of the Revolution. The restrictions on theatre by the Continental Congress, and anti-theatre sentiments by religious groups, saw to that. But gradually after the Revolution, professional and semi-professional acting troupes made use of converted buildings, and then built small theatres, and by the 1820s larger theatres were being planned or constructed to meet growing demand.[6] Famous English actors were hot property on the bill at the Park; with impressive facilities for staging productions and a transatlantic reputation, it was one of the leading theatres in the republic, let alone the city. At the same time, a German visitor to New York in 1818 remarked sniffily on what he saw as backward, colonial audience behaviour. Gentlemen, he declared, put their feet on the benches and spat out chewed tobacco but did not remove their hats; ladies, on the other hand, removed their bonnets even in such a public space! In short 'people so fond of liberty lay themselves under very little restraint at the theatre'.[7] Yet these same theatres welcomed London luminaries such as Charles Matthews, Mr and Madame Vestris, Charles Kemble and Fanny Kemble, Edmund Kean and Charles Kean, and Dickens' friend William Macready, who were well accustomed to acting before the frequently rambunctious audiences at home.[8]

The London stage and the New York stage were not so very different. American theatre pioneer William Dunlap hoped in 1832 that America would develop its own distinctive national theatre, but for now, he sighed, 'the favorites of England were the favorites of the colonies'.⁹ You could find occasional performances in other languages in towns with, say, French- or German-speaking populations, but overall most productions in the new United States were in the English language and of British origin. As theatre historian Jeffrey H. Richards puts it, even 'the few American dramas in English that did make it to theatres all show the marked use of British templates in their construction, even if the matter and setting appear to be "native" to American locations and situations'.¹⁰ In other words, 'Billy Waters' travelled around Britain and America as part of 'a transatlantic theatre culture in which acts, actors, and audiences circulated continually'.¹¹

'Billy Waters' did not translate entirely smoothly into this new context, however. Waters was still something of a local Character, and the fascination with the precise specificity of the Cadgers' scene did not always readily translate. In a move we might recognise today, sometimes the name of the Cadgers' scene was changed to be more understandable by US theatregoers. One New York edition of Moncrieff's *Tom and Jerry* only mentions the 'Cadgers' of St Giles in passing, and skips straight on to All-Max and 'African Sal'. Waters is excised from this version of the play entirely.¹² But 'Billy Waters' must have appeared on stage in some New York productions as our next clue to its circulation comes from an 1824 edition of *Tom and Jerry*. Printed in Philadelphia, it claims to be 'as performed at the Boston, New York, and Philadelphia theatres'. This script has a reduced speaking part for 'Billy Waters' when compared with the editions printed in London and in Edinburgh, but the fundamentals (his fiddle playing and his involvement in bullying the landlord for better food) remain largely unchanged. *Tom and Jerry* reached Philadelphia on Friday 25 April 1823, where 'it made a most tremendous hit' at both the Chestnut Street and Walnut Street (also known as the Olympic) theatres. Some loved the Chestnut Street version and said it was even better than the New York Park, and some flocked to the Walnut Street production where the cast and team were used to mounting circus shows as well as dramatic ones.[13]

As in Britain, the choice of actor was significant. The cast list for the prestigious Chestnut Street Theatre Company shows that Waters was played by Mr J. Jefferson.[14] The Jeffersons were a hugely important American acting family, whose most famous member was Joseph 'Rip Van Winkle' Jefferson III (1829–1905), celebrated for his portrayal of a well-loved character of the late nineteenth-century American stage. But even before the third Joseph Jefferson was born, the Jeffersons were American stage royalty. Their presence all over the *Tom and Jerry* cast list tells us a great deal about the status of the play. Mr Joseph Jefferson I (1774–1832), a talented actor-manager, appeared as 'Bob Logic' next to the famous English actor Henry Weymss as 'Tom'. Also in the cast were the Jefferson boys: Thomas (as 'Dick Trifle'), and either John or Joseph II (or perhaps both of them) as 'Jemmy Green' and 'Billy Waters'.[15] As in London, 'Billy Waters' was a blackface role: there is no evidence yet that in Philadelphia a Black actor was given the opportunity to explore on stage the rich cultural heritages behind Waters' signature performing style.

Not only that, but the role of 'Billy Waters' was reduced in significant ways from the London version. Act 2 scene 6 has no special entrance for 'Billy': he is 'discovered' on stage at the start of the scene along with all the other Cadgers. Now not an individual the playgoers are at all likely to have met in person, 'Billy' is much less in charge of the scene and instead the power shifts to 'Little Jemmy' (usually played by a child actor), who even gets 'Waters'' original last orders, 'Carry me out!' Where 'Billy's' dialogue does survive he is made to look even worse: his contemptuous instruction to the

Landlord to 'give the broken wittals' gifted by kindly passers-by 'to some genteel dog vot pass your door' becomes simply an order to give the donated food 'to de dog'.

Novelist and critic Toni Morrison highlights what she calls a prevalence of 'Africanism' within American culture:

> Africanism is the vehicle by which the American self knows itself as not enslaved, but free; not repulsive, but desirable; not helpless, but licensed and powerful; not history-less, but historical; not damned, but innocent; not a blind accident of evolution, but a progressive fulfilment of destiny.[16]

In other words, what Morrison calls Africanist characters are Black characters whose function is little more than to define and set off the white characters. In his American context in particular, 'Billy Waters' helped to establish the ideal American citizen – white, middle-class male, able-bodied, and neither comic nor gullible – as the young Republic struggled to form and formulate itself. As Jeffery H. Richards points out, British-authored plays looked different when performed in an American context. Even though most plays on the American stage between 1775 and 1825 were British-authored, 'the popularity of some dramas offers insights as to what mirror was being held to the audiences'.[17] Less skilled, less vocal, and less powerful, the version of Waters that appeared on the Philadelphia stage was less attached to audience memories of the real person and much more aligned to the stereotypes of the lazy and ungrateful 'Comic Black'.

Before long the Chestnut Street company was in Baltimore on tour as they regularly were, and they took 'Billy Waters' with them.[18] The first airing of the Moncrieff version was advertised for Monday 19 May 1823, and it kept being shown throughout 1823 (a few weeks before that, at the Baltimore Circus on 31 March 1823, there was a production with a 'Poney Race' that might perhaps have been based on the ones at London's Astley's or Sadler's Wells).[19] The Chestnut Street company kept the same cast and script. By now, however, neither Egan's nor Moncrieff's names made the title page. This was now a play that had been 'Performed with Unbounded Applause in London and America', according to the published script.[20] It was becoming just as much a part of the American theatre scene as it was the British one. Charles Durang, a well-known nineteenth-century Philadelphia-born writer, actor, and theatre historian, called it a 'dramatic monstrosity', which endangered both the taste and the morals of the new Republic, but even he had to admit that wherever the play was put on, the Chestnut Street company had a hit on its hands:

> We had a racy group of *Toms, Logics, and Jerrys*, which sprang from its vicious froth *instanter*, in every city where it was represented. Tavern haunts and mixed drinks were created, and christened 'Tom and Jerry', to suit the vitiated new-born taste.[21]

It wasn't just 'Billy Waters' who was adapted to suit new local contexts. Spin-offs first performed in London appeared in Baltimore: if you wandered into Robinson's Circulating Library in the city in May 1823, you could buy *The Treadmill, or Tom and Jerry at Brixton*. Six months later you could look forward to Robinson's publication of *Death of Life in London*, which had already been performed at the Baltimore Theatre on 2 October and was clearly popular enough for the Library to be confident that the script would sell.[22] Meanwhile, *Tom and Jerry* itself was still onstage at the Baltimore Theatre throughout the winter season; indeed, Acts 1 and 2 of *Tom and Jerry* were on at Baltimore's Holliday Street Theatre ten years later.[23] The craze brought the Jeffersons' version of 'Billy Waters' to Baltimore as part of a play which quickly acquired local popularity and local meanings. But again, the right to perform as Waters was a white actor's privilege. Was that all it was ever going to be?

By the closing days of 1823, 'Billy Waters' reached Boston (somewhat to the consternation of the *Boston Commercial Gazette*, which worried about *Tom and Jerry*'s potential bad influence on Boston's youthful citizens).[24] An advertisement in the *Columbian Centinel* proudly announced the arrival at the Boston Theatre, 'a lofty and spacious edifice' built solidly out of brick.[25] The *Centinel* trumpeted approvingly that the production would use the 'Manuscript, Original Music, and Prints of the Costumes' received from the Philadelphia and Baltimore theatres.[26] Ironically, despite the many versions and copies and changes associated with this play, and the use of blackface in the portrayal of 'Billy Waters' and 'African Sal', it's the authenticity of the production that is emphasised. As Durang rather sarcastically notes about early American theatrical practices, 'much stage business is finally settled, through the appeal to the actors of the *"original!"*, no matter how absurd it may be'.[27]

Indeed, the published Boston playscript makes a bid for a special kind of transatlantic authenticity. The title page announces that the play was 'Performed with unbounded applause in London, New-York, Philadelphia and Boston', and furthermore:

> The Publisher feels confident that a piece which has been exhibited with so much success upon the 'Boston Boards', cannot fail to please the public; and under this impression, has at great expense procured a Copy from London, and ventures to launch it forth upon the sea of public favor, and to risk it among the waves of the enlightened metropolis of New England.

It's upon Boston theatrical success plus the lure of a London printed text that publisher E. K. Allen stakes this commercial decision. Yet this script is identical to the Philadelphia and Baltimore ones, with the same cuts made to the London version. Perhaps because his name recognition was not quite the same outside of Britain, where any visitor to London's West End could be reasonably sure to have seen Waters in person, 'Billy Waters' is not mentioned on the playbill ('African Sal' is played by Mr Waugh). The scene in 'Life in Rags . . . Beggars' Hall in St Giles' is there in some detail though.[28] 'Billy Waters' appears in the cast list in the Boston edition of the play.

Bostonians could go to various spin-off entertainments on the *Life in London* theme, and 'Billy Waters' was named in the adverts. In February 1824 the Boston Circus advertised 'Pony Races . . . or, Tom and Jerry at Epsom', where live races were interspersed with 'Singing, Dancing, Fighting, and all the incidental humors of the racecourse'. The circus floor was fitted out like a racecourse and an exciting part of the bill of fare promised to be the 'Race for a Silver watch, between Dusty Bob, tied up in a Sack, and Billy Waters, mounted on a Donkey'. On certain nights the evening's entertainment concluded with a performance of *Tom and Jerry*.[29] The year after, at the more upmarket Boston Theatre, 'Billy Waters' reappeared in the advert for their production of *Death of Life in London*, which was clearly the same script as the London and Baltimore versions.[30] *Tom and Jerry* was playing in 1834 at Boston's Warren Theatre, where 'Billy Waters' was played by a Mr Adams. *Tom and Jerry* also made it to Washington and as far as Charleston in South Carolina: these were both productions using Moncrieff's text, 'As performed at the Adelphi Theatre, London, for the unprecedented time of 150 nights, and in New York, Philadelphia and Baltimore, with unexampled applause'. Given that they list 'Beggars' among the cast members, as well as 'Life in Rags: Beggar's Hall in St Giles' on the list of scenes, it's highly likely that 'Billy Waters' was still on stage like he was in the Boston production.[31]

In 1837 the *Penny Satirist* reprinted a piece from the New York *Weekly Herald* that purported to be an account of a meeting of the Loco-Foco Party. Despite its eccentric name, this was a serious early American radical political organisation, most active in the 1830s.[32] Here 'Black Billy Waters' appears as a representative of both rowdy lower-class gatherings and dark(ened) faces: his association with the St Giles Cadgers has moved out of the US playhouse and into US popular allusion:

> The room, as we entered, would have put the people of Babel to the blush ... We were never present at a meeting of the Neapolitan *Lazzaroni*, Italian *Carbonari*, the German *Illuminati*, the French *Infuriati*, or the St Giles' Loaferati; but one meeting of the illustrious Locofocoati of New York, is richer in rioting rowdyism, and incongruous incidents, than the whole of the above combined.
>
> Shades of Massaniello, Robespierre, Danton, Marat, and Black Billy Waters, 'hide your diminished heads' whilst we detail the doings of the determined democratic *Locosfocos* at the *Civil and Military Hall* on Monday night.[33]

This journalist attempts to neutralise radical politics by describing it as just lower-class 'loafing'. Repetitive rhythms distance the reader from serious consideration of the Loco-Focos' political discussion and turn the scene into something out of *Life in London*'s comic prose. The threatening bodies of the Loco-Focos are reduced to an anonymous crowd of dirty faces and dirty shirts. 'All sorts and all sizes were there – all ages and complexions, grades and shades, from "Snowy white to sooty",' we're told, 'Not that we mean seriously to assert there were any negroes present; oh no! ... but there were divers and sundry souls in that assemblage, whose bodies unquestionably betokened then as belonging to the body of "Great unwashed".' Again there's that nasty association being made between Blackness and dirtiness. Working-class New Yorkers are depicted as almost Black because they are unwashed. It's the 'Billy Waters' reference that anchors some of these ideas.

Until at least 1848, as the last enslaved New Yorkers finally received their freedom, you could make a throwaway reference to 'Billy Waters' and expect people to make the connection. For example, Benjamin Baker's hit musical farce *A Glance at New York* (1848) establishes its own low-life scene through the convenient short-hand of the name Billy Waters, and relies for much of its effects upon audience knowledge of Egan's *Life in London* or Moncrieff's *Tom and Jerry*.[34] *A Glance at New York* had its own knowing townie, who takes his country cousin on a tour of New York. The production also introduced 'Mose', the Black character who later featured in several other musical pieces written by Baker. Act 1 scene 5 is set in 'the Loafer's Paradise', a New York version of the 'Beggars' Opera'. Stage directions call for '*A dirty Bar-room*' with '*A number of LOAFERS about*'. The loafers are slightly different to the Cadgers – for instance, one of their number is '*MAJOR GATES, a literary loafer*'. But the Loafer's Paradise occupies the same function in the play as the Cadgers scene: it is a place of low-life and misrule. What's striking about the scene for our purposes is the off-hand reference to 'Billy Waters', by which name one of the loafers is twice addressed. 'Billy Waters' does not appear as a character with a spoken part but just a mention of the name is enough, it seems, to conjure up the atmosphere required. It's possible that the playwright did not even consciously realise what name he'd given one of his 'loafers'. The ideas associated with 'Billy Waters' spread far beyond their London context and shifted beyond their London meanings.

William Waters was dead; but 'Billy Waters' refused to die, and instead continued to circulate through transatlantic popular culture. Theatre historian Peter Reed argues that a 'print-performance culture' spread around the Atlantic world, following the same routes as many of the people it portrayed. Reed suggests that this produced and shaped ideas about the lower-classed, the disenfranchised, and the poor, but also celebrated their energy.[35] His fellow theatre historian Jenna Gibbs agrees that transatlantic popular culture reveals a public sphere that was 'far more expansive' than just male, pale, and stale, and which acknowledged the diversity visible daily in the streets of the Atlantic world.[36] However, Marvin McAllister points out that this was a white-dominated culture, which looked very different from the perspective of Black performers and audiences. Sure, says McAllister, white performers and audiences 'understood blackface as a vehicle for challenging respectability and subverting the status quo'. But that doesn't mean Black performers and audiences felt the same way. White performers assumed that they were entitled to play 'Billy Waters' on stage, but we have no hard evidence that any Black performer was ever allowed the same privilege. In other words, 'unequal access to representation' prevented blackface minstrelsy 'from becoming a genuine site of interracial exchange and reduced that national art form to a demeaning, white supremacist endorsement of "Negro" inferiority'.[37] 'Billy Waters' spread throughout the Atlantic world in part as a celebration of his skill and virtuosity but it also reduced that skill to something white actors and audiences could contain, control, and perform.

There is an intriguing gap in the printed evidence of the Boston production of *Tom and Jerry*. There is no named actor listed against the role 'Billy Waters' in the Boston edition, nor is there one for 'African Sal'. Both these roles, of course, were Black characters. The printed cast list is silent about performers who definitely would have been on stage. What was going on here? There are two possibilities. Perhaps the producers wanted to play with ideas of authenticity, and suggest that it was in fact the 'real' Waters and Sal who were on stage. In which case this silence in print is actually a double silencing: white male actors played Black characters and then their names were not given. There is another, albeit very faint possibility: did the Boston Theatre get away with having Black performers on stage for these roles, but didn't want to shout about it? We cannot know. 'Billy Waters' represented a threat. His most immediate legacy was one in which his skill and agency were silenced into white-performed clowning. Perhaps that was the biggest compliment that transatlantic popular culture was ready to give him. Fortunately, as the Boston edition of the play intimates, this is not quite the whole story.

The Precarious Atlantic

The dignity, skill, and virtuosity displayed by Waters was a reality and an idea hidden within the blackface roles in *Tom and Jerry*: buried deep, maybe, but never entirely extinguished. Waters had his carefully constructed act stolen from him. But Black American performers found ways to grab it back. They faced deadly racism and were usually forced to conform to blackface stereotypes as they navigated an Atlantic world which for them could only ever feel precarious. But in recognising these problems and limitations we must be careful not to fall into the trap of looking *at* nineteenth-century Black Americans, rather than *with* them. As theatre historian Jeffrey Richards notes, even the unsurprising can be surprising in a new context.[1] Black performance was snuffed out on the white-controlled stage by the rise of minstrelsy. But was there more to 'Billy Waters' than minstrelsy?

To seek out Waters' legacy to Black performers, we might begin with the African Company's 1823 adaptation of *Tom and Jerry* into *Tom and Jerry: Life in New York* (Figure 65). The African Company was a mostly Black, mostly amateur acting company founded by retired ship-steward William Brown. Another Black American (possibly originally from the West Indies) who earned a living from the sea, Brown used his retirement as an opportunity for entrepreneurship. His first venture in 1821 was a pleasure garden open to Black New Yorkers (and white citizens as well). Dubbed the 'African Grove' by one unsympathetic journalist, this pleasure garden offered free and enslaved workers the chance to access the kind of leisure pursuits previously denied them – music, shows, and fireworks – all in an attractive outdoor space. Indeed, Marvin McAllister argues that this daring idea was much more than a pleasure garden: it was a rehearsal for substantial social and political change as emancipation gathered pace.[2] Perhaps that was why the garden was closed down by anxious City authorities after only one month. Undaunted, Brown turned to theatre. There had been some kind of short-lived 'African Theatre' in New York by 1801; if Brown knew of it, he was determined to recreate it.[3]

From Brown's cramped upstairs apartment at 38 Thomas Street, New York, in September 1821, his Company mounted its first production. Their choice of play was striking: Shakespeare's *Richard III*. Black actors played white kings and queens on an American stage in an assertion of dignity and equality; New York newspapers reacted with stunned mockery.[4] But Brown had even bigger plans. A series of moves saw him and his Company attempt to establish a full-scale theatre in New York, first in Greenwich Village, then next door to the Park itself, then back in Greenwich Village. Brown's theatre changed name from the 'Minor Theatre' to the nationalistic 'American Theatre', and by 1822 Brown advertised his troupe as the 'African Company': Brown's answer to Du Bois' twentieth-century question 'Am I American or am I a Negro? Can I be both?' would have been a resounding 'Yes!'[5] Brown's vision was of a city and a United States where Black Americans could manage, run, and perform plays just like their white counterparts at the by-now prestigious Park Theatre. While the Park Theatre was busy mounting a series of plays which featured various blackface 'stage Africans' as comic foils within a vision of a white-dominated society,

Brown's Theatre and Company offered representations of all kinds of characters: white, Native American, and Black. Productions at Brown's theatre were a powerful statement of what a truly racially inclusive American culture might look like.[6] With leading male actor James Hewlett and leading ladies S. Welsh and Williams, Brown and his thirty or so performers tested the logic of emancipation on stage, night after night. Did this new United States really mean to offer cultural and social participation to all? Could Black and white citizens freely borrow and share and revise culture between each other, or was Blackness something only whites could perform on stage? One of the test cases for these questions was their production of *Tom and Jerry*.

The African Company and its Black actors rewrote *Tom and Jerry* to include a scene 'On the Slave Market', contextual-

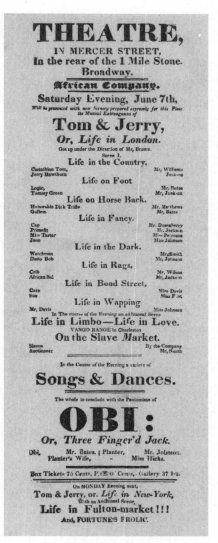

65. *African Company playbill* (1823).

ising the Black characters already within the play. We have no more information on their versions of *Tom and Jerry* than the surviving playbill, but the bill promises that in their *Tom and Jerry: Life in London* the scene 'Life in Rags' will be included. 'Billy Waters' is not mentioned in the cast list, but 'African Sal' is, played, as had now become convention, by a man. However, given that so few characters are named on the playbill, and most of the scenes in *Tom and Jerry* required numerous extras in order to work, it's not unreasonable to speculate whether 'African Sal' danced to the music of a Black fiddler in a feathered hat. The African Company's adaptation of *Tom and Jerry: Life in New York* went further. With its promise of 'an Additional Scene, Life in Fulton Market!!!', the production appears to have adapted the scenes of waterfront market dance and song in New York, which inspired Waters' own performances in the first place. This was a transatlantic network of popular culture where the most striking features were its 'mobile actors, scripts, and scenes', but also its mobile echoes and influences, threaded together at will by a mobile population.[7] People migrated around this Atlantic world, on forced and unforced journeys, and carried ideas and Characters, meme-like, with them. We need to be alert to that circulation. Only then can we see how 'Billy Waters' returned to the birthplace of William Waters to challenge and disrupt the norms of the country in which Waters was born.

The *Life in London* craze opened up to some Black American performers a new imaginative space in which to display their own abilities and resilience. Ira Aldridge (whom we met on stage in London) was one of Brown's protégés; another was a man called James Hewlett who worked as a ship steward in between acting to supplement his income. Both went on to act on other stages. Always enterprising, Hewlett saw the rise of minstrelsy in the United States and headed for Trinidad, taking ideas from *Tom and Jerry* with him. At Port of Spain's Royal Victoria Theatre he headlined for several nights during the run-up to Christmas 1837, and advertised in the *Port of Spain Gazette* that he would be writing a piece about Port of Spain, 'a sort of "Tom and Jerry" affair, light and lively, full of entertainment and fun. It is in him, he knows, and out it must come, and will during the holidays.'[8] Like Brown before him, Hewlett spotted the *Life in London* craze as an opportunity to showcase agency and creativity. The system that destroyed Waters did not allow them much room for success and the African Company was short-lived; by 1822 a riot in its Greenwich Village theatre led to its closure. For the most part theatregoers patronised 'the theatres in all cities where imitation black was favoured over the presence of the real thing and where mockery of people of African ancestry was not only possible but encouraged'.[9] Beyond the efforts of the African Company, however, the *Life in London* craze offered an opportunity for another Black performer, known only to the historical record as Old Corn Meal.

The evidence of Waters' legacy to Black performers takes us next over 1,000 miles south of Boston, New York, Philadelphia and Baltimore, to New Orleans in Louisiana. It was here that Old Corn Meal achieved what Waters never did: he performed as himself on stage.[10] Like Waters, Old Corn Meal was a local celebrity before he became one in print: New Orleans' leading paper the *Picayune* declared in 1837 that 'every man, woman and child in the city, white, black, and colored, are acquainted with, and fully appreciate' his talents 'as he has appeared in public daily for years'.[11] Old Corn Meal (sometimes referred to as 'Signor Cornmeali') was a street seller of corn meal who drove a pony and cart full of meal to Camp Street and the Exchanges. To announce his wares he performed comic songs in a voice that ranged from deep bass to striking falsetto, as well as his song, or 'cry', of 'Fresh Corn Meal'. In his sixties by the last years of the 1830s, the facts about Old Corn Meal's life are shrouded in even more obscurity than those of Waters, although the *Picayune* had its office in Camp Street where Old Corn Meal performed, and the paper featured Old Corn Meal in its pages again and again. The only image we have of him is a cheap and generic woodcut first provided by the *Picayune*, a silhouette rather than a portrait, a space where the 'real' man disappears (Figure 66).

66. Old Corn Meal.

The *Picayune* was fascinated by Old Corn Meal's vocal skills, declaring him 'so quick from tenor to bass and from bass to falsetto. He has a great compass of voice.'[12] Given his occupation and activities it's probable that he had free status, but the *Picayune* does not say. His name was provided by his occupation and his street cry; it could have been the only one he gave his street audiences, or it may have been conferred upon him in this slaveholding city. New Orleans only joined the United States in 1803 when the colony of Louisiana was sold by Napoleon for the princely sum of $15 million. But by the time William Waters left the British Navy it was a powerhouse of national and international trade. Its lavish slave market was a major centre for the slave trade in nineteenth-century America, while the city itself was a multi-racial, multi-lingual urban centre. This made it both an attractive but also a dangerous place to be a free Black man, where that free status was something that could be snatched from you at any point.[13] Against this backdrop, Old Corn Meal's successes are even more admirable.

Waters and Old Corn Meal are connected through the circulation and spread of the *Life in London* craze. By the 1830s, numerous American-based playwrights were starting to tinker with the basic premise to adapt the idea for their own audiences. One of the most successful stage versions was celebrated Bohemian writer John Brougham's *Tom & Jerry in America, or Life in Boston* (on a double bill in May 1848 at the Boston Adelphi Theatre with Mr Baker's *A Glance at New York in 1848*); amusingly, the playbill claimed that this production was 'Original! No Piracy'.[14] This 'interplay between transatlantic exchange and the contingent local adaptations', Jenna Gibbs tells us, 'was what produced a British-American popular culture'.[15] New Orleans was no exception. The rowdy port city was already famed for its spectacular entertainments, from prize fights to masquerades, and musical productions at the impressive St Charles Theatre (opened in 1835 and one of the finest, if not the finest, US theatre of its time). Commentators might have decried New Orleans' lack of 'high culture' but the punters flocked there for a good time regardless.[16]

In May 1837 the *Picayune* announced excitedly that 'an *old* actor is to appear in a *new* line of business':

> Old '*Corn Meal*' is to drive across and around the stage in his real 'dug-out', and sing his favorite melodies. Himself, horse and cart are to be introduced in a new piece entitled 'Life in New Orleans', in which many public characters are also to figure. It is needless for us to call upon our citizens to attend the St Charles tonight. We state but the circumstances – they will go without asking.[17]

The *Picayune* takes on the role of cheerleader and unofficial publicist for its Camp Street neighbour here, managing to exhort the public to go to the stage production, even as it boasts that it has no need to do so – presumably because Old Corn Meal is not only so well known, but known to be so good. This 'celebrated *sable satellite*', as the paper calls him in another issue, 'will appear in character, with his Horse and Cart, and sing his well-known

Extravaganza': intriguingly, Old Corn Meal will be both himself and in character.[18] The lines between authenticity and theatricality are well and truly blurred.

They were blurred in the play itself, too. Until now we haven't really known what the 'highly successful, comical, tragical and local drama of *Life in New Orleans!*' was like, but although the play itself is lost, I discovered two playbills for it in the Harvard Theatre Collection. The playbills reproduce the small woodcut from the *Picayune*, and give the full title as *Life in New Orleans! Or, Things As They Are!*, starring a Mad Author, a Kentuckian, a New York Dandy, a Mad Actor from the St Charles Theatre, O'Rourke the Irish watchman, and at least two non-white characters in addition to Old Corn Meal himself. What it lacked in subtlety it made up for in action and extravaganza. The plot of this 'new and local Melo-Drama' shared *Tom and Jerry*'s episodic structure. Its six scenes gave a picaresque tour of the main hits of this vibrant, dangerous, disreputable new city, including a bar-room scene which treated the audience to a whirlwind of New Orleans attractions: 'mint juleps – brandy – bankrupts – prize fighting, &c'. Corn Meal's scene followed straight after, in which 'Negroes without passes' were arrested by Watchman O'Rourke. No doubt much supposedly comic business ensued, to be resolved when 'CORNMEAL appears (mounted) with his Horse and Cart, and sings his celebrated Extravaganza': his two main hits 'Sich a Gittin Up the Stairs' and 'Rosin the Bow', sung in his incredibly flexible voice, which could switch from bass to falsetto and tenor, as if he was duetting with himself.[19] The final scene was a Grand Masquerade. The second performance was due to be on 16 May, but unfortunately disaster struck: Old Corn Meal's horse fell off the stage and was killed, leading to the cancellation of any further nights.[20] This was not the end of his theatre career: he appeared at the Camp Street Theatre twice in 1840 (minus the horse), and along with blackface minstrelsy performer Mick Saunders in the characters of 'Ginger

Blue' and 'Pompey Squash'.[21] As Waters had already found out in London, blackface did not allow Black performers much space on the stage.

In *Life in New Orleans*, to be American is to be ideally white and male. Indeed, judging by the playbills, the other Black characters in the scene were white performers in blackface (they appear on other playbills where it seems unlikely they would have been Black actors). However, Corn Meal's presence complicates this. Corn Meal bursts into song to disrupt the white watchman's capture of the 'Black' characters Jim and Johnson. He pivots the action away from potential tragedy (New Orleans had a propensity for mob violence against Black men perceived to be breaking the rules) and towards the 'dances and songs' of the Grand Masquerade scene.[22] Corn Meal makes a musical and political intervention, which shows up both the realities of inhumane treatment towards Black people and also the appropriations of Black cultures inherent in blackface. Corn Meal's skilful 'celebrated Extravaganzas' are shown to be part of 'Life As It Is!'; they demonstrate and validate his virtuosity on stage for the audience. In the process they undercut stereotyping and racist violence. The creativity of Black performers such as Waters found a new outlet in Corn Meal's inclusion in *Life in New Orleans*. The fact that his act ended in the death of his horse highlights the hazards of this endeavour, however.

Old Corn Meal combined the techniques of street cries and blackface minstrelsy to create something new, yet not new. For the *Picayune* it is 'not the barrel-looking body, the happy phiz, the aguish go-cart, nor the pig-like squeak of his falsetto voice that commends *Old Corn-meal* to our esteem; he has won our regard because he is an original'.[23] He faced competition from other street sellers in the city, with their own distinctive cries, but it was Old Corn Meal whose performances were so notable that they made the papers as far as Georgia and New Hampshire.[24] Like Waters he made himself into a unique Character to survive

67. *A Mardi Gras procession passes the St Charles Theatre.*

economic precarity. At the same time it was his compilation of multiple influences that, like Waters, made him 'original'. The *Picayune* likened Old Corn Meal's 'wheel about' voice to the dance moves of T. D. Rice,[25] who early in the 1830s invented the blackface character 'Jim Crow' to wide transatlantic acclaim. Rice sang the song 'wheel about and turn about and jump Jim Crow' while he danced in an exaggerated fashion in the persona of a Southern, disabled, enslaved, Black man. Rice sang 'Rosin the Bow' and 'Sich a Gittin Up the Stairs' as part of his 'Jim Crow' act. Neither Old Corn Meal nor Waters were allowed to stand apart from blackface minstrelsy. If anything, performance scholar Ayanna Thompson argues, minstrelsy was an angry response to such success.[26] In 1836 (the year that T. D. Rice first toured the UK and danced and sang as 'Jim Crow'), *Cleave's Weekly Police Gazette* explained that 'The original "Jim Crow" was a Transatlantic "Billy Waters".'[27] The February 1839 Mardi Gras procession featured a blackface 'Old Corn Meal';

like Waters, Old Corn Meal was turned into a masquerade costume for white fun.[28] But Old Corn Meal sang minstrel favourites as a Black performer: he imitated the imitation, giving white-generated stereotypes back to white audiences in audacious and triumphant fashion.

The tension between authenticity and theatricality in this transatlantic culture opened up a chink of creative space for performers like Waters and Corn Meal to exploit. And exploit it they did. Despite the power of blackface, there was a moment where other possibilities floated, bubble-like, to the surface. Old Corn Meal performed at a large and significant urban theatre, using the *Life in London* craze in order to do it. Waters' gift to the otherwise anonymous 'Old Corn Meal' was the space to push the blackface defence of authenticity to its logical end and to perform on the stage.

Waters' legacy was used by white performers and musicians, too. One notable figure to take Waters' image and shift it in the direction of minstrelsy was the popular composer W. H. Montgomery. Montgomery directed theatre music and published sheet music for his quadrilles in Britain and America. The quadrille was a popular middle-class partner-dance by the 1850s in a period where the publication of songs and dances designed to be played around a piano at home was big business.[29] Amongst the hundreds of booklets of quadrille music printed in the 1850s with Montgomery's name on the cover (with titles such as *Evening Party Quadrille*, *The Saxe Gotha Quadrilles*, and *New York N—r Quadrilles*) was a booklet called *Negro Melody Quadrilles*.[30] The image of the cover (Plate XVI) is one very familiar to us: a version of Thomas Busby's engraving of Billy Waters. This time the image is of a dead man, not a living one; it is also the image of an idea and a Character that has been pushed and pulled in so many different directions, that has proved itself to be so very flexible and transportable, and that is very much alive.

Negro Melody Quadrilles gives us access to a legacy of Waters' performances for white but also for Black dancers of quadrilles. The cover image is vivid and the lines of the engraving are delicately done. The details are poignant: his sleeve pokes out at his elbow, his shirt doesn't cover his chest, his hands curl around the violin. But his face is the squashed caricature of Busby's picture. It's another attempt to trade off the qualities that in life made Waters so striking: his music, dancing, and costume, all as delineated in his supposed 'Last Will and Testament'. The caption below the image – 'First Progenitor of Promenade Concerts – He Died About Twenty Years Ago' – uses alliteration to make Waters sound special. It assigns him musicality, and suggest that he is the founding father of a musical movement. The vague inclusion of 'about' in the caption is also significant, suggesting as it does that it's the mythmaking that's important, not the facts, not the 'real' Waters, though Waters' skills appear to be celebrated.

However, the verse on the cover (printed on other side of Montgomery's name) and the choice of music inside the booklet reveal that something unpleasant is going on. The verse addresses Billy Waters in mock-heroic style as 'Thou Child of Genius! Who with wooden leg, / Wert doomed to stroll – to scrape thy way & beg', in 'humble imitation' of a laudatory poem to a French popular musician called M. Jullien. While the poem to Jullien calls him 'Godlike', able to 'sway the tide of Music at Command', this version for Waters reduces him to a 'Child of Genius', an untutored talent, a 'noble savage'. 'Hadst thou been spared to these enlightened days / Thy Triumph sure would be a perfect blaze,' we're told, which seems at first glance to express admiration. But Waters is only to be admired as a novelty, no more: 'For tho' thy skill in music – was all stuff / Thy garb – thy antics now would be enough.' The verse actually not-so-subtly undercuts him, reduces him to conductor of a 'Monstrous Monstre Band', very different to the 'Godlike' statues accorded to the white Frenchman Jullien. The printed music itself is a mixture of traditional favourites and songs from the standard minstrelsy repertoire, including Old Corn Meal's 'Rosin the Beau (Bow)' and 'Sich a Gittin Up the Stairs'. The generic title of 'Negro-Melody' music changes the context of the Busby image and turns Waters' idea into just another 'Negro' representation. It blurs the boundaries between Black performance and blackface, a technique that Ayanna Thompson lambasts as the 'consistent exculpatory fiction' of blackface, that it pays homage to real life.[31] The legacy of Waters' skill is framed by the white composer and white commentary, and shaped into minstrelsy stereotypes. The music (which doesn't include 'Polly Will You Marry Me') is for middle-class consumers to perform. His movement and sound are frozen in time into a captured image.

But what if we look *with* other dancers who also enjoyed the quadrille? Dance historian and dancer Rodreguez King-Dorset has found visual evidence from nineteenth-century London and nineteenth-century Philadelphia that at so-called 'Black Balls' organised and attended by free servants and workers, dancers danced the quadrille with 'their body weight forward and in something of a crouched position which is associated with African dance' (he uses the very general term 'African' with reservations). King-Dorset makes an even bigger argument: that dance was vital to enslaved Africans as they navigated the impact and traumatic legacies of enslavement. African rhythms endured but also changed as enslaved people in the Caribbean, in America, and in Britain encountered European and other dance styles and imitated them or incorporated them into their own dances. So we can visualise the quadrille as danced by nineteenth-century Black Londoners as 'European with a difference, an African difference', interpreted by white commentors as ineptitude but in fact a sophisticated and sometimes humorous or mocking response to the creolisation of culture created by the forced migrations of the slave trade.[32] In other words, King-Dorset's research offers the possibility that the pianist picking up *Negro Melody*

68. *'The Wandering Minstrel for Westminster'* (1847).

Quadrilles in order to play the next dance, and the dancers gathered in the room ready to make up their sets, were not always white – nor they were they always taking the dances, the music or the images on the sheet-music title pages at face value.

Waters' legacy, then, circulated within both Black and white popular cultures. We might also catch glimpses of its after-echoes in less tangible places. One shows us the unpleasant aspects that enabled Waters' memorialisation. One shows us the power of endurance. Waters was not the first person to be turned into china statuettes, printed images and stage roles. Nor was 'Billy Waters' the first fictional character to get the same treatment. Regency Britons and post-Revolutionary Americans might have statuettes of Nelson or Portsmouth Poll on their mantelpieces, and prints of Dr Syntax or Davy Crockett on their walls. John Liston's version of the stage role 'Paul Pry' in the 1820s, and Charles Dickens' 'Samuel Pickwick' in the 1830s, developed lives of their own, sometimes (as in the case of Pickwick) transatlantic ones. Because Waters was both real and imagined, a living person and a fictionalised character, he breathed an extra kind of life into the memes of Regency and early Victorian culture. In turn this meant that it was easier for nineteenth-century transatlantic audiences to accept the idea that popular Characters might develop a life of their own. In 1847, *Punch* magazine ran a short series of articles which mocked prospective MP Charles Cochrane for a strange stunt in which he dressed as a 'Spanish Minstrel' and travelled the country in disguise. *Punch* used a procession of meme-like characters as an illustration to the first article (Figure 68). 'Billy Waters' is the only real person depicted; but it's not the real person we see here at all.

Not all that survives of us, however, is memes. As he lay dying, Waters must have worried that the future looked bleak for his children. In Regency London the death of a father – a breadwinner – was a devastating blow, sometimes emotionally and always financially. Waters must have worried that the legacy he left them was one of worse poverty, increased danger, and few prospects.

Undoubtedly this was true. But he left them more than that. By showing what was possible as a Black disabled street performer in a white-dominated society, he contributed yet more unavoidable evidence (in addition to the numerous other life stories touched on in this book) that the people who earned a living in city streets deserved better than poverty, exclusion, and tokenism as they negotiated with skill and professionalism the precarious Atlantic world in which they found themselves. His career was evidence that not every white Briton looked at Black performers with derision. Indirectly Waters helped to develop a platform for Ira Aldridge, James Hewlett, and 'Old Corn Meal' (to name a few individuals). His presence at the heart of the *Life in London* craze showed that Black citizens were not only depicted in transatlantic popular cultures, they were busy shaping them. It went further than that: when folk-music collectors Alan Lomax and Shirley Collins recorded African American blues player, songwriter, and bandleader Sid Hemphill at Hemphill's home in Senatobia, Mississippi in September 1959, Hemphill sang them a version of 'Polly Will You Marry Me' on a homemade banjo. Son of an enslaved fiddle player and now blind, Hemphill was described to Lomax as 'the best musician in the world'.[33] The recording is freely available online via the Lomax Digital Archive: 'It's an ooold song,' says Hemphill.[34] As Waters lay dying, he had already left his children one of the greatest gifts from any parent to their child: the hope of a broader future.

Epilogue
Who Tells Your Story?

What became of Billy Waters? Do these street heroes die the death of men – in bed, and with friends near them; or do they generally find their fate at last in the workhouse or the gaol; and get buried no one knows when or by whom or where?

I cannot agree with Mr Dickens that 'no one knows for certain' about such persons '*because* no one cares'. Indeed Mr D.'s philosophy and practice are at variance in this matter. He makes his own sketch of 'the little mad old woman', because he feels that it will interest. How more would the original could we get at it! But the truth is, these people are as mysterious as the fireman's dog. They 'come like shadows, so depart': leaving behind them on so many ineffaceable impressions.

Alfred Gatty, 'London Street Characters' (1852)

A lfred Gatty knew that precarity was a key theme of Waters' story. Regency and early Victorian popular culture frequently destabilised the real people it touched. Like a reality TV star who plays a caricatured version of themselves only to find their image further manipulated by exterior forces, Waters built his image but

301

he couldn't control its power. It eventually destroyed him. The image lived on.

Waters' fame faded as the Victorian era unfurled. Journalist Edmond Yeats asked in 1877: 'who is aware now that half a century ago Billy Waters was a well-known London beggar?'[1] Yet reproductions of original nineteenth-century 'Billy Waters' figurines were still being produced for sale in the twentieth century (which tells us as much about that era's acceptance of racial stereotypes as it does about Waters). Revivals of *Tom and Jerry* brought the characters to whole new generations: in 1870 Mr Joseph A. Cave produced a revival of the Adelphi version at the Surrey Theatre, in which 'Billy Waters' – 'a well-known character' – was played by Mr F. Mitchell. This ran for nine weeks with 'distinguished success', so Mr Conquest, of the Grecian, and Mrs Lane, of the Britannia, spied a business opportunity and staged their own revivals straight afterwards. The Surrey Theatre got in on the act a few years later in 1877. In May 1886 Mr Cave re-launched *Tom and Jerry* again at the Elephant and Castle Theatre with 'All the Original Music, Songs, Duets, Chorusses and Dances Produced from the Original Adelphi Manuscript' and 'All the Noted Characters in Costumes of the time'.[2] The *Telegraph* reminisced in 1901 about the Old Adelphi and mused how 'now and then something inexplicably becomes a "rage". So it was with *Tom and Jerry*,' while a magazine article from 1925 re-explained 'Billy Waters' to its readers. For the *Telegraph* writer, *Tom and Jerry* is wrapped up with nostalgia for a theatrical past of melodrama and simple comedy:

'Tom and Jerry', in book form, with all its coloured plates and antique fooling, seems poor stuff, but it brought fame and fortune to the Adelphi in 1821. The last time we saw the play was just eight and twenty years ago, when the late 'Daddy' Harris, of Liverpool, played Corinthian Tom and Mr E. M. Robson Billy Waters – the one-legged musical negro who had fiddled successfully through the streets of the metropolis, and who was literally ruined as a charitable object by his introduction into Moncrieff's adaptation.[3]

This nostalgia (for the *Telegraph*) is inextricably associated with loss: the loss of the Adelphi Theatre (now 'faded from the Strand') and the loss of Billy Waters. The survival of documents about Waters has been more a process of historical accident than anything else. It's amazing that we know about him at all. He stands out as exceptional rightly because of his talents; but he also must stand for the innumerable thousands of ordinary Black Britons and Americans who are lost to us in the archives. As I chased Waters' shadow, every fact had its contradiction and its myth. His absences as much as his presence in these pages show how powerful the myths became.

Waters demonstrated astonishing resilience in the face of multiple challenges. He wasn't like George Bridgetower, or the Chevalier de Saint-Georges, or Ira Aldridge. He didn't have access to royalty, aristocracy, famous composers, or the Shakespearean stage. What he did have was the ability to harness spectacle and play to a crowd. He knew he had to perform in certain ways to get noticed and to be appreciated, regardless of his 'real' life. He understood the edges on which he danced and he used this knowledge to support his family, initially to great success. Regency and early Victorian popular culture thrived on the gap between reality and the stories people told, and this gap was something Waters realised he could usefully exploit.

But it was also a gap that was turned against him by more powerful people with their own agendas, to devastating effect. The Cruikshank brothers, Moncrieff, the Mendicity Society, Catnach, the Jefferson family, and the British Navy took what they needed from Waters. They were able to do so because so many people were willing to view Waters not as a unique and vulnerable individual

69. Two twentieth-century 'Billy Waters' figurines.

(aren't we all?) but as a Character: 'Jack Tar', the 'King of the Beggars', the 'Stage Black'. Popular culture was Waters' ultimate nemesis, even though it was also the source of his widest fame. It consumed some of the very people off whom it fed. In the Regency and early Victorian period, popular culture was shifting from something that still could be generated by what we'd now call folk traditions to something that was more capitalist and commercial, driven increasingly by a mainstream mass market for plays, books, visual images, and celebrity memorabilia. Waters found himself caught in that shift. It leaves us all with a responsibility to seek out, in the memorabilia that survives, the traces of the man himself. All portraits of people are a kind of biography.[4] Sometimes they are all we have of autobiography, too.

More survives, though, than just memorabilia. We are more than the sum of our memes. In the ceramic figurines made of Waters at least as early as 1825, he's frozen, his face a featureless mask, his individuality nominally celebrated but essentially lost. It's the ultimate capture. This is explored in 'Staffordshire Figurine, 1825', a poem by Rita Dove – the first African American woman to be United States Poet Laureate since the title was changed to Poet Laureate, and the second African American to receive the Pulitzer Prize for Poetry – about 'Billy Waters' memorabilia. Dove's poem highlights how these figurines close down nuance when:

> The rest
> is shrouded in that profoundest
> of neglects, the haze
> of centuries.[5]

Confronted by these figurines – survivors from the past when many of the details of Waters' actual historical life are lost – it's easy to feel that these are the last word on Waters. Waters was caught in the ultimate tension of celebrity: his uniqueness was what sold his brand, but his brand was also endlessly imitable, serial, and meme-like. It's easy to feel that Waters, for all his skills, has survived as little more than a series of identical memorabilia (Figure 69).

Rita Dove resists precisely this kind of defeatism in her poem 'Black Billy Waters, at His Pitch' (from her 2009 poetic biography of George Bridgetower, *Sonata Mulattica*) by giving Waters back the voice which he was never allowed:

> All men are beggars, white or black;
> some worship gold, some peddle brass.
> My only house is on my back.

I play my fiddle, I stay on track,
Give my peg leg – thankee sire! – a jolly thwack;
all men are beggars, white or black.

And the plink of coin in my gunny sack
is the bittersweet music in a life of lack;
my only house is on my back.

Was a soldier once, led a failed attack
in that greener country for the Union Jack.
All men are beggars, white or black.

Crippled as a crab, sugary as sassafras:
I'm Black Billy Waters, and you can kiss my sweet ass!
My only house weighs on my back.

There he struts, like a Turkish cracker jack!
London queues for any novelty, and that's a fact.
All men are beggars, white or black.

And to this bright brown upstart, hack
among kings, one piece of advice: don't unpack.
All the home you'll own is on your back.

I'll dance for the price of a mean cognac,
Sing gay songs like a natural-born maniac;
all men are beggars, white or black.

So let's scrape the catgut clean, stack
the chords three deep! See, I'm no quack –
though my only house is on my back.
All men are beggars, white or black.

Dove's 'Billy Waters' addresses the reader in the first person, mixing Regency references with twenty-first-century slang as he comments on young George Bridgetower. This 'Billy Waters' knows full well the stakes of the uncertain game he and Bridgetower are playing as people of colour in a white world, but he also gives no ground: in Dove's poem 'Pretty Boy', Bridgetower encounters 'Old Black Billy Waters, / peg leg and fiddle / just a-going, laughing as if to say / *Whatcha gonna do with that stare?* / and tossing it / back'. Waters enables Dove to explore the differences between looking at and looking with the subjects of her poems. When the outlines of historical Black presences are left unrealised by bare facts, Dove shows us how poetic reimaginings are a deft tool to shade in those outlines.

At the time of writing there are more questions than answers regarding the details of Waters' life. A movement is underway now to address his historical neglect: on the 200th anniversary of his death, Waters received a blue plaque in a building in London's Dyott Street, site of the slum where Waters lived with his family; the anniversary was also noted in the UK Parliament by something called an Early Day Motion, which recognised Waters' contribution to Black British history. But the thoughts and feelings of the 'real' William Waters are likely to remain forever elusive. As the scholar Alain Corbin once wrote about the subject of his own piece of research, 'may he forgive me for this fleeting resurrection, and for the various ways in which the reader may, because of what I have written, imagine the man he was'.[6] If we keep asking questions about Waters and his world, Billy Waters is dancing. I like to picture him dancing with Elizabeth.

Acknowledgements

This project was possible because of groundbreaking work on Black history by scholars such as Peter Fryer, Gretchen Gerzina, and Paul Gilroy, among others. The incredible generosity shown by all kinds of people during the course of writing this book has been a constant source of heart-warming surprise to me. No one I have approached for help or advice has been too busy; everyone has been happy to share their expertise and ideas. Special votes of thanks appear below, but so many people have been integral to the writing of this book.

It was Brian Maidment, David Vincent, and Caroline Radcliffe who first said, 'You do realise this could be a book, don't you?' From that moment on they have continued to cheerlead it. I'm so grateful. Brian combed his book collection and gave me permission to publish many treasures.

The Leverhulme Trust and the Research Society for Victorian Periodicals generously funded almost two years of research leave at a crucial time. I must thank the University of Roehampton for allowing me to take it up. Anna Grundy at the Leverhulme Trust was very supportive during challenging circumstances. The Paul Mellon Fund and Harvard University enabled research trips to

Oxford and Boston; Dale Stinchcomb, Vanessa Wilkie, and Alison Fitzgerald helped to make my Houghton Library Fellowship at Harvard an amazing intellectual adventure. Dale helped me to locate the playbill for Old Corn Meal and provided all kinds of assistance. Clare McManus supported this research from the very beginning.

My editor Julian Loose took the time to teach me so much about the writing of non-fiction. His belief in this project (and his patience with writerly ticks) has been more important than he realises. His assistant Frazer Martin has been a model of efficiency and professionalism, especially on thorny issues of images. The whole team at Yale have been fantastic and a joy to work with: special thanks to Heather Nathan, Lucy Buchan, Rachael Lonsdale, Rachel Hunter and Leah Jacobs-Gordon. My assistant Ardyn Tennyson has handled the paperwork for all eighty-five images in this book with panache, even when I changed the figure numbers – again. Thanks also to the anonymous readers at Yale whose comments made this a better book.

There were other readers, too: Lars Atkin, Joanne Begiato, Mike Brown, Alex Bubb, Hannah Cusworth, Maria Damkjaer, Linda K. Hughes, Claire Hynes, Jasmine Jagger, Oskar Jensen, Mathelinda Nabugodie, Kate Newey, Laura Peters, Caroline Radcliffe, Leone Ross, Julia Thomas, Tash Thomas, all gave of their time and knowledge. Ingrid Alexander, Sarah Anderson, Kathleen Chater, Rita Dove, Miles Grier, Rebecca Fogg, Joseph Harley, Colin Merrell, the Race and Transimperialism Reading Group, the RootsChat forum and the UK Disability History and Heritage Hub provided references or talked though ideas. Ian Haywood and Rohan McWilliam were firm supporters, as always.

Fortunately, given the gaps in our knowledge of Waters' life, there is a growing network of enthusiasts hot on the trail, including artist and Rookery historian Jane Palm-Gold, music journalist Tony Montague, and curator, educator and activist Emily Momoh. Curator Suchitra Chatterjee, musicologist Oskar Jensen, disability scholar Elena Ghiggino, musician Angeline Morrison and historian Ben Marsh bring their particular areas of expertise to the quest. I am grateful for their companionship; this book is my contribution.

I have benefited from the expertise of numerous fantastic archivists and librarians in the UK and US: Robert Blyth (National Museums Greenwich), Daniel Croughton (Camden Local Studies Centre), Mark Dunton and Kate Fox (National Archives Kew), Rhonda Evans (Schomburg Center for Research in Black Culture), Tiffany Hore (Vaughan Williams Library), Lauren Rogers (University of Mississippi), Jasmine Smith (Philadelphia Library Company), Claire Titely (London Metropolitan Archives), and Amanda Zimmerman (Library of Congress). The staff of the London Library, British Library, British Museum, Bodleian Libraries, Black Cultural Archives, Westminster Archives Centre, New York Public Library, and the National Maritime Museum's Caird Library have been such a source of knowledge and assistance.

To Julia for London Library Wednesdays, Emma for Writing Club and Bea for wise words on biography: thank you. Thank you also to my parents for endless support. As ever, it's my family and friends who keep me dancing.

Notes

Prologue

1. Anon, 'N—er Minstrelsy', *Saturday Review of Politics, Literature, Science and Art* (11 May 1861): 477–8 (477).
2. For more on Moncrieff's career see Cox, *Reading Adaptations*.
3. 'Pierce Egan . . . after the publication of the first number of "Tom and Jerry", with coloured plates by George Cruikshank, awoke one morning and found himself famous; found that his bookseller was overwhelmed with orders . . . With each new number the furore increased' (Baker, 'The Home of the Melodrama').
4. Maidment, *Dusty Bob*, 59.
5. For the history of what we now call 'The West End', see Bratton, *Making of the West End*; Davis and Emeljanow, *Reflecting the Audience*; McWilliam, *London's West End*.
6. Also rendered as 'Kitty Will You Marry Me?'.
7. Waters is discussed briefly in Jensen, *Vagabonds*, Maidment, *Dusty Bob*, and Hindley, *True History*. He makes a two-sentence appearance in Ramdin's *Making of the Black Working Class*, and in Fryer's *Staying Power*. His transatlantic resonances are discussed in Gibbs, *Performing the Temple of Liberty*. He is also mentioned in Reed, *Rogue Performances*, Waters, *Racism*, and Jensen, *Ballad-Singer*. I wrote the first article on him (Shannon, 'The Multiple Lives of Billy Waters'). The prints and texts that immortalised him are increasingly referenced as part of Black British history collections at the London Metropolitan Archives, Victoria and Albert Museum, the National Portrait Gallery, the National Archives, Chatham Historic Dockyard and the National Maritime Museum. Music journalist Tony Montague wrote an article for the *Guardian* ('An O-o-ld Song') with important new facts. But there has been no sustained treatment of Waters in the context of his place in literary history, and many sources are inaccurate.

8. The terms 'popular', 'culture' and 'popular culture' are, of course, far from straightforward. Scholars debate them back and forth and they are 'used to mean so many different things at different times and across different disciplines' (see Bell, *Spring-Heeled Jack*, 3–4). For full discussion of how I am defining popular culture, see Chapter 1.

9. *Ceres* and *Ganymede* Musters. ADM 37/3274; 3229.

10. On the Black population of London in this period, see Fryer, *Staying Power*; Myers, *Reconstructing the Black Past*; Chater, *Untold Histories*.

11. Moncrieff, 'Tom and Jerry', 8.

12. Hindley, *Life and Times*, 135.

13. Catnach, *The Death, Last Will, and Funeral of Black Billy*; Jerrold, 'The Ballad Singer', 225.

14. Hindley, *True History*; Busby, *Costume*.

15. See Garland-Thomson, *Staring*.

16. As Reid puts it, 'To say that *Life in London* was a phenomenal success is not to exaggerate' (*Bucks and Bruisers*, 73).

17. Hepburn, *Scattered Leaves*, 1: 33; 2: 308–11.

18. Carlson, *Performance*, 4–5. Carlson emphasises that performance is 'an essentially contested concept' (5) over which scholars wrangle, but argues that all kinds of actions made deliberately for an audience class as performance, even if the audience is only oneself.

19. Esterhammer, *Print and Performance*.

20. Hindley, *True History*, 10.

21. There was even a French translation of Egan's text: *Diorama Anglais* (1823).

22. There is a growing body of work on Georgian and Regency celebrity culture: see Inglis, *Short History of Celebrity*; Lilti, *Invention of Celebrity*; Luckhurst and Moody, eds, *Theatre and Celebrity*; McPherson, *Art and Celebrity*, Mole, *Byron's Romantic Celebrity*; Mole, ed., *Romanticism and Celebrity Culture*. As a Black disabled man, however, Waters' relationship to celebrity culture doesn't quite fit these models.

23. On *Tom and Jerry* as old-fashioned see 'Advertisements & Notices', *Era* (6 Mar. 1870): 8.

24. 'Saturday's Police', *Lloyd's Illustrated Newspaper* (21 Jul. 1844): 7.

25. [Edmund Yates], 'Burlesque: Past and Present', *Time* (May 1880): 127; 'Advertisements & Notices', *Era* (2 Aug. 1884): 14. There was a well-known boxer called Billy Waters in the second half of the century, but it is generally very clear which Billy Waters is being used as a reference point given that our Billy Waters had such a distinctive physical and visual presence.

26. Corbin aims for the 'evocation of a life' (212); Turner's book connects women's life stories to the fictional Wife of Bath; Hartman has led the way in how to work 'with and against' the silences of the archive with reference to enslaved Black people (see *Wayward Lives*, xiii, and 'Venus in Two Acts', 10–12).

27. Other writers have paid close attention to popular characters such as Harlequin, Mr Punch, Three-Finger'd Jack, Paul Pry, Dusty Bob the dustman (another well-loved character from the *Life in London* craze), Sweeney Todd, Jim Crow, Dolly Varden (a popular 1840s Dickens character now largely forgotten) and, of course, Mr Pickwick. See Maidment, *Dusty Bob*; Mack,

Sweeney Todd; Bell, *Spring-Heeled Jack*; Scriven, 'The Jim Crow Craze'; Vincent, *I Hope I Don't Intrude?*; Botkin, *Thieving Three-Fingered Jack*; Abraham, 'Plagiarizing Pickwick'. Lifeguardsman John Shaw was turned into a popular hero after his death at Waterloo, but Waters became a meme during his lifetime (Begiato, *Manliness*, 120–7).

28. See Abraham, *Plagiarizing*, and MacFarlane, *Original Copy*. Bolter and Grusin gave us the term 'remediation', Cordell calls nineteenth-century newspapers 'viral texts' (viraltexts.org), and novelist Jasper Fforde's term 'bookhopper' describes characters who jump out of their original context. Lissette Szwydky emphasises how 'eighteenth and nineteenth-century theatre and print industries thrived on adaptation, appropriation, and other forms of storytelling' (*Transmedia Adaptation*, 6), and uses Henry Jenkins' terms 'transmedia storytelling' and 'convergence culture' to describe this prevalence of adaptation (15). Paul Davis came up with the term 'culture-text' for narratives that, driven by adaptation, exist in the cultural imagination as a popular concept. But no one has used the framework of the meme for nineteenth-century popular characters or images of real historical people.

29. For a definition of memes in literature, see Cooper, *The English Romance*, 3. See also 'meme, n.', OED Online.

30. Cooper reminds us that 'There is a word for such things now: a "meme", an idea that behaves like a gene in its ability to replicate faithfully and abundantly, but also on occasion to adapt, mutate, and therefore survive in different forms and cultures' (*The English Romance*, 3). She is drawing upon ideas from evolutionary biologist Richard Dawkins and psychologist Susan Blackmore. The word 'meme' was first proposed by Dawkins as genes' equivalent in human culture; Blackmore and others took up this word to propose an entire new field of cultural study, mimetics (Dawkins, *Selfish Gene*, 206; 'meme, n.', OED Online; Blackmore, *Meme Machine*). Theatre historian Louise George Clubb coined the related term 'theatergram', which proved to be highly influential (Clubb, *Italian Drama*). For the subsequent use of this term to analyse the histories of blackface, see Hornback, *Racism and Early Blackface*, 35.

31. Stereotypes, then, might be considered to act more like the inert cliché, 'which replicate[s] the familiar without change' (Cooper, 15), while tropes, which can change and adapt, act more like the agile meme.

32. In ways that made 1830 literary commentators especially anxious: see MacFarlane, *Original Copy*.

33. Olusoga, *Black and British*, 28.

34. Otele, *African Europeans*, 203.

35. In taking this approach I acknowledge my debt to work by cultural historians such as Kathleen Chater and Paul Gilroy, literary critics such as Gretchen Gerzina, art historians such as Denise Murrell, and cultural geographers such as Caroline Bressey. They paved the way in arguing that we have not yet fully appreciated the importance of non-white participants in nineteenth-century culture. Rosemary Ashton reminds us that 'Microhistory, the study in depth and detail of historical phenomena, can uncover hitherto hidden connections, patterns, and structures' (*One Hot Summer*, 5).

36. There are authoritative studies of disability and wooden legs in the long nineteenth century but not in relation to ordinary Napoleonic sailors (Dickie, *Cruelty and Laughter*; Holmes, *Fictions of Affliction*; Sweet, *Prosthetic Body Parts*); there are excellent studies of Napoleonic veterans (Brown and Begiato, eds, *Martial Masculinities*) but accounts of cultural representations of Black and white mariners in Britain tend to focus on nautical melodrama (e.g. Burroughs and Waters) while Gilje has focussed on the US 'Tar' only.

37. Key authorities on the representation of St Giles and London beggars are Mayne, *The Imagined Slum*; Dyos, 'The Slums of Victorian London'; Makdisi, *Making England Western*, Chapter 1; Crymble, 'Decline and Fall'; Hitchcock, *Down and Out*; Jensen, *Vagabonds*; on Black communities in St Giles try Martin's novel *Incomparable World*.

38. Fryer argued that in the eighteenth century 'the working people of London' saw in black slaves 'fellow-victims of their own enemies', and were therefore regularly willing to help runaways (*Staying Power*, 73–4). Three years later, David Dabydeen's *Hogarth's Blacks* (1987) turned to art history to suggest that Hogarth's work in particular reveals 'a solidarity between blacks and lower-class whites which overrides racial division'. Recently Laura Michelle Keigan argued that 'issues of class were central to how people understood those of race [in the 1830s], and . . . this connection requires further study if we are to better understand both' ('Intersections', 12; 262).

39. The exceptions are Keigan and Miles Grier, who investigate 1830s Othello burlesques, some of which include Black crossing-sweepers. Jeremy Goheen has looked at race and chimney-sweeps ('Soot in One's Soup').

40. See, for example, James, *Fiction for the Working Man*; Thompson, *Making of the English Working Class*.

41. We know the novelist W. M. Thackeray did, for instance, because he wrote about it (see 'Wig'). Adults probably did as well.

42. In using the term network I am developing work by Maidment and Vincent on Dusty Bob and Paul Pry, as well as ideas I have already expressed (Shannon, 'The Multiple Lives of Billy Waters') that draw upon Robert Darnton's influential idea of the book history 'communications circuit' of author-printer-publisher-bookseller-reader, and Darnton's work on networks of people communicating through gossip, poems and songs. Waters is the most complete demonstration of this network in action yet considered.

Hat

1. For Bob, Ned and Jack, see De Voe, *Market Book*, I: 344–5.

Childhood

2. Moncrieff, 'Billy Waters', 3:121–3.
3. For more on this see Waters, *Racism*. Hindley's compilation of all sorts of materials about *Life in London* and its various offshoots and imitations was not published until 1888, some decades after Waters' death.
4. *Ceres* Muster. ADM 37/3274; Burial Register DL/T/36/47.
5. Douglass, *Bondage*, 35.

6. This is according to the dates given on his Royal Navy muster records and his burial record. While the muster records are not specific as to whether this is New York City, New York State or even New York the hamlet in Lincolnshire, a comparison with entries for other sailors suggests that the records were intended to reflect American origin. *Ganymede* Muster ADM 37/3229. There are several William Waters listed in the New York State census for 1790 and 1800, but these are all free white men, one of whom is a slaveholder.

7. The Declaration of Independence was agreed to by Congress on 4 Jul. 1776. For the New York Manumission Society see Harris, *Shadow of Slavery*, 55.

8. Scudder, ed., *Recollections*, 90.

9. White, *Somewhat*, 14.

10. Frederic, *Travels*, 2:457–8.

11. Strickland, *Journal*, 63.

12. See White, *Somewhat*, 3–23 and 153–5; Harris, *Shadow of Slavery*, 73–4; Foote, *Black and White Manhattan*.

13. Coventry, 'Memoirs of an Immigrant (1789)', 69; 145. Quoted in White, *Somewhat*, 16.

14. White, *Somewhat*, 88–9.

15. Ibid., 89.

16. 'To Be Sold: A Negro Man', *New York Journal* (2 Jun. 1774): 3.

17. Dunlap, *Diary*, 1:118.

18. Harris, *Shadow of Slavery*, 62.

19. Jacobs, *Incidents*, 16.

20. Wilson, *Our Nig*.

21. See Odumosu, *Africans in English Caricature*, 40–89, 138, 129. For more on Sall's dance with the Dustman see Maidment, *Dusty Bob*.

22. Jerrold, *St Giles and St James*, Chapter 17; for Ralph grown up see also Chapter 29.

23. See, for example, as well as Maidment, Vickers and Bell: Reay, *Popular Cultures in England*; Gilroy, *Black Atlantic*; Bailey, *Popular Culture and Performance*.

24. See Nicholson, 'Transatlantic Connections', 164.

25. Habib, *Black Lives*, 270; 272; 18.

Community

1. Southern, *Music of Black Americans*, 30–9.

2. Harris, *Shadow of Slavery*, 76–7; White, *Somewhat*, 178.

3. White, *Somewhat*, 94.

4. De Voe, *Market Book*, I: 344–5; Harris, *Shadow of Slavery*, 69; White, *Somewhat*, 96.

5. Howell and Tenny, *History*, 725. White calls this festival 'one of the most important and revealing cultural phenomena in the history of the black experience of America'; Harris sees it as 'an attempt to mitigate the isolation and hardships of slavery' (White, *Somewhat*, 96; Harris, *Shadow of Slavery*, 69).

6. Harris, *Shadow of Slavery*, 88–9.

7. Gilroy, *Black Atlantic*, 15. For some of the many responses to this concept see Oboe and Scacchi, eds, *Recharting the Black Atlantic*, and Ledent and Cuder-Domínguez, eds, *New Perspectives on the Black Atlantic*.

8. Dewulf, *The Pinkster King*, 39.

9. As Harris points out, 'these dances continued the African traditions that emphasized the centrality of dance to community and religious celebrations' (*Shadow of Slavery*, 69).

10. The major primary sources for our knowledge of Pinkster are: two contemporary sources – [Aimwell], 'A Pinkster Ode', and A. B., 'Pinkster', available in White, 'Pinkster' – and one antiquarian piece by Eights, 'Pinkster Festivities'.

11. A. B., 'Pinkster'.

12. Eights, 'Pinkster Festivities'.

13. 'A Glimpse of an Old Dutch Town', *Harpers New Monthly Magazine* 62 (Mar. 1881): 525–52.

14. Eights, 'Pinkster Festivities'.

15. [Aimwell], 'A Pinkster Ode'; Eights, 'Pinkster Festivities'. Jubilee had specific radical and abolitionist connotations in this period: see Linebaugh and Rediker, *Many-Headed Hydra*.

16. King-Dorset (citing K. A. Opoku), *Black Dance*, 47.

17. See Lewis, *Journal*, 33. On Jonkonnu as resistance see Reed, *Rogue Performances*, 117–20.

18. White, *Somewhat*, 101.

19. Stuckey, *Going Through the Storm*, 66–8; 53. Stuckey explains that so-called 'ring dances' traditionally had a spiritual element to them; he emphasises the possible connections between Pinkster dances and the ring dances on Southern plantations and in the nineteenth-century Caribbean.

20. A. B., 'Pinkster'; Stuckey criticises Shane White for taking the sources on Pinkster too much at face value and not interrogating the racist language (Stuckey, *Going Through the Storm*, 61–3).

21. Eights, 'Pinkster Festivities'.

22. Ibid.; Stuckey, *Going Through the Storm*, 64. Dewulf suggests that there might also be a link between Pinkster and dance performances in Haiti that celebrated a 'king' ('Pinkster', 263).

23. Munsell, *Collections on the History of Albany*, 2:56.

24. Stuckey, *Going Through the Storm*, 78.

25. Coventry, 'Memoirs of an Immigrant (1789)', 44; Dewulf, 'Pinkster', 246, 266; Sponsler, *Ritual Imports*, 63.

26. Southern, *Music of Black Americans*, 57.

27. De Voe, *Market Book*, I: 344–5.

28. *New York Times*, 9 Aug. 1992. Quoted in Stuckey, *Going Through the Storm*, 77, who also speculates whether King Charles ever visited New York City, as he reportedly visited Troy, NY. For more on the African Burial Ground, see Harris, *Shadow of Slavery*.

29. A. B., 'Pinkster'.

30. White, *Somewhat*, 104; Dewulf, 'Pinkster', 249.

31. *New York Public Advertiser* (23 May 1809). Although the author of the article may have been confusing the Whitsun Festival with May Day, known in London since the mid-eighteenth century as the 'Chimney-Sweep's Holiday'.

32. For discussion of the links between sweeps, race and class, see 'Wig'.

33. [Aimwell], 'A Pinkster Ode'.

34. *Albany Balance, and State Journal* (14 Jun. 1811): 178; *Albany Gazette* (29 Jun. 1815): 2.
35. Even if King Charles' role in Pinkster was not formalised until around 1800, as one historian thinks is possible, the parade and ceremonials did not spring up from nowhere (Sponsler, *Ritual Imports*, 51).
36. As described by cultural theorist Mikhail Bakhtin and subsequent historians: see *Rabelais and His World*.
37. White, 'Pinkster': 70.
38. [Aimwell], 'A Pinkster Ode'.
39. Eights, 'Pinkster Festivities'.
40. Stuckey, *Going Through the Storm*, 53–4.
41. Catnach, 'Life of Billy Waters', from *The Death, Last Will, and Funeral of Black Billy*.
42. [Hodgson], *Cries of London*.
43. For more on Cooke see https://www.rmg.co.uk/stories/blog/childhood-drawings-edward-william-cooke.
44. Moncrieff, 'Billy Waters', 123.
45. Jerrold, 'The Ballad-Singer', 5:225.
46. For a full discussion of beggars, street sellers and ballads, see 'Fiddle', as well as Jensen, *Ballad-Singer*.
47. Smith, *Vagabondiana*, image 6. Jensen's excellent discussion of Johnson and nineteenth-century sailors more generally (169–89) has informed my thinking on Waters' cultural influences in all kinds of helpful ways.
48. [Waterhouse], *Journal*, 164.
49. Richard Tynt [Jack Rag], *Streetology*, 13.
50. Qureshi, 'Displaying Sara Baartman'; Qureshi, *Peoples on Parade*; Holmes, *The Hottentot Venus*. There is no consensus on how to render Baartman's name: historians call her Sarah, Sara, Saartje and Saartjie; Baartman, Bartman and Bartmann.
51. See Waters, *Racism*; on human zoos see Qureshi, *Peoples on Parade*. On freak shows and ethnological showbusiness see Bogdan, *Freak Show*; Garland-Thomson, ed., *Freakery*; and Lindfors, *Africans on Stage*.
52. Gerzina, 'Introduction', *Black Victorians/Black Victoriana*, 4.
53. Davis, *Comic Acting and Portraiture*; McPherson, *Art and Celebrity*.
54. The painting was sold on the open art market in 1971 and again in 1994 as a work by Wilkie, before eventually being bought by the National Maritime Museum from a private collector. In the auction catalogues the painting appeared as *Portrait of Bill Waters*. Christie's, Lot 123 'Portrait of Bill Waters', *English Pictures c. 1700–1850* (Friday 18 Jun. 1971), 36; Christie's, Lot 99 'Portrait of Bill Waters', *English Pictures* (Friday 11 Nov. 1994), 99.
55. 'Hatton-Garden'.
56. Dr Nicholas Tromans, author of the only monograph on Wilkie to date (email, 31.10.2019). It is not impossible that the artist painted a study of Waters, and he had a London studio. The glorious golden background is unlike anything else by Wilkie, however, and no larger work exists for which this might have been a study. See Tromans, *David Wilkie*; Marsh, ed., *Black Victorians*.

57. The National Maritime Museum dates it as circa 1815 (https://www.rmg. co.uk/collections/objects/rmgc-object-254220).
58. The nineteenth-century art world's curious preoccupation with 'the Black man in red' is identified by art historians Adrienne L. Childs and Susan H. Libby in *The Black Figure in the European Imaginary*, 20–3.
59. See Honour, *Image of the Black in Western Art*, vol. IV/1 *Slaves and Liberators*, vol. IV/2 *Black Models and White Myths* (1989). On artists' networks in London see Shannon, 'Artists' Street', 243–66.
60. Murrell, *Posing Modernity*, 7. By contrast see Odumosu on Western depictions of Black women in caricature.
61. Dewulf, 'Pinkster', 245. Sponsler and White take different positions on this question.
62. The borders between 'mass culture' (often understood as commercial and driven by new media such as the newspaper) and 'popular culture' (sometimes coded as vernacular or bubbling up from 'below', deriving from old media such as ballads and oral culture) are messy and interesting. On mass culture and new media see Zieger, *Mediated Mind*; Teukolsky, *Picture World*.

Sailor Jacket
Going Aboard

1. Equiano, *Interesting Narrative*, 83–4; Douglass, *Life and Times*, 198–9.
2. There is no scholarship that combines the study of Black and white sailors in British popular culture (beyond nautical melodrama). Although there are useful scholarly accounts of Black mariners and of sailors in print and visual culture from a US perspective (Bolster, *Black Jacks*; Gilje, *Swear Like a Sailor*), there is relatively little scholarship on Black sailors in Nelson's Navy. Notable exceptions are: Costello, *Black Salt*; Foy, 'Britain's Black Tars'; Caputo, *Foreign Jack Tars*. The major authorities on Regency and Victorian caricature, apart from Odumosu, are Haywood (*Romanticism and Caricature*; *Rise of Victorian Caricature*) and Maidment (*Comedy, Caricature and the Social Order*), but none of these scholars specifically explore the cultural history of Black 'Jack Tars'.
3. Moncrieff, 'Billy Waters', 121.
4. Bryant, *Account of an Insurrection*.
5. 'The three most popular names for white men (John, William and Thomas) were also the three most popular for Black men throughout the entire long eighteenth century' (Chater, *Untold Histories*, 187).
6. Bolster, *Black Jacks*, 216.
7. Equiano, *Interesting Narrative*, 64; Foy, 'Britain's Black Tars', 79.
8. Dancy, *Myth of the Press Gang*, 3.
9. Harris, *Shadow of Slavery*, 80; White, *Somewhat*, 159.
10. Ibid.
11. White, *Somewhat*, 159.
12. Bolster, *Black Jacks*, 5–6.
13. Ibid., 21–6.
14. Ibid.; *Virginia Gazette* (12 Jun. 1778), quoted in Bolster, *Black Jacks*, 25.

15. Foy, 'Britain's Black Tars', 68.
16. 'Imprisonment of Colored Seamen', *National Anti-Slavery Standard* (30 Dec. 1841): 2.
17. Rogers, *Press Gang*, 14.
18. White, *Somewhat*, 127.
19. Cutbush, *Observations*, 126–7. See also Rodger, *Command of the Ocean*, 504.
20. Marrant, *Narrative*, 9.
21. Emidy settled in Truro in Cornwall and raised a family; he taught music, composed works and organised a successful biennial concert. He endured and triumphed. We know this because of the account by one of his students, an anti-slavery campaigner and politician: Buckingham, *Autobiography*, 163–72. See also McGrady, 'Joseph Emidy'.
22. Olmstead, *Incidents of a Whaling Voyage*, 115.
23. Marryat went on to write, among other things, *Mr Midshipman Easy* (1836), a hugely popular and influential sea story about the fortunes of the teenage Jack Easy and his companion the Black servant and ex-slave Mesty. See Brantlinger on race in Marryat's naval fiction in Chapter 2 of *Rule of Darkness*.
24. [Waterhouse], *Journal*, 167.
25. Rodger, *Command of the Ocean*, 504; Liddell Hart, ed., *Letters of Private Wheeler*, 47.
26. Hay, ed., *Landsman Hay*, 94. The sea-shanty's 'late eighteenth-century origins corresponded with rising numbers of black sailors, and the period of the shanty's greatest development after 1820 was one of black prominence at sea' (Bolster, *Black Jacks*, 217).
27. Bolster, *Black Jacks*, 217; Evans, 'Black Fife and Drum Music'.
28. Mageean, 'Black Origins of Sea Shanties'.
29. Bolster, *Black Jacks*, 35.
30. Jensen, *Ballad-Singer*, 193; 11.
31. Sharpe, *In the Wake*, 2; 16; 62.
32. Linebaugh and Rediker, *Many-Headed Hydra*, 144.
33. Gilroy, *Black Atlantic*, 4; 16; 17.
34. Bolster, *Black Jacks*, 21. For Sharpe, too, there is still room for agency 'in the wake' of tragedy, and for the survival and resilience that she calls 'wake work' (11; 13).
35. King, *Black Shoals*, 2.

Press'd?

1. Douglas-Fairhurst, *Turning-Point*, 31.
2. Zimmerman, *Impressment*, 179.
3. Useful modern studies of the British press gang are Dancy, *Myth of the Press Gang*, and Rogers, *Press Gang*.
4. Caputo, *Foreign Jack Tars*, 65.
5. Brown, *Life*, 26.
6. 'Pennsylvania, Philadelphia, Seamen's Proofs of Citizenship, 1791–1861', https://familysearch.org. For more on Philadelphia and Protection Certificates, see Newman, *Embodied History*.
7. Nagle, *Nagle Journal*, 189.
8. Dancy, *Myth of the Press Gang*, 144.

9. Brunsman, 'Subjects vs. Citizens', 580. Brunsman estimates that 'By 1812, about 15 percent of the seamen in [the Royal Navy] were from outside Britain' and approximately 10,000 American sailors were impressed between 1793 and 1812 (571–2).

10. Zimmerman, *Impressment*, 22.

11. Waters was one of only eight men taken from the *Ceres* on 23 Nov. 1811 in one batch of a hundred men who were listed as volunteers. Another was Peter Brown, who may also have been Black. But names are notoriously bad guides about race (see Chater, *Untold Histories*, 236). *Namur* Muster ADM 37/2805.

12. See Dancy, *Myth of the Press Gang*; Nagle, *Nagle Journal*, 189.

13. Nagle, *Nagle Journal*, 17.

14. Gilje, *Swear Like a Sailor*, 43–64.

15. Lamire, 'A Question of Trousers'.

16. Ennis, *Enter the Press-Gang*, 84.

17. Russell, *Theatres of War*, 9.

18. Begiato, *Manliness*, 122. The phrase 'nail your colours to the mast' entered idiomatic language around this time.

19. Begiato, 'Tears and the Manly Sailor'.

20. Ennis, *Enter the Press-Gang*, 84.

21. See Bratton, 'Dancing the Hornpipe', drawing upon Emmerson, 'The Hornpipe' and Inglehearn, 'The Hornpipe'.

22. Douglass, *Life and Times*, 198.

23. On stereotypes of 'Jack Tar' in Britain see Land, *War*; in the US see Gilje, *Swear Like a Sailor*. On the 'comic' stage Black in nautical melodrama see Waters, *Racism*.

24. Kafer and Kim, 'Disability and the Edges of Intersectionality', 123; 136.

25. In eighteenth-century pamphlets see Ennis, *Enter the Press-Gang*; in pro-war 1810s US periodicals see Brunsman, 'Subjects vs. Citizens'; in 1820s–40s nautical melodrama see Burroughs, 'Sailors and Slaves', and Waters, *Racism*.

26. [Oglethorpe], *Sailor's Advocate*, 8.

27. *Western Eagle* (4 Feb. 1814), quoted in Brunsman, 'Subjects vs. Citizens', 583.

28. 'Treatment of Sailors', *National Anti-Slavery Standard* (28 Jan. 1841): 3.

29. Hanley, 'Slavery and the Birth of Working-Class Racism in England'. For the opposite view see Linebaugh and Rediker, *Many-Headed Hydra*.

30. Lee, *American Slave Narrative*.

31. Douglass, *Heroic Slave*; Wedderburn, *Horrors of Slavery*; see Hoermann, 'Fermentation will be universal'.

32. Ennis, *Enter the Press-Gang*, 116.

33. Hay, *Landsman Hay*, 47.

34. See Winfield, *British Warships*, 15. The *Namur* will form the topic of my next book.

35. *Namur* Captain's Log. ADM 51/2619.5.

Life Aboard

1. Begiato, 'Tears and the Manly Sailor'.

2. Ganymede Pay Book. ADM 35/3489.

3. Winfield, *British Warships*, 242; threedecks.org; *Ganymede* Muster ADM 37/3229. *Ganymede* was later refitted as a frigate and then retired as a convict ship in 1819.
4. Found 'partly guilty . . . in practising the summary punishment of "starting", he was warned by the court to change his conduct' (Pope, *Nelson's Navy*, 213).
5. *Namur* Muster. ADM 37/2805; *Ganymede* Muster. ADM/37/3229.
6. *Ganymede* Muster. ADM 37/3229.
7. *Ganymede* Pay Book. ADM 35/3489. See also Caputo, *Foreign Jack Tars*, on cosmopolitan British Navy crews.
8. Robert Wilson, in Thursfield, ed., *Five Naval Journals*, 246. For the role of quarter gunner see Adkins and Adkins, *Jack Tar*, 15; Lavery, *Royal Tars*, 262–3; Lavery, *Nelson's Navy*, 103 and 136. They were not always utilised properly: one captain bemoaned the fact that 'the gunner's crew in a ship appears to be a class much neglected. For instead of making them skillful artillery men, and retaining them principally for that service, they are often suffered to remain totally ignorant of it, and only perform that part of the duty of seamen which is attached to their station' ([A Naval Captain], *Observations and Instructions*, also pirated in America).
9. Lavery, *Nelson's Navy*, 103; [Falconer], *Universal Dictionary*, 239.
10. Nicol, *Life and Adventures*, 170; 174.
11. Bechervaise, *Thirty-Six Years of a Seafaring Life*, 120.

A Veritable Jack Tar

1. 'To Correspondents', *The Mirror of the Stage*, 2:24 (14 Jul. 1823): 194. On Incledon, see Barry, 'Charles Incledon'.
2. Bolster, *Black Jacks*, 4.
3. Hammon, *Narrative*, 11.
4. Equiano, *Interesting Narrative*, 83–4.
5. Marrant, *Narrative*, 38.
6. Costello, *Black Salt*, 60–8; 68.
7. Ibid., 1. See, for example, Daniel Maclise's famous oil painting *Death of Nelson*, 1864.
8. The (probably fictional) story of William Brown, 'a female African' sailor, is one where skill was emphasised from the start (Taylor, 395; Costello, *Black Salt*, 39). Black boxers could also be Regency celebrities: American Tom Molineaux was portrayed in prints and figurines, himself meme-like.
9. These include Jamaican-born Captain John Perkins (d. 1812), who was probably mixed race, and African American merchant captain Paul Cuffe (1759–1817): Costello, *Black Salt*, 98–100.
10. See Gatrell, *Conspiracy*.
11. Miles, 'Characterising the Nation', 107.
12. Add. MS 42966 (2) BL Lord Chamberlain's plays.
13. See Newman et al., eds, *Charles Dibdin*, 1–20.
14. 'Amusements', *The Herald* (20 May 1837): 3.
15. Dibdin, *Songs*, 58, 56, 59, 96.
16. Bolster, *Black Jacks*, 31, 70, 113–17; Ennis, *Enter the Press-Gang*, 133.

17. Equiano, *Interesting Narrative*, 77; Hammon, *Narrative*, 12; Ennis, *Enter the Press-Gang*, 129.
18. 'Imprisonment of Colored Seamen', *National Anti-Slavery Standard* (30 December 1841): 2.
19. Gilroy, *Black Atlantic*, 12; see also Linebaugh and Rediker, *Many-Headed Hydra*, 321–2, and James, *Black Jacobins*.
20. Mageean, 'Black Origins of Sea Shanties'.
21. Lamire, 'A Question of Trousers'.
22. Moncrieff, 'Back Slums in the Holy Land', 113.
23. Scott, *Weapons of the Weak*, xvii.
24. Lee, *American Slave Narrative*, 22.

Wooden Leg
Crisis

1. *Ganymede* Captain's Log. ADM 51/2392.
2. There are authoritative studies of disability and wooden legs in the long nineteenth century but not in relation to ordinary Napoleonic-era sailors (Dickie, *Cruelty and Laughter*, Holmes, *Fictions of Affliction*, Sweet, *Prosthetic Body Parts*); there are excellent studies of Napoleonic-era soldiers and sailors (Brown and Begiato, eds, *Martial Masculinities*); but accounts of cultural representations of Black and white mariners in Britain tend to focus on nautical melodrama (e.g. Burroughs and Waters), while Gilje has focussed on the US 'Tar' only.
3. Smith, *Theory of Moral Sentiments*, I:301.
4. Moncrieff, 'Billy Waters', 121–2; Busby, *Costume*, 1; Hindley, *True History*, 105.
5. Naval historian and author Dudley Pope notes that competition between ships in a fleet to be fastest at sail drill led to many accidents (*Nelson's Navy*, 198).
6. See Brockliss et al., *Nelson's Surgeon*, 13–15.
7. *Ganymede* Pay Book. ADM/35/3489; Haslar Muster. ADM 102/296.
8. I have based my account of Waters' operation on Kirkup, *History of Limb Amputation*, Brown, *Emotions and Surgery*, Kelly, *Mr Foote*, 231–2, Brockliss et al., *Nelson's Surgeon*, and Northcote, *Marine Practice*.
9. Richardson, *A Mariner of England*, 131. See Kennaway, 'Celts under the Knife' and 'Military Surgery', on this phenomenon.
10. Amputation Foundation website, https://amputationfoundation.org. Accessed 28.01.23.
11. *Ganymede* Captain's Log. ADM 51/2392. Haslar Muster. ADM 102/296.
12. Allen, *History of Portsmouth*, 178–81; 'A Visit to Haslar Hospital', *Illustrated Magazine of Art*, 4:24 (1854): 329–31 (329); Lewis, *Illustrated Hand-Book of Portsmouth*, 93; 95.
13. Haslar Muster. ADM 102/296.
14. Haslar Pay List. ADM 102/392.
15. Haslar Governor's Orders. ADM 305/37.
16. Disability theorist Tobin Siebers argues for the importance of recognising the realities of physical pain for certain disabled people (*Disability Theory*, 64, 68),

as does Lindsey Row-Heyveld (*Dissembling Disability*, Introduction, paragraph 9.3).

17. George Spearing, 'The Sufferings of Lieut. Geo. Spearing, in a Coal Pit, 1769', *Gentleman's Magazine*, 63:2 (Aug. 1793): 697–700 (700). I've also drawn on Mayhew, *A Heavy Reckoning*, for my account of recovery.
18. Haslar Muster. ADM 102/296.

Overboard

1. See 'Life of Billy Waters', in Catnach, *The Death, Last Will, and Funeral of Black Billy*; 'Dramatic Necrology', 386; Hindley, *Life and Times*, 136.
2. Salaries and Pensions, ADM 22/274, 287, 300, 313, 332 (the pre-1815 Register for W. does not survive); Ellis, 'A Black "Jack Tar"'; Snell, *Annals of the Labouring Poor*, 413; Hunt, 'Industrialization and Regional Inequality', 964; https://www.measuringworth.com/calculators/ukcompare/relativevalue.php; https://www.nationalarchives.gov.uk/currency-converter/#currency-result; https://www.oldbaileyonline.org/static/Coinage.jsp#reading; Howell, *State Trials*, 33, cols 1554–8.
3. Moncrieff, 'Billy Waters', 122.
4. [The Peripatetic], 'The Peripatetic no. V', *Literary Chronicle*, 20:209 (17 May 1823): 312–13.
5. 'Death of Billy Waters'.
6. Mayhew et al., *London Labour*, 3:203.
7. King-Dorset, *Black Dance*, 73; 51.
8. Ibid., 51; 158.
9. Odumosu, *Africans in English Caricature*, 30.
10. For more see Michals, 'Invisible Amputation and Heroic Masculinity', and *Lame Captains & Left-Handed Admirals*. Waters would not have been described as a 'veteran' in his day: this term was reserved specifically for those with twenty to thirty years' military service. See Appendix in Joshua, *Physical Disability*.
11. Richardson, *A Mariner of England*, 107–8.
12. Dickie, *Cruelty and Laughter*, 93.
13. Hazlitt, 'On Wit and Humour', 4.
14. Stott, *Comedy*, 61.
15. On amputees as feminised, see Neilsen, 'Chelsea Out-Pensioners', 193.
16. Jerrold, 'The Ballad-Singer', 295.
17. Parkes, 'Wooden Legs and Tales of Sorrow Done', 191.
18. For more on Victorian sentimentalism about sailors see Begiato, *Manliness*. On the US see Gilje, *Swear Like a Sailor*. On amputees and prostheses in the Victorian period see Sweet, *Prosthetic Body Parts*.
19. The event was reported in *The Times* (8 December 1818): 2: 'Yesterday morning, the curiosities, &c., brought from Baffins-bay, by Captain Ross, were landed at Whitehall-stairs, from the boats of the Isabella and Alexander discovery ships ... Among the curiosities was an amazingly large skin of white bear, about 7 feet in length: a sledge of bone, about 5 feet long and 2 high, with the whip, &c. used by the newly-discovered inhabitants; specimens of mineralogy and botany, and some very remarkable star-fish. The

whole of the productions were conveyed to the British Museum, for the inspection of the public' (Patten, *George Cruikshank*, 1: 196).

20. Mitchell and Snyder, *Narrative Prosthesis*, 51.
21. 'The Wandering Minstrel for Westminster', *Punch* (20 Mar. 1847): 122.
22. *History of Andrew Whiston, King of the Beggars*, 15–17. Hou.
23. 'Dramatic Necrology'.
24. *Society for the Suppression of Mendicity*. Accessed 01/06/22; Mendicity Society, *Sixth Report*, 31.
25. *The Progress of Cant*. British Museum. Museum No. 1977, U.453.
26. Dickie, *Cruelty and Laughter*, 67.
27. 'On Seeing the Incomparable Mons. Timbertoe Dance at Mother Midnight's Oratory', *General Advertiser* (22 May 1752). Quoted in Dickie, *Cruelty and Laughter*, 67.
28. Kelly, *Mr Foote*, 377.
29. *European Magazine, and London Review* (Jan. 1794), quoted in Kelly, *Mr Foote*, 246.
30. O'Keefe, *Recollections*, 1: 328.
31. Mayhew et al., *London Labour*, 3: 203.
32. Kriegel, 'The Cripple in Literature', 45.
33. See Gabel and Peters, 'Presage of a Paradigm Shift?'
34. See, for example, Mitchell and Snyder, *Narrative Prosthesis*, 2, and Sandahl and Auslander, 'Disability Studies', 1.

Finding Poll

1. 'Police'; 'Hatton-Garden'. I am indebted to Suchitra Chatterjee for finding these reports.
2. Hindley, *True History*, 103.
3. Hindley, *Life and Times*, 136. An early twentieth-century antiquarian collector of folk tunes remembered hearing a song called 'Kitty will you marry me?' when growing up in Ireland, and recorded the verse thus:

   Oh, Kitty, will you marry me? or Kitty I will die;
   Then Kitty, you'll be fretting for your loving little boy.
   Oh, Kitty, can't you tell me will you marry me at all;
   Or else I'll surely go to sleep inside the churchyard wall (Joyce, *Old Irish Folk Music and Songs*, 37).

   There are other sources for this tune title, including Scots Musical Museum, 5:459, 473. digital.nls.uk/special-collections-of-printed-music/archive/87803522.

4. It appears in the Vickers manuscript, now owned by the Newcastle Society of Antiquaries and freely accessible via the online FARNE archive.
5. Dibdin, *Songs*, 23, 1, 20, 34, 41, 14, 12.
6. There are several prints in the British Museum's collections of the sailor and his lass, and in several figurines from the 1800s onwards in the collections of the Royal Museums Greenwich.
7. Pinckard, *Notes on the West Indies*, 1: 36–8; Stark, *Female Tars*, 37.
8. *An Excellent New Song, Entitled a Hot Engagement between a French Privateer and an English Fire-Ship*, https://ebba.english.ucsb.edu/ballad/33079/image. Accessed 01/04/22; Gilje, *Swear Like a Sailor*, 142.

9. For a discussion of how these stereotypes play out in contemporary American culture, see Curry, 'This Nigger's Broken'.
10. Ennis, *Enter the Press Gang*, 144.
11. *Tom and Jerry*. Davies' Amphitheatre Adaptation. Library of Congress, Washington.
12. 'Easter Amusements', *London Reader of Literature, Science, Art and General Information*, 28:729 (21 Apr. 1877): 580.
13. Dibdin, *Songs*, 19.
14. Nicol, *Life and Adventures*, 175.
15. Salaries and Pensions. ADM 22/332.

Surviving the Storm

1. [The Peripatetic], 'The Peripatetic no. V', *Literary Chronicle*, 20:209 (17 May 1823): 312–13.
2. Gilroy, *Black Atlantic*, 74.
3. 'The Arts', *Leader* (24 Jul. 1858): 719.
4. 'Music and the Drama', *London News* (8 Aug. 1858), p. 3. Reprinted in 'Music and the Drama', *North Wales Chronicle* (7 Aug. 1858).
5. Jerrold, 'The Ballad-Singer', 297.
6. Moncrieff, 'Billy Waters', 123; Hindley, *True History*, 106.
7. King-Dorset, *Black Dance*, 83.
8. Ibid., 120, 80, 158, 117.
9. Ndiaye, *Scripts of Blackness*, 233–4; King, *Black Shoals*, 7.
10. See Levine, 'Black Laughter'.
11. See MacKenzie et al., eds, *Comedy and Critical Thought*.
12. Fanon, *Black Skin, White Masks*, 140.
13. Carpio, *Laughing Fit to Kill*, 7.

Fiddle

The Notorious Slum

1. Gatrell, *Conspiracy*, 137.
2. Of course, they also saw their images appropriated by others, but their social position was very different. For a good overview of existing models, see Mole, ed., *Romanticism and Celebrity Culture*. Oskar Jensen began to think through street performers and celebrity in 'The Diminution of "Irish" Johnstone', but the topic demands further investigation, and is complicated by Waters' race and disability.
3. For scholars who do, see Ashton, *142 Strand*; Gatrell, *First Bohemians*; Shannon, *Dickens, Reynolds and Mayhew*.
4. 'Dramatic Necrology', 386; 'Death of Billy Waters'.
5. Denford and Hayes, eds, *Streets of St Giles*, 34.
6. Crymble, 'Decline and Fall', 327, 319; Hepburn, 'Introduction' to *Scattered Leaves*, 1: 33. On St Giles see also Dobie, *History of the United Parishes*; Beames, *The Rookeries of London*; Godwin, *London Shadows*; Thornbury, *Old and New London*.

7. Church Street and Church Lane are swapped around on various maps from the period, so they were probably considered pretty interchangeable. See LMA Insurance and Land Tax records, and St Giles Poor Rates records, Camden. For more on the history of landowning and of Irish immigration to the parish see Crymble, 'Decline and Fall'. My thanks to Jane Palm-Gold for sharing her extensive knowledge of the Rookery.

8. Denford and Hayes, eds, *Streets of St Giles*, 59.

9. Ibid., 34–6.

10. *The Olla Podrida*, 29 (Sep. 1787), 171. On Rookery living conditions see Beames, *The Rookeries of London*, 26, and Crymble, 'Decline and Fall', 323–8.

11. 'Minutes', 128.

12. 'Police'; 'Hatton-Garden'. Consensus amongst experts I consulted is that Waters' widow would have had to prove her status through documentation in order to get paid that final pension instalment. Unfortunately, no such documentation survives. Surviving documentation for 1832–6 (ADM 22 54–5 NAK), however, reveals a meticulous system of inspectors, examinations and certification by parish officers, before a widow could receive any money. All sums are carefully receipted. It seems unlikely that the Navy would have been more careless about money in the 1820s. See Pappalardo, *Tracing Your Naval Ancestors*, 158; Lincoln, *Naval Wives & Mistresses*, 44–5.

13. London, Marriages and Banns, 1754–1938, www.ancestry.com. Thanks to Jane Palm-Gold for this information.

14. See Lincoln, *Naval Wives & Mistresses*, 157, 159–62.

15. Busby, *Costume*, 1.

16. Catnach, *The Death, Last Will, and Funeral of Black Billy*; 'Death of Billy Waters'.

17. There is one potential marriage record of a William and Elizabeth Waters in St George's parish, neighbouring St Giles, in 1816, but what if they were married outside the metropolis? There are few indications from available records as to where that might have been. A Jane Elizabeth Waters was christened by her parents William and Elizabeth Waters on 23 Nov. 1817, so within the right time frame, but the christening took place in St Andrew Undershaft in the City (London, Marriages and Banns, 1754–1938; C of E Births and Baptisms 1813–1923, www.ancestry.com).

18. Oddly, this William Waters dies in the November of the same year as William 'Billy' Waters (London, C of E Births and Baptisms 1813–1923; Workhouse Admissions and Discharge Records, 1764–1930, www.ancestry.com).

19. Gerzina, *Black England*, 3.

20. Olusoga, *Black and British*, 81

21. Smith, *Vagabondiana*, 36.

22. Olusoga, *Black and British*, 226–7.

23. Sancho, letter XLVII, 140. There is a growing literature on the Black population of London in the Georgian, Regency and Victorian periods, but places to start are Bressey, 'The Next Chapter' and Fryer, *Staying Power*, who describes mixed-race marriages (239).

24. Odumosu, *Africans in English Caricature*, 170-2-2.

25. *Cobbett's Weekly Political Register* (16 Jun. 1804): 935.

26. 'In London, being friendless and despised, on account of their complexion, and too many of them being really incapable of any useful occupation, they sink into abject poverty and soon become St Giles's black-birds' (Wadström, *Essay on Colonisation*, 2:228). Historians tend to agree that 'erroneous assumptions have been made about the whole concept of a black community' (Myers, *Reconstructing the Black Past*, 132–5, Chater, *Untold Histories*, 163); 'Historians have searched without great success for the black "communities" of Georgian London' (Olusoga, *Black and British*, 81). For the opposite view, see King-Dorset, *Black Dance*, 104–5 and 114–15.
27. Chater, *Untold Histories*, 50, 162; Old Bailey Proceedings Online, 1785–6, no. 559; Jensen, *Vagabonds*, 145; Fryer, *Staying Power*, 73.
28. Gerzina, *Black England*, 76.
29. Olusoga, *Black and British*, 237.
30. Garland-Thomson, *Extraordinary Bodies*, 10.
31. This was 'a state of things which was finally put an end to by driving New Oxford Street through the midst. At the same time several of the old streets were abolished, and some of those which remained had their names altered' (Riley and Gomme, eds, *Survey*, 145–6).
32. Parton, *Some Account*, 153–4.
33. Douglas, *Purity and Danger*, 35.
34. See Jensen, *Ballad-Singer*.
35. On its Early Modern origins see Row-Heyveld, *Dissembling Disability*.
36. Hepburn, *Scattered Leaves*, 1: 142–5.
37. Timbs, *Curiosities*, 378.
38. Makdisi, *Making England Western*, 52.
39. 'The Last Farewell to Poor St Giles's' can be found at https://digital.nls.uk/english-ballads.
40. Forster, *Life*, 1:11.
41. Harley, 'Consumption and Poverty'.
42. Holmes argues that 'the historical connection between stage melodrama and disability' led to 'the spread of a melodramatic mode of representing disability' across literary and non-literary genres (*Fictions of Affliction*, 5).
43. See Diggle, ed., *Theophrastus*.
44. I am drawing on Teukolsky, *Picture World*, and Freeman, *Character's Theater*.

Public Enemy No. 1

1. Old Bailey Proceedings Online, Feb. 1787, t17870221-29.
2. Hitchcock, *Down and Out*, 49.
3. Bezer's autobiography is reproduced in Vincent, ed., *Testaments of Radicalism*, 153–88.
4. Jensen makes a similar point about Joseph Johnson (*Vagabonds*, 177).
5. Hindley, *True History*, 105.
6. Rose, *Rogues and Vagabonds*, 47.
7. Reeves, 'Lines on Billy Waters'; Busby, *Costume*, 1; 'Death of Billy Waters'; 'Dramatic Necrology', 386; 'The Wandering Minstrel for Westminster', *Punch* (20 Mar. 1847): 122; 'Police'; 'Hatton-Garden'; [Moncrieff], 'Billy Waters; or,

Two Richmonds': 3 (my thanks to Tony Montague for this reference). For the stories that Waters performed outside the Adelphi, see: Gibbs, *Performing the Temple of Liberty*, 123; Hepburn, *Scattered Leaves*, 1: 33, Myers, *Reconstructing the Black Past*, 76; Reed, *Rogue Performances*, 129; and my article. A print of Waters pasted into an extra-illustrated copy of *History of Vauxhall Gardens* suggests a link with Waters (TS 952.2, Hou). Rohan McWilliam's *London's West End* is the definitive history.

8. *The English Metropolis*, 18. I'm drawing on Jensen's work for how street performers might have turned the street into a performance space: see *Vagabonds*, 169–70.

9. Paul E. W. Roberts is the authority on this topic: see 'English Fiddling 1650–1850'; Roberts' Village Music Project (www.village-music-project.org.uk) is an important resource.

10. Jensen, *Ballad-Singer*, 154 and *Napoleon*, 115; T. L., 'Yankee Doodle or the Negroes Farewell to America' (*c.* 1775), BL Music Collections G.310.(163.); http://ballads.bodleian.ox.ac.uk/view/edition/19293 (thanks to Oskar Jensen for these references).

11. Roberts, 'English Fiddling 1650–1850'.

12. Baker, 'The Home of the Melodrama', 141–3.

13. Blanchard, 'The Playgoer's Portfolio', 1.

14. *Picture of London for 1820*, 71; Gatrell, *Conspiracy*, 70.

15. Charles Lamb, letter to Wordsworth, *Letters*, vol. 1.

16. *The English Metropolis*, 10.

17. *Picture of London for 1820*, 256–7, 262–3, 284–97.

18. See Odumosu, *Africans in English Caricature*.

19. There is extensive scholarship on this genre, but especially useful is Shesgreen, *Images of the Outcast*.

20. Writing about the mid- to late Victorian period, theatre historian Lyn Voskuil argues that concepts of theatricality and authenticity looked different in the Victorian period to how they do now, but I'm arguing that this started long before the mid-1800s (*Acting Naturally*, 3).

21. Davis, 'Theatricality and Civil Society', in Davis et al., *Theatricality*, 145–6. This is different to more modern notions of 'performativity', where speech and action create a new reality for the *performer* (Butler, *Bodies that Matter*, xii).

22. A similar complex positioning of spectator and performer was established at Freak Shows: see Bogdan, *Freak Show*, and Garland-Thomson, *Extraordinary Bodies*, Chapter 3.

23. Ibid., 1. For more on Waters' naval service see 'Sailor Jacket' and 'Wooden Leg'.

24. This is the same for the presentation of known figures in *Vagabondia*, e.g. Joseph Johnson, Charles McGee and 'Cranky Jem'.

25. Wood, *Slavery*, 16.

26. See Roberts, 'Reshaping the Gift Relationship'; Gatrell, *Conspiracy*; Lees, *Solidarities of Strangers*, 83. On Peterloo see Poole, *Peterloo*.

27. Busby, *Costume*, 1.

28. Hitchcock, *Down and Out*, 98; Elia [Lamb], 'A Complaint', 262.

29. Siebers calls this the 'masquerade' that all disabled people, at one time or another, have to perform (*Disability Theory*, Chapter 5). See also Row-Heyveld, *Dissembling Disability*.
30. Hepburn, *Scattered Leaves*, 2: 301.
31. Row-Heyveld, *Dissembling Disability*.
32. 'Hatton-Garden'.
33. 'Select Committee on Mendicity in the Metropolis: Final Report', *Parliamentary Papers* 5 (1816): 393–6, 401.
34. 'Minutes', 128–30.
35. Moncrieff, 'Beggars, or Cadgers', 114.
36. 'Minutes', 131–2.
37. 'Reports from the Select Committee on the State of Mendicity in the Metropolis', *Parliamentary Papers* 5 (1816): 391–416.
38. See *Society for the Suppression of Mendicity*. Accessed 01/06/22; Roberts, 'Reshaping the Gift Relationship'; Society for the Suppression of Mendicity: Minute Book, BL Add MS 50136. Annual reports held in BL (1819 onwards).
39. 'Ode to H. Bodkin, Esq.', *The Mirror of Literature, Amusement, and Instruction* 5 (1825): 310.
40. 'Dramatic Necrology', 386; 'Hatton-Garden'. See also Montague, 'An O-o-ld Song'.
41. 'The Music Of The Streets', *Chambers' Edinburgh Journal*, 584 (8 Apr. 1843): 89–90 (89).
42. [Henry Mayhew], 'Labour and the Poor', *Morning Chronicle* (16 May 1850): 5.

The Beggar's Opera

1. Moncrieff, 'Billy Waters', 122. *The Drama* puts Waters' election as King of the Beggars only 'A short time prior to his death . . . in consequence of his notoriety' ('Dramatic Necrology', 386). The publisher of broadside ballads, James Catnach, also put the date of Waters' supposed election 'A short time before he died' (Catnach, *Death, Last Will, and Funeral of Black Billy*).
2. 'Hatton-Garden'.
3. https://www.exclassics.com/carew/carew.pdf; Wilson, *Decency and Disorder*, 231–2.
4. *History of Andrew Whiston* (1826) Hou; Brine, *King of the Beggars*; 'Death of the King of the Beggars', *The Age*, 2:48 (9 Apr. 1826): 379. Hindley tells us that 'Subsequently to the death of BILLY WATERS, the notorious black mendicant fiddler, . . . "LITTLE JEMMY" acquired the soubriquet of The King of the Beggars' (*True History*, 109–10).
5. Garland-Thomson, *Extraordinary Bodies*, 8.
6. Ibid., 44.
7. 'Minutes', *Quarterly Review*, 129. LMA Insurance records CLC/B/192/F/001/MS11936.
8. Ibid., 130.
9. Reid, *Bucks and Bruisers*, 69; 'Spirit of the Public Journals: London Ballad-Singers' (pt 2), *The Mirror of Literature, Amusement, and Instruction* (16 Jul. 1825): 54. Thanks to Jane Palm-Gold and to Oskar Jensen for these references.

10. Cummins, *Life and Career*, 18.
11. Hindley, *Catnach Press*, 28.
12. 'Minutes', 130.
13. *Real Life in London*, I: 181–2. Additional page numbers given in brackets.
14. [Westmacott], *The English Spy*, 2: 33.
15. *Doings in London*, 113. Other page numbers given in brackets.
16. 'Dramatic Necrology'; 'Minutes'; *History of Andrew Whiston*; 'History of the Beggars', *The Casket* 6: 287 (8 Jun. 1832).
17. Egan, *Finish to the Adventures of Tom, Jerry, and Logic*, 10.
18. Mole, *Byron's Romantic Celebrity*, 81.
19. These Derby- and Staffordshire-ware ceramics, with their reproduction of the kinds of racial stereotyping found in contemporary caricature and their often crudely done colouring, tended to emphasise Waters' Blackness, although they were, on the whole, much more individuated than the depersonalised figurines of Black bandsmen popular from the 1760s onwards (Beddoe, *Potted History*, 183).

Becoming 'Billy Waters'

1. Guede, *Monsieur de Saint-George*, 98. For famous eighteenth- and nineteenth-century British musicians who were Black see Fryer, *Staying Power*; Olusoga, *Black and British*.
2. Bridgetower, *Six Pathetic Canzonets*. Thanks to Oskar Jensen for telling me about this composition.
3. Roberts, 'English Fiddling 1650–1850', 27–8.
4. 'Dramatic Necrology', 386; Busby, *Costume*, 1.
5. Fawcett, *Spectacular Disappearances*, 4. See also Mole, 'Celebrity and Anonymity'.
6. Reeves, 'Lines on Billy Waters'.
7. Hitchcock, *Down and Out*, 210; 232.
8. Jensen, *Vagabonds*, 161, 137, 158.
9. Gikandi, *Slavery*, 266.
10. Incog., 'A Sentimental Journey, from Islington to Waterloo Bridge, in March, 1821', *London Magazine*, 4:23 (Nov. 1821): 508–15 (508).
11. Mee, 'Keyword: Performance'; Maidment, *Robert Seymour*, 23, 25.
12. Fawcett, *Spectacular Disappearances*, 214. See also Marcus, *The Drama of Celebrity*.
13. Wilson, *Decency and Disorder*, xiv.
14. Mayhew et al., *London Labour*, 2: 556–9.
15. Daniel, *Merrie England*, 365.

Wig
Tom and Jerry

1. [Bysh], *Cries*.
2. McAllister, *Whiting Up*, 1.

3. Boz, *Memoirs*, 20; Highfill et al., *Biographical Dictionary*, 11: 237–9; For images of Senior Paulo, see MS Thr 942, Hou, and John Genest, *Some Account of the English Stage*, after 536. TS 937 H4, Hou.

4. Clown sometimes shared the stage with Harlequin in his black mask, and the image of Waters as 'Folly' in Figure 16 draws on clowning traditions ('Advertisement', *Theatrical Observer* (7 Oct. 1822): 4). See Pickering, *Blackface Minstrelsy*, 144–58, and Hornback, *Racism and Early Blackface*, for discussions of blackface, clowning, Folly and Harlequin.

5. Abraham and Woolf, *Black Victorians*, 164.

6. Hartman, *Scenes of Subjection*, 26; King, *Black Shoals*, 25.

7. Grier, 'Inkface'.

8. Scott, 'Blackface Minstrels', 270; 273; Thompson, *Blackface*, 40; 50–2.

9. [An Occasional Correspondent], 'Recollections of the Stage', *Era* (10 Sep. 1898): 9.

10. Ibid.

11. [Moncrieff], 'Billy Waters; or, Two Richmonds'; 'Advertisement', *Theatrical Observer*, 279 (7 Oct. 1822): 4.

12. 'Easter Amusements', *London Reader*, 28:729 (21 Apr. 1877): 580.

13. Baker, 'The Home of the Melodrama', 144–5; 'White Conduit House', *Theatrical Journal*, 2:93 (Sep. 1841): 309.

14. For Moncrieff's career see Cox, *Reading Adaptations*, 126–62.

15. V&A. Adelphi 1821. Playbill.

16. Hindley, *Catnach Press*, 113; Hindley, *True History*, 8; 5.

17. Quoted in Clarke, *Every Night Book*, 801.

18. V&A. Adelphi 1821. Playbill.

19. As Cox puts it, '[t]he centrality of the "illustration-tableau" in the adaptations of this period clearly indicates the importance the playwrights give to the visual elements of the original volumes' (*Reading Adaptations*, 143).

20. See Shannon, 'Dickens in Byron's Chair', on this strategy in relation to 'Boz' and to the characters Tom and Jerry.

21. Moncrieff, 'Tom and Jerry', 8. Further page numbers are given in the text.

22. See Baker, 'The Home of the Melodrama', 144; Hindley, *True History*, 5–7; as Reed points out, audiences in America were 'less likely to have confused Waters for a real street performer, given his London origins' (*Rogue Performances*, 130). Hindley declares that Billy Waters 'possessed abilities/ that as an actor would have rendered him a *shining* ornament to the stage' (*True History*, 106–7). Critics continue to be confused to this day.

23. See, for another example of this kind of deliberately racialised blackspeak, Cesar the black footman in Douglas Jerrold, *St Giles and St James*.

24. Holder, 'Other Londoners', 34.

25. Murray, 'That "Weird and Wonderful Posture"'; Ndiaye, *Scripts of Blackness*. There is extensive scholarship in Rice and 'Jim Crow': a good starting point is Lhamon, *Jump Jim Crow* (although I think Lhamon exaggerates to call Crow-mania the 'First Atlantic Popular Culture', given *Life in London* preceded Crow by a decade).

26. Siebers, *Disability Theory*, 114.

27. Grant, *Sketches in London*, 38–42.

28. [Moncrieff], 'Billy Waters; or, Two Richmonds', reprinted in *Bell's Life in Sydney*, and Sydney *Freeman's Journal*, Oct. 1851; for 'Moll in the Wad/Wood' see https://thesession.org/tunes/12262.

29. Playbill, Royalty Theatre, 13 May 1822. For the Egan version see Hindley, *True History*, 86–7. For the Davis's version see: Playbill, Monday 8 Apr. 1822, pasted inside *Tom and Jerry, or, Life in London*, London: John Lowndes (1822). Library of Congress, Washington. https://lccn.loc.gov/2014657236. For the Olympic version see: Playbill, Thursday 28 Mar. 1822, http://www.arthurlloyd.co.uk/Olympic.htm; 'Advertisement', *Theatrical Observer*, 390 (17 Feb. 1823): 3; Dibdin jnr, *Life in London*. Maidment counts 'at least six different versions, to say nothing of minor variations and new productions of [Moncrieff's version]' (59). See also Hindley, *True History*, 92–3 and *Catnach*, 120; Gibbs, *Performing the Temple of Liberty*, 131; Reed, *Rogue Performances*, 129–30.

30. Hone, 'Fantoccini', 7.

31. 'King's Theatre', *Mirror of the Stage* (24 Feb. 1823): 46; 'The Drama', *European Magazine, and London Review* 83 (Feb. 1823): 180–3 (180); 'Fancy Dress Ball, and Grand and Novel Masquerade', *Theatrical Journal*, 2:63 (Feb. 1841): 70.

32. Hill, *Playing About*, 1: 215–17.

33. Wilson, *Danciad*, 35; 48.

34. Daniel, *Merrie England*, 1:57.

35. Moncrieff, 'Billy Waters', 122.

36. 'Dramatic Necrology'.

37. [Moncrieff], 'Billy Waters; or, Two Richmonds'.

Ludgate Hill

1. Waters, *Racism*, 61; 14; 202; [Moncrieff], 'Billy Waters; or, Two Richmonds'.

2. See Fryer, *Staying Power*, for foundational discussions of race and class in Britain.

3. On childhood and family relationships in the 1790s and 1800s see Griffin, *Bread Winner*, but also Humphries, *Childhood and Child Labour*.

4. 'Negro Melody – "Song of a Sweep"', in 'Mr Dyce Sombre, and Sir James Lushington,' *The Age* (5 Mar. 1843): 5.

5. Visram, *Ayahs, Lascars and Princes*, 57–60.

6. [Sans Souci], 'The Two Obelisks; Or, Double Double U, a Colloquial Cantata', *The Age* (20 Oct. 1833): 334.

7. 'Crossing-Sweepers', *Daily News* (8 Dec. 1884): 3.

8. For an example of McGee's fame, see [Thomas Hood], 'Twenty-One Elegiac Stanzas, to the Black Man who swept the Crossing at the Obelisk, Black Friars, and who lately Died of Age', *London Magazine and Review* (Apr. 1825): 585–7. Tim and David Hitchcock, and Oskar Jensen, have written on McGee.

9. Smith, *Vagabondiana*, 33–4. There is an additional portrait of McGee in Smith's book, which can be found in the V&A collections online at https://collections.vam.ac.uk/item/O70010/print-smith-john-thomas.

10. Treloar, *Ludgate Hill*, 120.

11. [Bysh], *Cries*.

12. Treloar, *Ludgate Hill*, 118.

13. Tucker, *Racial Sight*, 13.
14. Examples include *The N—er What Sweeps the Crossings* (Royal Victoria Theatre, 1838, poster in the University of Bristol Theatre Collection) and Edward Fitzball, *The Negro of Wapping* [1838?]. The few studies so far include: Intro. to Stanley Wells, *Nineteenth-Century Shakespeare Burlesques*, 2; Keigan, 'Intersections'.
15. See Matthew D. Morrison, 'Race, Blacksound', Ndiaye, *Scripts of Blackness*, Murray, 'That "Weird and Wonderful Posture"', and Siebers, *Disability Theory*.
16. Lott, *Love and Theft*; Johnson, 'Death and the Minstrel', 97; Thompson, *Blackface*, 23; Morrison, 'Race, Blacksound'; Johnson, *Appropriating Blackness*; Bhabha, 'Of Mimicry and Man'.
17. Frederick Douglass, 'The Hutchinsons', *North Star* (27 Oct. 1848).
18. See Makonnen, 'Even in the Best Minds'.

Dirty Faces?

1. 'Mr Dyce Sombre, and Sir James Lushington', *The Age* (5 Mar. 1843): 5.
2. That such individual entertainments in the 'character' of Billy Waters did take place is attested to by several newspaper accounts of a performance in 1858 of nightly performances by a Mr J. G. Ford who 'causes roars of laughter by the ridiculous adventures of "Billy Waters"' at the Canterbury Hall on Westminster Bridge Road ('Music and the Drama', *London News*, 7 Aug. 1858).
3. Fisher, *Inordinately Strange Life of Dyce Sombre*, 215.
4. DeVere Brody, *Impossible Purities*, 13.
5. Briefel, *The Racial Hand*, 2.
6. For the Sons of Africa see Olusoga, *Black and British*, 212.
7. 'Lord Brougham and the Blacks', *Figaro in London* (17 Mar. 1838): 43.
8. Thompson, *Blackface*, 35.
9. See Waters, *Racism*, Draudt, 'Critical Introduction', and Keigan, 'Intersections'.
10. 'Theatricals', *Figaro in London* (22 Sep. 1832): 168.
11. From the 1850s and especially from the 1870s onwards the popularity of theatrical productions of Harriet Beecher Stowe's hit abolitionist novel *Uncle Tom's Cabin* changes the possibilities for black performers on stage. See Bressey, 'The Next Chapter', 318–21.
12. 'Theatricals', *Figaro in London* (6 Apr. 1833): 55–6 (56).
13. 'Theatricals', *Figaro in London* (25 May 1833): 83–4 (84).
14. This is another cheaply produced text that has not yet enjoyed much critical attention. The exception to this is Abraham, *Plagiarizing*. Page numbers in brackets.
15. Thackeray, 'De Juventute', 71–2; 82–4; Thackeray, 'On the Genius of George Cruikshank', cited in the bookseller John Camden Hotten's introduction to his 1869 edition of *Life in London*.
16. Brody calls her rightly 'the most important of the several black and mulatto/a characters in *Vanity Fair*' (*Impossible Purities*, 27). For in-depth analysis on race in *Vanity Fair*, this book is the best place to start.

The Triumph of Joseph Jenkins

1. 'Theatricals', *Figaro in London* (13 Apr. 1833): 60.
2. 'Theatricals', *Figaro in London* (18 May 1833): 79–80 (79).
3. [Moncrieff], 'Billy Waters; or, Two Richmonds'.
4. *Streetology*; Jensen, *Vagabonds*, 257–8.
5. Mayhew et al., *London Labour*, 2:556–60.
6. Prizel's article 'The Dead Man Come to Life Again' reproduces the book in full.
7. Brown, *American Fugitive*, 268–75.
8. Tucker, *Racial Sight*, 17.
9. Goheen, 'Soot in One's Soup'.
10. 'Black and White', *The Englishman's Magazine* (May 1831): 191–2 (191).
11. Blanchard, 'The Playgoers Portfolio', 2.
12. Reeves, 'Lines on Billy Waters'; 'Police'.
13. 'Dramatic Necrology'; Hindley, *True History*, 105–6.

Performance
Workhouse

1. Now the site of Dudley Court, a large block of housing. You can read about the workhouse in Parton's *Some Account*.
2. In 1818. Between 1795 and 1834, poor relief was an astonishing 2 per cent of national product (compare 1.5 per cent for Netherlands, Belgium and France): Green, *Pauper Capital*, 76; 3–4.
3. Parton, *Some Account*, 234.
4. More people entered the workhouse in London in the early nineteenth century than in any other part of the country, but still the vast majority of paupers getting help from their parish were not inmates of a workhouse (Green, *Pauper Capital*, 38).
5. Brundage, *English Poor Laws*, 14.
6. *Case of the inhabitants of the parish of St Giles in the Fields*. BL 816 m9-65.
7. *The Workhouse Cruelty*. BL 816 m9-78, 80.
8. In another London workhouse, St Margaret's, 'almost 38% of applicants . . . cited illness or injury as the reason they applied' (Siena, 'Contagion, Exclusion', 20).
9. *Picture of London*, 70–1.
10. Parton, *Some Account*, 319.
11. Ibid., 233–4.
12. Upton, *Birmingham Parish Workhouse*, 68. For the names of the master and matron see P/GG/PO/6/2, Camden.
13. *Hints and Cautions for the Information of the Churchwardens and Overseers of the Poor of the Parish of St Giles in the Fields . . . 1797 edn*, 6. Quoted in Hitchcock, *Down and Out*, 114.
14. Upton, *Birmingham Parish Workhouse*, 4. See also Ellis, 'Left to the Streets and the Workhouse'.
15. *An Account of the Workhouses of Great Britain* (London: 1786, 3rd edn); P/GG/PO/9, Camden.

16. Parton, *Some Account*, 320.
17. Harley, 'Material Lives of the Poor', 86; 90.
18. Boulton et al., 'These ANTE-CHAMBERS OF THE GRAVE', 77.
19. P/GG/PO/6/3, Camden; Boulton et al., 'These ANTE-CHAMBERS OF THE GRAVE', 65.
20. 'Two Ounces Of Cheese', *The Satirist* (16 Apr. 1837): 538.
21. 'Dramatic Necrology'.
22. Hindley, *True History*, 102; Blanchard, 'The Playgoers Portfolio', 2. Waters' Navy records have him D. D. (discharged, dead) on 17 Mar.

Will and Testament

1. E.g. *Morning Advertiser*; 'Dramatic Necrology'.
2. Siena, 'Contagion, Exclusion', 31; Boulton et al., 'These ANTE-CHAMBERS OF THE GRAVE', 63. In 1827 in St Giles parish, for example, historians estimate that there were 1,235 pauper burials of which 353 were deaths in the workhouse (Boulton et al., 'These ANTE-CHAMBERS OF THE GRAVE', 61).
3. 'Rules and Orders', *An Account of the Work-Houses in Great Britain*, 3rd edn (London, 1786), 36–44 (41).
4. [Moncrieff], 'Billy Waters; or, Two Richmonds'.
5. [Westmacott], *English Spy*, 2: 34.
6. Parton, *Some Account*, 289.
7. Lamb, 'On Burial Societies'. For two conflicting views of pauper burials see: Laqueur, 'Bodies, Death, and Pauper Funerals'; Hurren and King, 'Begging for a Burial'; Strange, 'She Cried Very Little'.
8. Parton, *Some Account*, 289. Emery and Wooldridge, *St Pancras*.
9. Jensen, *Vagabonds*, 267–8.
10. 'Life of Billy Waters', J. C. 25 Mar. 1823. From *The Death, Last Will, and Funeral of 'Black Billy'* [Signed: J. C., i.e. James Catnach. Founded on Pierce Egan's 'Life in London'], 10th edn [1823?]. BL.
11. Lamb, 'On Burial Societies'.
12. Catnach, 'The merry Will & Testament of Master BLACK BILLY', in *Death, Last Will, and Funeral of Black Billy*.
13. Hindley, *True History*, 106; Moncrieff, 'Billy Waters', 122–3.
14. 'Raising the Dead', *London Magazine*, 10 (Oct. 1824): 398–400.
15. 'The Art Of Getting into Debt', *Monthly Magazine*, 1:3 (Mar. 1826): 253–7.
16. G. D., 'The Islington Garland', *Mirror of Literature* (10 Aug. 1839): 87–8.

'Billy Waters' On Tour

1. Hindley, *True History*, 96–7; Jerrold, *Life of George Cruikshank*, 85.
2. Greenwood, *Death of Life in London*.
3. John Johnson Collection. Bridgnorth Collection III.C. (56). Bod.
4. MS Thr 620, (4); MS Thr 620, (12); MS Thr 620, (14). Hou.
5. Undated playbill, [*c.* 1830s], John Johnson Collection. Entertainments folder 5 (10) – Provincial Venues. Bod.
6. MS Thr 620 (33); MS Thr 620, (33). Hou.

7. John Johnson Collection. Provincial Playbills folder 3 (108) – Lincoln; 4 (29) – Newcastle. Bod.
8. For Brighton, see Hindley, *True History*, 92–4; MS Thr 620 (4); MS Thr 620, (52). Hou.
9. *Tom and Jerry*. Edinburgh: 1824. THE HD 17477.39.6.31. Hou.
10. MS Thr 620, (22); MS Thr 620, (22). Hou.
11. Hindley, quoting the editor of the *Edinburgh Dramatic Review*, in *True History*, 95.
12. 'Surrey Theatre', *Weekly True Sun* (6 Jul. 1834): 356.
13. 'The Ring', *Bell's Life in London* (3 Aug. 1834), 3.
14. 'Adelphi Theatre'. *The Age* (5 Apr. 1835): 1.
15. 'White Conduit House', *Theatrical Journal* (Sep. 1841): 309; 'Advertisements & Notices', *Era* (10 Oct. 1841): 4.

'Billy Waters' Returns

1. Reed, *Rogue Performances*, 128.
2. Ibid.
3. 'Easter Amusements', *London Reader* (21 Apr. 1877): 580.
4. Reed wrote in 2009 that 'American playhouses have left less evidence of Tom and Jerry's rambles than did English theatres' (*Rogue Performances*, 128), but in fact Harvard University's Theatre Collection holds a fascinating range of materials on the *Life in London* craze as it travelled around the British Isles and America.
5. Reed, *Rogue Performances*, 127; Odell, *Annals*, 3:59.
6. Richards, *Drama, Theatre, and Identity*, 1.
7. 'Sketches of Society in the United States of North America', 1818, reprinted in the *Athenaeum* (20 Sep. 1834), 691, THE HD HTC Clippings 10, Box 2, Hou.
8. See undated newspaper clippings, THE HD HTC Clippings 10, Box 2, Hou.
9. Dunlap, *History*, 67–8.
10. Richards, *Drama, Theatre, and Identity*, 2.
11. Reed, *Rogue Performances*, 128.
12. Samuel French's New York edition of Moncrieff's *Tom and Jerry*, Act 2 scenes 4 and 5, 23–5.
13. Durang, *Philadelphia Stage*, Chapter 11. This first appeared in the *Philadelphia Sunday Dispatch* in 1854, and continued for a second series from 1856 and a third series from 1860. THE GEN TS 275 10 F. Hou.
14. *Tom and Jerry* (Philadelphia, 1824). AM 1824 Egan 2025.D.2 Philadelphia Library Company.
15. In the London playscript Jemmy Green and Billy Waters appear in the same scene, so would require different actors, but this wasn't the case in the Philadelphia version. John Jefferson was a talented actor who sadly died in his twenties, but Joseph is the one known for comic parts: see Winter, *The Jeffersons*, 145; Winter, *Life and Art*, 131. The whole family frequently acted together once they were old enough: see the 1831 cast list of *School for Scandal* in Moses, *Famous Actor Families in America*, 68.
16. Morrison, *Playing in the Dark*, 52.
17. Richards, *Drama, Theatre, and Identity*, 2; 17. See also Nathans, *Early American*, on theatre's role in forming an American 'nation'.

18. 'The managers of the Chestnut had a theatrical circuit which included Baltimore and Washington, and they were accustomed to make regular, periodical visits to those cities.' Winter, *Life and Art*, 70, n. 1.
19. *Baltimore Patriot* (17 May 1823): 2; *Baltimore Patriot* (31 Mar. 1823): 2.
20. *Tom and Jerry* (Baltimore: J. Robinson, Circulating Library and Dramatic Repository, 1825). THE HD 17477.39.6.31. Hou.
21. Durang, *Philadelphia Stage*, Chapter 11. THE GEN TS 275 10 F. Hou.
22. Copies in the Harvard Theatre Collection reveal that the printed text was the same as the London version, although one prompt copy from Baltimore has sections including the 'Billy Waters' part crossed out. THE HD 23497.71.27.35. Hou.
23. *Baltimore Patriot* (6 May 1823): 2; *Baltimore Patriot* (4 Nov. 1823): 2; Playbills, Holliday Theatre, 4 Mar. 1823 (TCS 68, Hou).
24. *Boston Commercial Gazette* (25 Dec. 1826): 4.
25. As described in the *Federal Orrery* (Oct. 1794), reprinted in Witham, ed., *Theatre in the United States*, 56.
26. 'Boston Theatre', *Columbian Centinel* (3 Dec. 1823): 4; Clapp, *Boston Stage*, 216.
27. Durang, *Philadelphia Stage*, Chapter 11. THE GEN TS 275 10 F. Hou.
28. Advertisement, *Boston Commercial Gazette* (8 Jan. 1824), and Playbill, 'Tom and Jerry', Boston Theatre, Boston, 4 Feb. 1824. America's Historical Imprints. Accessed 07.07.22. For the description of Act 2 scene 6 from the Adelphi playbill, see Adelphi Theatre playbill, MS Thr 621. Hou.
29. 'Circus', *Boston Commercial Gazette* (8 Jan. 1824): 3.
30. 'Boston Theatre', *Boston Commercial Gazette* (25 Apr. 1825): 3.
31. Playbill, 'Tom & Jerry', 7 Aug. 1823. https://lccn.loc.gov/2014657264; Playbill, 'Tom & Jerry', 21 Jan. 1825. https://lccn.loc.gov/2014657218. Library of Congress, Washington.
32. Recent scholarship has argued that their influence persisted into the 1870s: see Comegna, 'The Dupes of Hope Forever'.
33. 'GREAT MEETING of the Locofocos – Speeches and Votes – Rows and Riots – Confusion, Disorders and Shinplasters', *Penny Satirist* (18 Nov. 1837): 3.
34. 'By making a few geographical alterations, the manager or an actor could transform a quintessential English artisan into a representative American one' (Richards, *Drama, Theatre, and Identity*, 287).
35. Reed, *Rogue Performances*, 4–7; 129. See also Lhamon, *Raising Cain*.
36. Gibbs, *Performing the Temple of Liberty*, 9.
37. McAllister, *White People Do Not Know*, 162; 166; 181.

The Precarious Atlantic

1. Richards, *Drama, Theatre, and Identity*, 16.
2. Errol G. Hill estimates that around 1800 there were six thousand Black Americans in New York, of which half were enslaved; by 1820 there were only five hundred remaining in enslavement and ten thousand free Black New Yorkers ('The African Theatre to Uncle Tom's Cabin', in Hill and Hatch, *History of African American Theatre*, 24–60 (24)).
3. Richards, *Drama, Theatre, and Identity*, 211.

4. See McAllister, *White People Do Not Know*, Chapter 1. McAllister's book is the definitive history, but he does not make the link to Waters.

5. Du Bois, *Souls of Black Folk*. McAllister, *White People Do Not Know*, 71.

6. See McAllister, *White People Do Not Know*, on the various stages and productions of Brown's Company, including its rivalry with the Park.

7. Reed, *Rogue Performances*, 132.

8. Thompson, *Documentary History*, 222–4.

9. Richards, *Drama, Theatre, and Identity*, 213.

10. It's only really in the *Picayune* between 1837 and 1841 that we have any significant window into Old Corn Meal's world. These articles were first discussed by the historian Henry A. Kmen in 'Old Corn Meal'. I offer new information here to add to his account and to Reed's in *Rogue Performances* (144–6).

11. *Daily Picayune* (13 May 1837): 2.

12. *Daily Picayune* (28 Aug. 1839): 2.

13. Smith, *Southern Queen*, 19; 50; 94.

14. Playbill, *Tom & Jerry in America, or Life in Boston*, Bland's Boston Adelphi. America's Historical Imprints. Accessed 07.07.22. Also MS Thr 1076 Hou; Brougham, *Life in New York*. By 1856 Brougham reworked it as *Life in New York*, with local metropolitan colour.

15. Gibbs, *Performing the Temple of Liberty*, 9.

16. Smith, *Southern Queen*, 80–3.

17. *Daily Picayune* (13 May 1837): 2.

18. *Daily Picayune* (12 May 1837): 2.

19. Pratt, ed., *Galveston Island*, 93–4.

20. *Daily Picayune* (16 May 1837): 2.

21. *Daily Picayune* (13 Jun. 1840): 3.

22. On violence against Black men in New Orleans see Smith, *Southern Queen*, 87.

23. 'Original Characters', *Daily Picayune* (19 Jun. 1839): 2.

24. 'Old Corn Meal vs. The Dutch Broom Sellers', *Macon Georgia Telegraph* (16 Feb. 1841); Notice of the death of 'Old Corn Meal', *New Hampshire Gazette* (7 Jun. 1842).

25. *Daily Picayune* (28 Aug. 1839): 2.

26. Thompson, *Blackface*, 41.

27. 'Money Making', *Cleave's Weekly Police Gazette*, (1 Oct. 1836): 2. See also 'The Theatres', *Spectator* (12 Nov. 1836): 1084 ('*Jim Crow* ... is a sort of *Billy Waters*').

28. 'Mardi Gras', *Daily Picayune* (13 Feb. 1839): 2.

29. King-Dorset, *Black Dance*, 67–70.

30. Both the Levy Sheet Music Collection (Johns Hopkins University) and the John Johnson Collection (Bodleian, Oxford) have good holdings of Montgomery's sheet music, which you can see online. https://levysheetmusic.mse.jhu.edu; http://johnjohnson.chadwyck.co.uk.

31. Thompson, *Blackface*, 5.

32. King-Dorset, *Black Dance*, 151; 158.

33. Petrusich, 'The Devil's Dream', https://pitchfork.com/reviews/albums/17862-sid-hemphill-the-devils-dream-alan-lomaxs-1942-library-of-congress-recordings/. Accessed 26/10/19.

34. https://archive.culturalequity.org/field-work/southern-us-1959-and-1960/ senatobia-i-959/polly-will-you-marry-me-ii. Accessed 03/02/23.

Epilogue

1. [Edmond Hodgson Yeats], 'Burlesque Past and Present', *London Society* (3 May 1885): 127–32 (130).
2. Hindley, *True History*, xxx–xxxiii; 'Victoria Theatre', *Era* (6 Mar. 1870): 8; 'The Theatres', *Graphic* (19 Mar. 1870): 378–9 (379); 'Surrey Theatre', *London Reader* (21 Apr. 1877): 580.
3. 'Last of the Adelphi', *Daily Telegraph* (12 Aug. 1901). Clipping. London Playbills folder 1 (27) – Adelphi Theatre. Bod; M. Wilson Disher, 'Famous Characters of the Streets', *Nineteenth-Century and After* (Apr. 1925): 564–8.
4. Jordanova, 'Portraits, Biography and Public Histories', 159–75.
5. Rita Dove, 'Staffordshire Figurine, 1825', *Sonata Mulattica*, 187–8 (188).
6. Corbin, *Life of an Unknown*, 213.

Bibliography

Newspaper articles cited only appear once in the notes.

Archives

Bodleian Libraries, Oxford (Bod)

John Johnson Collection of Printed Ephemera

British Library, London (BL)

Mendicity Society Minute Book. 1818–1824. Add. MS 50136
*The Case of the inhabitants of the parish of St Giles in the Fields, as to their poor and a
   workhouse designed to be built.* 816 m9-65
The Nautical Tom and Jerry; or Life of a True British Sailor. Add. MS 42966
*Workhouse Cruelty; being a full and true account of one Mrs Mary Whistle, a poor
   woman . . . in the parish of St Giles in the Fields.* 816 m9-78, 80
'Yankee Doodle or the Negroes Farewell to America' (*c.* 1775), BL Music
   Collections G.310.(163.)

Caird Library, National Maritime Museum, Greenwich

HMS *Pomone, Watch, Station, and Quarter Bill. c.* 1812. WQB/49; MS1980/170

Camden Local Studies Centre, London

P/GG/PO/6 (Poor Expenditure Ledgers 1819–1825), P/GG/PO/9 (Treasurer's
   Account – poor 1820–1827), UTAH 123-4 1822-3 vol. D (St Giles Poor Rates)

Houghton Library, Harvard (Hou)

Durang, Charles. *History of the Philadelphia Stage, 1749–1855.* TS 275 10 F

Genest, John. *Some Account of the English Stage, from the Restoration to 1830.* 1832. TS 937 H4

History of Andrew Whiston, King of the Beggars. 1826. Hou Gen *44W – 1229

History of Vauxhall Gardens. 9 vols. 1890. TS 952.2

Playbills, images and the performance history of *Tom and Jerry*: TCS 68, MS Thr 1004, MS Thr 1076, MS Thr 620, MS Thr 62, TS 937 H4, HTC Clippings 10, TS 275 10 F., HD 17477.39.6.31., HD 23497.71.27.35

Playtexts: THE HD 17477.39.6.31., THE HD 23497.71.27.35

Library of Congress, Washington

Playbill, 8 Apr. 1822. https://lccn.loc.gov/2014657236

Playbill, 'Tom & Jerry', 7 Aug. 1823. https://lccn.loc.gov/2014657264

Playbill, 'Tom & Jerry', 21 Jan. 1825. https://lccn.loc.gov/2014657218

Tom and Jerry Davies' Amphitheatre Adaptation

Library Company of Philadelphia

Tom and Jerry (Philadelphia: 1824). AM 1824 Egan 2025.D.2

London Metropolitan Archives, London (LMA)

DL/T/36/47 (Burial records), MR/PLT (Land Tax records), CLC/B/192/F/001/ MS11936 (Insurance records)

National Archives, Kew (NAK)

ADM 37 (Ship's Musters), ADM 51 (Captain's Logs), ADM 35 (Ship's Pay Books), ADM 102 (Haslar Hospital), ADM 22 (Pension records)

Victoria and Albert Museum, London

Theatre Archives. Adelphi 1820–1825. Playbill. *Tom and Jerry.* December 1821

Other Primary Sources

A. B. 'Pinkster', in Shane White, 'Pinkster in Albany, 1803: A Contemporary Description', *New York History* 70 (1989): 191–9

An Account of the Workhouses of Great Britain, 3rd edn. 1786

[Aimwell, Absolom]. 'A Pinkster Ode', reprinted in Geraldine R. Pleat and Agnes N. Underwood, 'Pinkster Ode, Albany, 1803', *New York Folklore Quarterly* 8 (1952): 31–45

Allen, Lake. *The History of Portsmouth; Containing a Full and Enlarged Account of its Ancient and Present State* (1817)

Baker, H. Barton. 'The Home of the Melodrama', *London Society*, 47:278 (Feb. 1881): 143

Beames, Thomas. *The Rookeries of London.* 1850

Bechervaise, John. *Thirty-Six Years of a Seafaring Life* (Portsea: W. Woodward, 1839)

Billy Waters, the London Fiddler: A Laughable Farce in One Act Adapted for Presentation in the Galanty Show [c. 1861]

Blanchard, E. L. 'The Playgoer's Portfolio', *The Era Almanack* (Jan. 1877): 1–10

Boz [Charles Dickens], *Memoirs of Joseph Grimaldi*. 1846

Bridgetower, Frederic. *Six Pathetic Canzonets*. 1815

Brine, George Atkins. *The King of the Beggars: A True Story of Vagrant Life*. 1883

Brougham, John. *Life in New York: or, Tom and Jerry on a visit. A comic drama, in two acts, etc.* [1856?]

Brown, William J. *The Life of William J. Brown, of Providence, R.I.* 1883

Brown, William Wells. *The American Fugitive in Europe*. 1855

Bryant, Joshua. *Account of an Insurrection of the Negro Slaves in the Colony of Demerara*. 1824

Buckingham, James Silk. *Autobiography*. 1855

Busby, Thomas Lord. *Costume of the Lower Orders of London. Painted and engraved from nature by T. L. Busby* [1820]

[Bysh, J.]. *Cries of London. c.* 1818–21

Catnach, James. *The Death, Last Will, and Funeral of Black Billy; also the Tears of London for the Death of Tom and Jerry. c.* 1823

Clarke, William. *Every Night Book or Life After Dark*. 1827

Coventry, Alexander. 'Memoirs of an Emigrant: The Journal of Alexander Coventry M.D.'. Typescript prepared by the Albany Institute of History and Art and the New York State Museum, 1978

Cummins, Alicia Sarah. *The Life and Career of Mother Cummins, the Celebrated Lady Abbess of St Giles* [1820?]

Cutbush, Edward. *Observations on the Means of Preserving the Health of Soldiers and Sailors*. 1808

Daniel, George. *Merrie England in the Olden Time; Or, Peregrinations with Uncle Tim and Mr Bosky of Little Britain, Drysalter.* 2 vols. 1842

'Death of Billy Waters', *Morning Advertiser* (22 March 1823): 3

Dens of London Exposed. 1835

De Voe, Thomas Farrington. *The Market Book: Containing a Historical Account of the Public Markets in New York, Boston, Philadelphia, and Brooklyn.* 2 vols. 1862

Dibdin, Charles. *Songs Naval and Nautical*. 1841

Dibdin jnr, Charles. *Life in London, or, The Larks of Logic, Tom, and Jerry*. 1822

Dobie, R. *The History of the United Parishes of St Giles in the Fields and St George Bloomsbury*. 1829

Doings in London; or Day and Night Scenes of the frauds, frolics, manners and depravities of the Metropolis. 1828

Douglass, Frederick. *The Heroic Slave: A Cultural and Critical Edition*. 2015

—. *Life and Times of Frederick Douglass, Written by Himself*. 1881

—. *My Bondage and My Freedom*. 1855

Dove, Rita. *Sonata Mulattica: A Life in Five Movements and a Short Play*. 2009

'Dramatic Necrology. For 1823–4', *The Drama: or, Theatrical Pocket Magazine*, 5:7 (Feb. 1824): 385–93

Dunlap, William. *The Diary of William Dunlap, 1766–1839.* 3 vols. 1929–31

—. *History of the American Theatre*. 1832

Egan, Pierce. *The Finish to the Adventures of Tom, Jerry, and Logic, in their pursuits through Life In and Out of London*. 1869

—. *Life in London, Or, The Day and Night Scenes of Jerry Hawthorne, esq, and His Elegant Friend Corinthian Tom, Accompanied by Bob Logic.* 1821

Eights, James. 'Pinkster Festivities in Albany Sixty Years Ago', in *Collections on the History of Albany, from Its Discovery to the Present Time*, ed. Joel Munsell. 4 vols. 2: 323–7. 1865–71

The English Metropolis; Or, London in the Year 1820. 1820

Equiano, Olaudah [Gustavus Vassa]. *The Interesting Narrative and Other Writings*, ed. Vincent Carretta. 2003

[Falconer, William]. *An Universal Dictionary of the Marine.* 1780

Fitzball, Edward. *The Negro of Wapping, or, the Boat-Builder's Hovel! A melo-drama, in two acts* [1838?]

Forster, John. *The Life of Charles Dickens.* 2 vols. n.d.

Frederic, Francois Alexandre. *Travels Through the United States of North America, the Country of the Iroquois, and Upper Canada in the Years 1795, 1796, and 1777.* 2 vols. 1799

Gatty, Alfred. 'Street Characters', *Notes and Queries* (20 March 1852): 270–1

Godwin, George. *London Shadows.* 1854

Grant, James. *Sketches in London.* 1838

Greenwood, T. *Death of Life in London, Or, the Funeral of Tom and Jerry* [1823]

Haines, John Thomas. *My Poll and My Partner Joe*, Cumberland's Minor Theatre. vol. 9. 1828

Hammon, Briton. *Narrative of the Uncommon Sufferings, and Surprizing Deliverance of Briton Hammon, a Negro Man.* 1760

'Hatton-Garden', *London Chronicle* (22 Feb. 1822)

Hay, M. D., ed. *Landsman Hay: The Memoirs of Robert Hay, 1789–1847.* 1953

Hazlitt, William. 'On Wit and Humour', in *The Miscellaneous Works of William Hazlitt.* 5 vols. 1864. 4: 2–31

Hill, Benson Earle. *Playing About, Or Theatrical Anecdotes and Adventures.* 2 vols. 1840

Hindley, Charles. *History of the Catnach Press.* 1886

—. *The Life and Times of James Catnach (Late of Seven Dials), Balladmonger.* 1878

—. *The True History of Tom and Jerry* [1892]

[Hodgson], *The Cries of London.* c. 1824

Hone, William. 'Fantoccini', in *The Every-Day Book, Or, The Guide to the Year.* 1825. 1113–17

Howell, George R., and Jonathan Tenny. *History of the County of Albany, from 1609 to 1886.* 1886.

Howell, T. B. *A Complete Collection of State Trials and Proceedings for High Treason and Other Crimes and Misdemeanours from the Earliest Period to the Present Time* (1824). 1817. 33:1554–8

Jacobs, Harriet A. *Incidents in the Life of a Slave Girl, Written by Herself.* 1861

Jerrold, Douglas. 'The Ballad-Singer', in *The Heads of the People; or, Portraits of the English Drawn by Kenny Meadows. With Original Essays by Distinguished Writers.* 2 vols. 1840–1. I: 289–97

—. *The History of St Giles and St James.* 1851

Joyce, P. W. *Old Irish Folk Music and Songs.* 1909

Judd, Jacob, comp. and ed. *Correspondence of the Van Cortlandt Family of Cortlandt Manor, 1748–1800.* 1977

Kmen, Henry A. 'Old Corn Meal: A Forgotten Negro Folk Singer', *Journal of American Folklore*, 75:295 (Jan.–Mar. 1962): 29–34

[Lamb, Charles]. 'A Complaint of the Decay of Beggars in the Metropolis', in *Elia, Essays Which Have Appeared Under that Signature in the London Magazine*. 1823. 262–75

—. *Letters* vol. 1

—. 'On Burial Societies and the Character of the Undertaker', *The Reflector*, 3 (1811)

Lewis, H. *Lewis's Illustrated Hand-Book of Portsmouth, and Guide to the Royal Dockyard, Harbour, Haslar Hospital, Gosport, Fortifications, etc.* [*With introductory remarks by R. P.*]. 1860

Lewis, Matthew. *Journal of a Residence among the Negroes in the West Indies*. 1845

Liddell Hart, B. H., ed. *The Letters of Private Wheeler, 1809–1828*. 1951

Marrant, John. *A Narrative of the Lord's Wonderful Dealings With John Marrant, a Black*, 4th edn. 1785

Mayhew, Henry, et al. *London Labour and the London Poor*. 4 vols. 1861

Mendicity Society, *Sixth Report*. 1824

'Minutes of the Evidence taken Before the Committee ... to Inquire into the State of Mendicity and Vagrancy in the Metropolis and its Neighbourhood. Ordered to be Printed, July 11th, 1815', *Quarterly Review*, 14:27 (Oct. 1815): 120–45

Moncrieff, W. T. 'Back Slums in the Holy Land', in *Selections from the Dramatic Works of W. T. Moncrieff*. 3 vols. 1851. 3: 112–13

—. 'Beggars, Or Cadgers', in *Selections from the Dramatic Works*, 3:114–15

—. 'Billy Waters', in *Selections from the Dramatic Works*, 3:121–3

—. 'Billy Waters; or, Two Richmonds in the Field', *Sunday Times* (11 May 1851): 3

—. 'Tom and Jerry; Or, Life in London', in *Cumberland's British Theatre*. Vol. 33 [n.d.]

Munsell, Joel, ed. *Collections on the History of Albany, from Its Discovery to the Present Time*. 4 vols. 1865–71

Nagle, Jacob. *The Nagle Journal: A Diary of the Life of Jacob Nagle, Sailor, from the Year 1775 to 1841*, ed. John C. Dann. 1988

Naval Captain. *Observations and Instructions for the Use of the Commissioned, the Junior, and Other Officers of the Royal Navy*. 1804

Nicol, John. *The Life and Adventures of John Nicol, Mariner*, ed. Tim Flannery. 2000

Northcote, William. *The Marine Practice of Physic and Surgery*. 2 vols. 1770

[Oglethorpe, James]. *The Sailor's Advocate, First Printed in 1727–28*. 1777

'Oh! What Will Mother Say?', in *The Universal Songster; Or, Museum of Mirth*. 3 vols. 1826. 2: 281

O'Keefe, John. *Recollections of the Life of John O'Keefe*. 3 vols. 1826

Olmstead, Francis Allyn. *Incidents of a Whaling Voyage (1839–40)*. 1841

Parton, John. *Some Account of the Hospital and Parish of St Giles in the Fields, Middlesex*. 1822

The Picture of London for 1820. 1820

Pinckard, George. *Notes on the West Indies: Written during the Expedition under the Command of the Late General Sir Ralph Abercromby*. 3 vols. 1806

'Police', *London Packet* (20 Feb. 1822)

The Posthumous Papers of the Cadger's Club. 1838

Pratt, Willis W., ed. *Galveston Island; or a Few Months off the Coast of Texas: The Journal of Francis C. Sheridan, 1839–40.* 1954

Real Life in London; or, the Rambles and Adventures of Bob Tallyho Esq. and his Cousin, the Hon. Tom Dashall through the Metropolis. 2 vols. 1821–2

Reeves, W. 'Lines on Billy Waters', in Hindley, *True History,* 108

'Reports from the Select Committee on the State of Mendicity in the Metropolis', *Parliamentary Papers* 5 (1816): 391–416

Richardson, William. *A Mariner of England: An Account of the Career of William Richardson as Told by Himself,* ed. Colonel Spencer Childers. 1908

Riley, W. Edward, and Laurence Gomme, eds. *Survey of London: Volume 5, St Giles-in-the-Fields, Pt III.* 1914

Sauvan, Jean-Baptiste-Balthazar. *Diorama Anglais ou Promenades Pittoresques à Londres.* 1823

Scudder, H. E., ed. *Recollections of Samuel Breck with Passages from his Note-Books (1771–1862).* 1877

'Select Committee on Mendicity in the Metropolis: Final Report', *Parliamentary Papers* 5. 1816

Smith, Adam. *Theory of Moral Sentiments.* 2 vols. 1804

Smith, John Thomas. *Vagabondiana: or, Anecdotes of Mendicant Wanderers through the Streets of London; with Portraits of the Most Remarkable Drawn from Life.* 1817

'Spirit of the Public Journals: London Ballad-Singers' (pt 2), *The Mirror of Literature, Amusement, and Instruction* (16 July 1825): 54

Strickland, William. *Journal of a Tour in the United States of America, 1794–1795,* ed. J. E. Strickland. 1971

Thackeray, W. M. 'De Juventute', *The Works of William Thackeray: Roundabout Papers.* 1869. 69–86

—. 'On the Genius of George Cruikshank', cited in introduction to *Pierce Egan, Tom and Jerry. Life in London or the Day and Night Scenes of Jerry Hawthorn, Esq. and his Elegant Friend Corinthian Tom in their Rambles and Sprees through the Metropolis.* 1869

—. *Vanity Fair.* 1848

Thornbury, Walter. *Old and New London.* 6 vols. [1887]–93

Thursfield, H. G. ed. *Five Naval Journals 1789–1817.* 1951

Timbs, John. *Curiosities of London.* 1867

The tread mill, or Tom and Jerry at Brixton: a serio, comic, operatic, milldramatic, farcical, moral burletta in two acts: as performed originally at the Surrey Theatre [1822?]

Wadström, C. B. *An Essay on Colonisation, Particularly Applied to the Western Coast of Africa.* 2 vols. 1794

[Waterhouse, James]. *Journal of a Young Man of Massachusetts, Late a Surgeon on Board an American Privateer.* 1816

Wedderburn, Robert. *The Horrors of Slavery and Other Writings,* ed. Iain McCalman. 1991

[Westmacott, Charles Molloy]. *The English Spy.* 2 vols. 1826

Wilson, Harriet E. *Our Nig; or, Sketches from the Life of a Free Black.* 1859

Wilson, Thomas. *The Danciad; or, Dancer's Monitor.* 1824

Secondary Sources

Abraham, Adam. 'Plagiarizing Pickwick: Imitations of Immortality', *Dickens Quarterly*, 32:1 (March 2015): 5–20

—. *Plagiarizing the Victorian Novel: Imitation, Parody, Aftertext.* 2019

Abraham, Keshia N., and John Woolf. *Black Victorians: Hidden in History.* 2022

Adkins, Lesley, and Roy Adkins. *Jack Tar: Life in Nelson's Navy.* 2011

Ashton, Rosemary. *142 Strand: A Radical Address in Victorian London.* 2006

—. *One Hot Summer: Dickens, Darwin, Disraeli, and the Great Stink of 1858.* 2017

Bailey, Peter. *Popular Culture and Performance in the Victorian City.* 1998

Bakhtin, Mikhail. *Rabelais and His World.* Trans. Hélène Iswolsky. 1984

Barry, Anna Maria. 'Charles Incledon: A Singing Sailor on the Georgian Stage', in *Martial Masculinities: Experiencing and Imagining the Military in the Long Nineteenth Century*, ed. Brown and Begiato, 82–101. 2019

Beddoe, Stella. *A Potted History: Henry Willett's Ceramic Chronicle of Britain.* 2015

Begiato, Joanne. *Manliness in Britain, 1760–1900: Bodies, Emotion, and Material Culture.* 2020

—. 'Tears and the Manly Sailor in England, *c.* 1760–1860', *Journal for Maritime Research*, 17:2 (2015): 117–33

Bell, Karl. *The Legend of Spring-Heeled Jack: Victorian Urban Folklore and Popular Cultures.* 2012

Bhabha, Homi. 'Of Mimicry and Man: The Ambivalence of Colonial Discourse', *October*, 28 (Spring 1984): 125–33

Blackmore, Susan. *The Meme Machine.* 1999

Bogdan, Robert. *Freak Show: Presenting Human Oddities for Amusement and Profit.* 1988

Bolster, W. Jeffrey. *Black Jacks: African American Seamen in the Age of Sail.* 1997

Bolter, Jay David, and Richard Grusin. *Remediation: Understanding New Media.* 1999

Botkin, Frances R. *Thieving Three-Fingered Jack: Transatlantic Tales of a Jamaican Outlaw.* 2017

Boulton, Jeremy, Romola Davenport, and Leonard Schwarz. '"These ANTE-CHAMBERS OF THE GRAVE"? Mortality, Medicine, and the Workhouse in Georgian London, 1725–1824', in *Medicine and the Workhouse*, ed. Jonathan Reinarz and Leonard Schwarz, 58–85. 2013

Brantlinger, Patrick. *Rule of Darkness: British Literature and Imperialism 1830–1914.* 1988

Bratton, Jacky. 'Dancing the Hornpipe in Fetters', *Folk Music Journal*, 6:1 (1990): 66–82

—. *The Making of the West End Stage: Marriage, Management and the Mapping of Gender in London, 1830–1870.* 2011

Bressey, Caroline. 'The Next Chapter: The Black Presence in the Nineteenth Century', in *Britain's Black Past*, ed. Gretchen Gerzina, 315–29. 2020

Briefel, Aviva. *The Racial Hand in the Victorian Imagination.* 2015

Brockliss, Laurence, et al. *Nelson's Surgeon: William Beatty, Naval Medicine, and the Battle of Trafalgar.* 2005

Brown, Michael. *Emotions and Surgery in Britain, 1793–1912.* 2022

—, and Joanne Begiato, eds. *Martial Masculinities: Experiencing and Imagining the Military in the Long Nineteenth Century*. 2019

Brundage, Anthony. *The English Poor Laws, 1700–1930*. 2002

Brunsman, Denver. 'Subjects vs. Citizens: Impressment and Identity in the Anglo-American Atlantic', *Journal of the Early Republic*, 30:4 (Winter 2010): 557–86

Burroughs, Robert. 'Sailors and Slaves: The "Poor Enslaved Tar" in Naval Reform and Nautical Melodrama', *Journal of Victorian Culture*, 16:3 (Dec. 2011): 305–22

Butler, Judith. *Bodies that Matter: On the Discursive Limits of 'Sex'*. 1993

Caputo, Sara. *Foreign Jack Tars: The British Navy and Transnational Seafarers during the Revolutionary and Napoleonic Wars*. 2022

Carlson, Marvin. *Performance: A Critical Introduction*, 2nd edn. 2004

Carpio, Glenda R. *Laughing Fit to Kill: Black Humor in the Fictions of Slavery*. 2008

Chater, Kathleen. *Untold Histories: Black People in England and Wales during the Period of the British Slave Trade, c. 1660–1807*. 2009

Childs, Adrienne L., and Susan H. Libby. *The Black Figure in the European Imaginary*. 2017

Clapp, W. W. *A Record of the Boston Stage*. 1853

Clubb, Louise George. *Italian Drama in Shakespeare's Time*. 1989

Comegna, Anthony. '"The Dupes of Hope Forever"': The Loco-Foco or Equal Rights Movement, 1820s–1870s'. PhD diss., University of Pittsburgh. 2016

Cooper, Helen. *The English Romance in Time: Transforming Motifs from Geoffrey of Monmouth to the Death of Shakespeare*. 2004

Corbin, Alain. *The Life of an Unknown: The Rediscovered World of the Clog Maker in Nineteenth-Century France*. 2001

Costello, Ray. *Black Salt: Seafarers of African Descent on British Ships*. 2012

Coventry, Alexander. 'Memoirs of an Immigrant (1789)', in *A Beautiful and Fruitful Place: Selected Rensselaerswijck Seminar Papers*, ed. Nancy A. McClure Zeller, 38–47. 1991

Cox, Philip. *Reading Adaptations: Novels and Verse Narratives on the Stage, 1790–1840*. 2000

Crymble, Adam. 'The Decline and Fall of an Early Modern Slum: London's St Giles "Rookery", c. 1550–1850', *Urban History*, 49:2 (May 2022): 310–34

Curry, Tommy J. 'This Nigger's Broken: Hyper-Masculinity, the Buck, and the Role of Physical Disability in White Anxiety Toward the Black Male Body', *Journal of Social Philosophy*, 48:3 (Fall 2017): 321–43

Dabydeen, David. *Hogarth's Blacks: Images of Blacks in Eighteenth Century English Art*. 1987

Dancy, J. Ross. *The Myth of the Press Gang: Volunteers, Impressment and the Naval Manpower Problem in the Late Eighteenth Century*. 2015

Darnton, Robert. *Poetry and the Police: Communication Networks in Eighteenth-Century Paris*. 2010

—. 'What is the History of Books?', *Daedalus* (Summer 1982), 65–83

Davis, Jim. *Comic Acting and Portraiture in Late-Georgian and Regency England*. 2015

— and Victor Emeljanow. *Reflecting the Audience: London Theatregoing, 1840–1880*. 2001

Davis, Paul B. *The Lives and Times of Ebenezer Scrooge*. 1990

Davis, Tracy C. 'Theatricality and Civil Society', in *Theatricality*, ed. Davis and Postlewait, 127–55. 2003

Dawkins, Richard. *The Selfish Gene.* 1976

Deazley, Ronan, et al., eds. *Privilege and Property: Essays on the History of Copyright.* 2010

Denford, Steve, and David Hayes, eds. *Streets of St Giles: A Survey of Streets, Buildings and Former Residents in a Part of Camden.* 2012

DeVere Brody, Jennifer. *Impossible Purities: Blackness, Femininity, and Victorian Culture.* 1998

Dewulf, Jeroen. 'Pinkster: An Atlantic Creole Festival in a Dutch-American Context', *Journal of American Folklore*, 126:501 (Summer 2013): 245–71

—. *The Pinkster King and the King of Kongo: The Forgotten History of America's Dutch-Owned Slaves.* 2017

Dickie, Simon. *Cruelty and Laughter: Forgotten Comic Literature and the Unsentimental Eighteenth Century.* 2011

Diggle, James, ed. *Theophrastus: Characters.* 2003

Douglas, Mary. *Purity and Danger: An Analysis of Concepts of Pollution and Taboo.* 1966

Douglas-Fairhurst, Robert. *The Turning-Point: The Year That Changed Dickens, and the World.* 2021

Draudt, Manfred. 'Critical Introduction', in *Othello the Moor of Fleet Street*, ed. Manfred Draudt, 1–39. 1993

Du Bois, W. E. B. *The Souls of Black Folk.* 1903

Dyos, H. J. 'The Slums of Victorian London', *Victorian Studies*, 11:1 (1967): 5–40

Ellis, John D. 'A Black "Jack Tar": Samuel Michael, an Afro-American Sailor Late of the Napoleonic Navy and In-Pensioner of Greenwich Hospital'. Unpublished paper

—. '"Left to the Streets and the Workhouse": The Life, Visual Representation and Death of John Baptists, 3rd Scots Fusilier Guards', *Journal of the Society for Army Historical Research* 82 (Autumn 2004): 204–9

Emery, Phillip, and Wooldridge, Kevin. *St Pancras Burial Ground: Excavations for St Pancras International, 2002–3.* 2011

Emmerson, George S. 'The Hornpipe', *Folk Music Journal*, 2 (1970): 12–34

Ennis, Daniel James. *Enter the Press-Gang: Naval Impressment in Eighteenth-Century British Literature.* 2002

Esterhammer, Angela. *Print and Performance in the 1820s: Improvisation, Speculation, Identity.* 2020

Evans, David. 'Black Fife and Drum Music in Mississippi', *Mississippi Folklore Register*, 6:3 (1972): 94–107. Accessed via https://www.folkstreams.net/contexts/black-fife-and-drum-music-in-mississippi

Fanon, Frantz. *Black Skin, White Masks.* Trans. Charles Lam Markmann. 1968

Fawcett, Julia H. *Spectacular Disappearances: Celebrity and Privacy, 1696–1801.* 2016

Fisher, Michael H. *The Inordinately Strange Life of Dyce Sombre: Victorian Anglo-Indian MP and Chancery 'Lunatic'.* 2010

Foote, Thelma Wills. *Black and White Manhattan: The History of Racial Formation in Colonial New York City.* 2004

Fowler, Simon. *The Workhouse.* 2007

Freeman, Lisa A. *Character's Theater: Genre and Identity on the Eighteenth-Century Stage*. 2001

Fryer, Peter. *Staying Power: The History of Black People in Britain*. 1984

Foy, Charles R. 'Britain's Black Tars', in *Britain's Black Past*, ed. Gretchen Gerzina, 63–79. 2020

—. 'The Royal Navy's Employment of Black Mariners and Maritime Workers, 1754–1783', *International Journal of Maritime History*, 28:1 (2016): 6–35

Gabel, Susan, and Susan Peters, 'Presage of a Paradigm Shift? Beyond the Social Model of Disability toward Resistance Theories of Disability', *Disability & Society*, 19:6 (2004): 585–600

Garland-Thomson, Rosemarie. *Extraordinary Bodies: Figuring Disability in American Literature and Culture* (Twentieth Anniversary Edition). 2017

—, ed. *Freakery: Cultural Spectacles of the Extraordinary Body*. 1996

—. *Staring: How We Look*. 2009

Gatrell, Vic. *Conspiracy on Cato Street: A Tale of Liberty and Revolution in Regency London*. 2022

—. *First Bohemians: Life and Art in London's Golden Age*. 2013

Gerzina, Gretchen. *Black England: A Forgotten Georgian History*, rev. edn. 2022

—, ed. *Black Victorians/Black Victoriana*. 2003

Gibbs, Jenna M. *Performing the Temple of Liberty: Slavery, Theater, and Popular Culture in London and Philadelphia, 1760–1850*. 2014

Gikandi, Simon. *Slavery and the Culture of Taste*. 2014

Gilje, Paul A. *To Swear Like a Sailor: Maritime Culture in America, 1750–1850*. 2016

Gilroy, Paul. *The Black Atlantic: Modernity and Double Consciousness*. 1993

Goheen, Jeremy. '"Soot in One's Soup": Transitory Blackness in British Romantic Chimney-Sweep Literature', *Studies in Romanticism*, 61:2 (Spring 2022): 57–65

Green, David R., *Pauper Capital: London and the Poor Law, 1790–1870*. 2010

Grier, Miles. 'Inkface: The Slave Stigma in England's Early Imperial Imagination', in *Scripturalizing the Human: The Written as Political*, ed. Vincent L. Wimbush, Chapter 8. 2015

Griffin, Emma. *Breadwinner: An Intimate History of the Victorian Economy*. 2020

Guede, Alain. *Monsieur de Saint-George, Virtuoso, Swordsman, Revolutionary: A Legendary Life Rediscovered*. Trans. Gilda M. Roberts. 2003

Habib, Imtiaz. *Black Lives in the English Archives, 1500–1677: Imprints of the Invisible*. 2008

Hanley, Ryan. 'Slavery and the Birth of Working-Class Racism in England, 1814–1833. The Alexander Prize Essay', *Transactions of the Royal Historical Society* 26 (2016): 103–23

Hansen, David. *Dempsey's People: A Folio of British Street Portraits 1824–1844*. 2017

Harley, Joseph. 'Consumption and Poverty in the Homes of the English Poor, c. 1670–1834', *Social History*, 43:1 (2018): 81–104

—. 'Material Lives of the Poor and Their Strategic Use of the Workhouse during the Final Decades of the English Old Poor Law', *Continuity and Change*, 30:1 (2015), 71–103

Harris, Leslie M. *In the Shadow of Slavery: African Americans in New York City, 1626–1863*. 2003

Harris, T. ed. *Popular Culture in England, c. 1500–1850*. 1995

Hartman, Saidiya. *Lose Your Mother: A Journey Along the Atlantic Slave Route*. 2008

—. *Scenes of Subjection: Terror, Slavery and Self-Making in Nineteenth-Century America*. 1997

—. 'Venus in Two Acts', *Small Axe*, 12:2 (1 June 2008): 1–14

—. *Wayward Lives, Beautiful Experiments: Intimate Histories of Riotous Black Girls, Troublesome Women and Queer Radicals*. 2019

Haywood, Ian. *The Rise of Victorian Caricature*. 2020

—. *Romanticism and Caricature*. 2013

Hepburn, James G. *A Book of Scattered Leaves: Poetry of Poverty in Broadside Ballads*. 2 vols. 2000–1

Highfill, Philip H. et al. *Biographical Dictionary of Actors*. 16 vols. 1973–93

Hill, Errol G., and James V. Hatch. *A History of African American Theatre*. 2003

Hitchcock, Tim. *Down and Out in Eighteenth-Century London*. 2004

Hoermann, Raphael. '"Fermentation Will Be universal": Intersections of Race and Class in Robert Wedderburn's Black Atlantic Discourse of Transatlantic Revolution', in *Britain's Black Past*, ed. Gerzina, 295–314. 2020

Holder, Heidi J. 'Other Londoners: Race and Class in Plays of Nineteenth-Century London Life', in *Imagined Londons*, ed. Pamela Gilbert, 31–44. 2002

Holmes, Martha Stoddard. *Fictions of Affliction: Physical Disability in Victorian Culture*. 2004

Holmes, Rachel. *The Hottentot Venus: The Life and Death of Sarah Baartman*. 2007

Honour, Hugh. *The Image of the Black in Western Art*, vol. IV/1 *Slaves and Liberators*, vol. IV/2 *Black Models and White Myths*. 1989

Hornback, Robert. *Racism and Early Blackface Comic Traditions: From the Old World to the New*. 2018

Humphries, Jane. *Childhood and Child Labour in the British Industrial Revolution*. 2010

Hunt, E. H. 'Industrialization and Regional Inequality: Wages in Britain, 1760–1914', *Journal of Economic History*, 46:4 (1986): 935–66

Hurren, Elizabeth, and Steve King. '"Begging for a Burial": Form, Function and Conflict in Nineteenth-Century Pauper Burial', *Social History*, 30:3 (Aug. 2005): 321–41

Inglehearn, Madeleine et al. 'The Hornpipe', http://chrisbrady.itgo.com/dance/stepdance/hornpipe_conference.htm

Inglis, Fred. *A Short History of Celebrity*. 2010

James, C. L. R. *The Black Jacobins: Toussaint L'Ouverture and the San Domingo Revolution*. 1938

James, Louis. *Fiction for the Working Man*. 1963

Jensen, Oskar. *The Ballad-Singer in Georgian and Victorian London*. 2021

—. 'The Diminution of "Irish" Johnstone', in *Ireland, Enlightenment and the English Stage, 1740–1820*, ed. David O'Shaughnessy, 79–98. 2019

—. *Napoleon and British Song, 1797–1822*. 2015

—. *Vagabonds: Life on the Streets of Nineteenth-Century London*. 2022

Jerrold, Blanchard. *The Life of George Cruikshank*. 1883

Johnson, E. Patrick. *Appropriating Blackness: Performance and the Politics of Authenticity*. 2003

Johnson, Stephen. 'Death and the Minstrel: Race, Madness, and Art in the Last (W)Rites of Three Early Blackface Performers', in *Burnt Cork: Traditions and Legacies of Blackface Minstrelsy*, ed. Johnson, 73–103. 2012

Jordanova, Ludmilla, 'Portraits, Biography and Public Histories', *Transactions of the Royal Historical Society*, 32 (2022): 159–75

Joshua, Essaka. *Physical Disability in British Romantic Literature*. 2020

Kafer, Alison, and Eunjing Kim, 'Disability and the Edges of Intersectionality', in *The Cambridge Companion to Literature and Disability*, ed. Clare Barker and Stuart Murray, 123–38. 2017

Keigan, Laura Michelle. 'Intersections of Race and Class in 1830s Othello Burlesques'. PhD diss., Louisiana State University. 2014

Kelly, Ian. *Mr Foote's Other Leg: Comedy, Tragedy and Murder in Georgian London*. 2012

Kennaway James. 'Celts under the Knife: Surgical Fortitude, Racial Theory and the British Army, 1800–1914', *Cultural and Social History*, 17:2 (2020): 227–44

—. 'Military Surgery as National Romance: The Memory of British Heroic Fortitude at Waterloo', *War & Society*, 39:2 (2020): 77–92

Kennedy, Catriona. *Narratives of the Revolutionary and Napoleonic Wars: Military and Civilian Experience in Britain and Ireland*. 2013

King, Steven, and Alannah Tomkins, eds. *The Poor in England 1700–1850: An Economy of Makeshifts*. 2003

King, Tiffany Lethabo. *The Black Shoals: Offshore Formations of Black and Native Studies*. 2019

King-Dorset, Rodreguez. *Black Dance in London, 1730–1850: Innovation, Tradition, and Resistance*. 2008

Kirkup, John. *A History of Limb Amputation*. 2007

Kriegel, Leonard. 'The Cripple in Literature', in *Images of the Disabled, Disabling Images*, ed. Alan Gartner and Tom Joe, 31–46. 1987

Lamire, Beverly. 'A Question of Trousers: Seafarers, Masculinity and Empire in the Shaping of British Male Dress, *c.* 1600–1800', *Cultural and Social History*, 13:1 (2016)

Land, Isaac. *War, Nationalism, and the British Sailor, 1750–1850*. 2009

Laqueur, Thomas. 'Bodies, Death, and Pauper Funerals', *Representations*, 1 (Feb. 1983): 109–31

Lavery, Brian. *Nelson's Navy: The Ships, Men, and Organisation, 1793–1815*. 2012

—. *Royal Tars: The Lower Deck of the Royal Navy, 875–1850*. 2011

Ledent, Bénédicte, and Pilar Cuder-Domínguez, eds. *New Perspectives on the Black Atlantic: Definitions, Readings, Practices, Dialogues*. 2012

Lee, Julia Sun-Joo. *The American Slave Narrative and the Victorian Novel*. 2010

Lees, Lynn Hollen. *The Solidarities of Strangers: The English Poor Laws and the People, 1700–1948*. 1998

Levine, Lawrence W., 'Black Laughter', in *Black Culture and Black Consciousness: Afro-American Folk Thought from Slavery to Freedom*, 298–366. 2007

Lhamon, W. T. *Jump Jim Crow: Lost Plays, Lyrics, and Street Prose of the First Atlantic Popular Culture*. 2003

—. *Raising Cain: Blackface Performance from Jim Crow to Hip-Hop*. 1998

Lilti, Antoine. *The Invention of Celebrity: 1750–1850*. Trans. Lynn Jeffres. 2017

Lincoln, Margarette. *Naval Wives & Mistresses*. 2007

Lindfors, Bernth, ed. *Africans on Stage: Studies in Ethnological Show Business*. 1999

Linebaugh, Peter, and Marcus Rediker. *The Many-Headed Hydra: Sailors, Slaves, Commoners, and the Hidden History of the Revolutionary Atlantic*. 2000

Lott, Eric. *Love and Theft: Blackface Minstrelsy and the American Working Class.* 1993

Luckhurst, Mary, and Jane Moody, eds. *Theatre and Celebrity in Britain, 1660–2000.* 2005

McAllister, Marvin. *White People Do Not Know How to Behave at Entertainments Designed for Ladies and Gentlemen of Colour: William Brown's African & American Theater.* 2003

—. *Whiting Up: Whiteface Minstrels & Stage Europeans in African American Performance.* 2011

MacFarlane, Robert. *Original Copy: Plagiarism and Originality in Nineteenth-Century Literature.* 2007

McGrady, Richard. 'Joseph Emidy: An African Cornwall', *Musical Times*, 127:1726 (Nov. 1986): 619–23

Mack, Robert L. *The Wonderful and Surprising History of Sweeney Todd: The Life and Times of an Urban Legend.* 2007

MacKenzie, Iain, et al., eds. *Comedy and Critical Thought: Laughter as Resistance.* 2018

McPherson, Heather. *Art and Celebrity in the Age of Reynolds and Siddons.* 2017

McWilliam, Rohan. *London's West End: Creating the Pleasure District, 1800–1914.* 2020

Mageean, Jim. 'The Black Origins of Sea Shanties', https://www.jimmageean.co.uk/post/the-black-origins-of-sea-shanties

Maidment, Brian. *Comedy, Caricature and the Social Order, 1820–50.* 2013

—. *Dusty Bob: A Cultural History of Dustmen, 1780–1870.* 2007

—. *Robert Seymour and Nineteenth-Century Print Culture.* 2021

Makdisi, Saree. *Making England Western: Occidentalism, Race, and Imperial Culture.* 2014

Makonnen, Atesede. '"Even in the Best Minds": Romanticism and the Evolution of Anti-Blackness', *Studies in Romanticism*, 61:2 (Spring 2022): 11–22

Marcus, Sharon. *The Drama of Celebrity.* 2019

Marsh, Jan, ed. *Black Victorians: Black People in British Art 1800–1900.* 2005

Martin, S. I. *Incomparable World.* 1996

Mayhew, Emily. *A Heavy Reckoning: War, Medicine and Survival in Afghanistan and Beyond.* 2017

Mayne, A. *The Imagined Slum: Newspaper Representation in Three Cities, 1870–1914.* 1993

Mee, Jon. 'Keyword: Performance', in *Remediating the 1820s*, ed. Jon Mee and Matthew Sangster, 109–12. 2023.

Michals, Teresa. 'Invisible Amputation and Heroic Masculinity', *Studies in Eighteenth-Century Culture*, 44 (2015): 17–39

—. *Lame Captains & Left-Handed Admirals: Amputee Officers in Nelson's Navy.* 2021

Miles, Ellie. 'Characterising the Nation: How T. P. Cooke Embodied the Naval Hero in Nineteenth-Century Nautical Melodrama', *Journal for Maritime Research*, 19:2 (2017): 107–20

Mitchell, David T., and Sharon L. Snyder. *Narrative Prosthesis: Disability and the Dependencies of Discourse.* 2000

Mole, Tom. *Byron's Romantic Celebrity: Industrial Culture and the Hermeneutic of Intimacy.* 2007

—. 'Celebrity and Anonymity', in *The Oxford Handbook of British Romanticism*, ed. David Duff, 464–77. 2018

—, ed. *Romanticism and Celebrity Culture, 1750–1850*. 2009

Montague, Tony. 'An O-o-old Song', https://www.theguardian.com/music/2023/mar/21/billy-waters-the-african-american-musician-who-captivated-1820s-london

Morrison, Matthew D. 'Race, Blacksound, and the (Re)Making of Musicological Discourse', *Journal of the American Musicological Society*, 72:3 (2019): 781–823

Morrison, Toni. *Playing in the Dark: Whiteness and the Literary Imagination*. 1992

Moses, Montrose J. *Famous Actor Families in America*. 1906

Mullan, John, and Christopher Reid, eds. 'Introduction' to *Eighteenth-Century Popular Culture: A Selection*, 1–28. 2000

Murray, Sean. 'That "Weird and Wonderful Posture": Jump "Jim Crow" and the Performance of Disability', in *The Oxford Handbook of Music and Disability Studies*, ed. Blake Howe et al., 357–70. 2015

Murrell, Denise. *Posing Modernity: The Black Model from Manet and Matisse to Today*. 2018

Myers, Norma. *Reconstructing the Black Past: Blacks in Britain c. 1780–1830*. 1996

Nathans, Heather S. *Early American Theatre from the Revolution to Thomas Jefferson: Into the Hands of the People*. 2003

Ndiaye, Noémie. *Scripts of Blackness: Early Modern Performance Culture and the Making of Race*. 2022

Neilsen, Caroline Louise. 'The Chelsea Out-Pensioners: Image and Reality in Eighteenth-Century and Early Nineteenth-Century Social Care'. PhD diss., University of Newcastle. 2014

Newman, Ian, Oskar Jensen, and David Kennerly, 'Introducing Mr Dibdin', in *Charles Dibdin and Late Georgian Culture*, 1–20. 2018

Newman, Simon P. *Embodied History: The Lives of the Poor in Early Philadelphia*. 2003

Nicholson, Bob. 'Transatlantic Connections', in *The Routledge Handbook to Nineteenth-Century British Periodicals and Newspapers*, ed. Andrew King, Alexis Easley and John Morton, 163–74. 2016.

Oboe, Annalisa, and Anna Scacchi, eds. *Recharting the Black Atlantic: Modern Cultures, Local Communities, Global Connections*. 2008

Odell, George. *Annals of the New York Stage*, 13 vols. 1927

Odumosu, Temi. *Africans in English Caricature 1769–1819: Black Jokes, White Humour*. 2017

Olusoga, David. *Black and British: A Forgotten History*. 2016

Otele, Olivette. *African Europeans: An Untold History*. 2020

Pappalardo, Bruno. *Tracing Your Naval Ancestors*. 2002

Parkes, Simon. 'Wooden Legs and Tales of Sorrow Done: The Literary Broken Soldier of the Late Eighteenth Century', *Journal for Eighteenth-Century Studies*, 36:2 (June 2013): 191–207

Patten, Robert L. *George Cruikshank's Life, Times, and Art*. 2 vols. 1992

Petrusich, Amanda. 'The Devil's Dream: Alan Lomax's 1942 Library of Congress Recordings', https://pitchfork.com/reviews/albums/17862-sid-hemphill-the-devils-dream-alan-lomaxs-1942-library-of-congress-recordings/

Phillips, George L. 'May-Day Is Sweeps' Day', *Folklore*, 60:1 (Mar. 1949): 217–27

Pickering, Michael. *Blackface Minstrelsy in Britain.* 2008

Poole, Robert. *Peterloo: The English Uprising.* 2019

Pope, Dudley. *Life in Nelson's Navy.* 1981

Prizel, Natalie. '"The Dead Man Come to Life Again": Edward Albert and the Strategies of Black Endurance', *Victorian Literature and Culture*, 45:2 (2017): 293–320

Qureshi, Sadiah. 'Displaying Sara Baartman, the "Hottentot Venus"', *History of Science*, 42:2 (June 2004): 233–57

—. *Peoples on Parade: Exhibitions, Empire, and Anthropology in Nineteenth-Century Britain.* 2011

Ramdin, Ron. *The Making of the Black Working Class in Britain.* 1987

Reay, Barry. *Popular Cultures in England, 1550–1750.* 1998

Reed, Peter P. *Rogue Performances: Staging the Underclasses in Early American Theatre Culture.* 2009

Reid, J. C. *Bucks and Bruisers: Pierce Egan and Regency England.* 1971

Richards, Jeffrey H. *Drama, Theatre, and Identity in the American New Republic.* 2005

Roberts, M. J. D. 'Reshaping the Gift Relationship: The London Mendicity Society and the Suppression of Begging in England 1818–1869', *International Review of Social History 1991*, 36:2 (1991): 201–31

Roberts, Paul E. W. 'English Fiddling 1650–1850: Reconstructing a Lost Idiom', in *Play It Like It Is: Fiddle and Dance Studies from Around the North Atlantic*, ed. Ian Russell and Mary Anne Alburger, 22–32. 2006

Rodger, N. A. M. *The Command of the Ocean: A Naval History of Britain 1649–1815.* 2004

Rogers, Nicholas. *The Press Gang: Naval Impressment and Its Opponents in Georgian Britain.* 2007

Rose, Lionel. *Rogues and Vagabonds: Vagrant Underworld in Britain 1815–1985.* 1988

Row-Heyveld, Lindsey. *Dissembling Disability in Early Modern English Drama.* 2018.

Russell, Gillian. *The Theatres of War: Performance, Politics, and Society, 1793–1815.* 1995

Sandahl, Carrie, and Philip Auslander. 'Introduction: Disability Studies in Commotion with Performance Studies', in *Bodies in Commotion: Disability and Performance*, ed. Carrie Sandahl and Philip Auslander, 1–12. 2005

Scott, Derek B. 'Blackface Minstrels, Black Minstrels, and Their Reception in England', in *Europe, Empire, and Spectacle in Nineteenth-Century British Music*, ed. Rachel Cowgill and Julian Rushton, 265–80. 2006

Scott, James C. *Weapons of the Weak: Everyday Forms of Peasant Resistance.* 1987

Scriven, Tom. 'The Jim Crow Craze in London's Press and Streets, 1836–9', *Journal of Victorian Culture*, 19:1 (Mar. 2014): 93–109

Shannon, Mary L. 'Artists' Street: Thomas Stothard, R. H. Cromek, and Literary Illustration on London's Newman Street', in Ian Haywood, Susan Matthews and Mary L. Shannon, eds, *Romanticism and Illustration*, 243–66. 2019

—. 'Dickens in Byron's Chair: Authenticity, Author Portraits, and Nineteenth-Century Visual Culture', *Victorian Literature and Culture*, 46:1 (2018): 57–81

—. *Dickens, Reynolds and Mayhew on Wellington Street: The Print Culture of a Victorian Street.* 2015

—. 'The Multiple Lives of Billy Waters: Dangerous Theatricality and Networked Illustrations in Nineteenth-Century Popular Culture', Special Edition of *Nineteenth Century Theatre and Film*, 46:2 (Nov. 2019): 161–89

Sharpe, Christina. *In the Wake: On Blackness and Being.* 2016

Shesgreen, Sean. *Images of the Outcast: The Urban Poor in the Cries of London.* 2002

Siebers, Tobin. *Disability Theory.* 2008

Siena, Kevin. 'Contagion, Exclusion, and the Unique Medical World of the Eighteenth-Century Workhouse: London Infirmaries in their Widest Relief', in Jonathan Reinarz and Leonard Schwarz, eds. *Medicine and the Workhouse*, 19–39. 2013

Smith, Thomas Ruys. *Southern Queen: New Orleans in the Nineteenth Century.* 2011

Snell, K. D. M. *Annals of the Labouring Poor: Social Change and Agrarian England, 1660–1900.* 1985

Southern, Eileen. *The Music of Black Americans: A History*, 2nd edn. 1983

Sponsler, Claire. *Ritual Imports: Performing Medieval Drama in America.* 2004.

Stark, Suzanne J. *Female Tars: Women Aboard Ship in the Age of Sail.* 1996

Storey, John. *Inventing Popular Culture: From Folklore to Globalization.* 2003

Stott, Andrew. *Comedy.* 2003

Strange, Julie-Marie. '"She Cried Very Little": Death, Grief and Mourning in Working-Class Culture, *c.* 1880–1914', *Social History*, 27:2 (May 2002): 143–61

Stuckey, Sterling. *Going through the Storm: The Influence of African American Art in History.* 1994

Sweet, Ryan. *Prosthetic Body Parts in Nineteenth-Century Literature and Culture.* 2022.

Szwydky, Lissette Lopez. *Transmedia Adaptation in the Nineteenth Century.* 2020

Taylor, Stephen. *Sons of the Waves: The Common Seaman in the Heroic Age of Sail.* 2020

Teukolsky, Rachel. *Picture World: Image, Aesthetics, and Victorian New Media.* 2020

Thompson, Ayanna. *Blackface.* 2021

Thompson, E. P. *The Making of the English Working Class.* 1963

Thompson, George A., Jr. *A Documentary History of the African Theatre.* 1998

Treloar, William Purdie. *Ludgate Hill: Past and Present.* 1881

Tromans, Nicholas. *David Wilkie: The People's Painter.* 2007

Tucker, Irene. *The Moment of Racial Sight: A History.* 2012

Turner, David M. *Disability in Eighteenth-Century England: Imagining Physical Impairment.* 2012

—. 'Disability and Prosthetics in Eighteenth- and Early Nineteenth-Century England', in *The Routledge History of Disease*, ed. Mark Jackson, 301–19. 2017

Upton, Chris. *The Birmingham Parish Workhouse 1730–1840.* 2019

Vincent, David. *I Hope I Don't Intrude? Privacy and its Dilemmas in Nineteenth-Century Britain.* 2015

—, ed. *Testaments of Radicalism: Memoirs of Working Class Politicians 1790–1885.* 1977

Visram, Rozina. *Ayahs, Lascars and Princes: Indians in Britain 1700–1947.* 1986

Voskuil, Lyn. *Acting Naturally: Victorian Theatricality and Authenticity.* 2004

Waters, Hazel. *Racism on the Victorian Stage.* 2007

Wells, Stanley, ed. *Nineteenth-Century Shakespeare Burlesques.* 5 vols. 1978

White, Shane. 'Pinkster: Afro-Dutch Syncretization in New York City and the Hudson Valley', *Journal of American Folklore* 102:403 (Jan.–Mar. 1989): 68–75

—. 'Pinkster in Albany, 1803: A Contemporary Description', *New York History* 70 (1989): 191–9

—. *Somewhat More Independent: The End of Slavery in New York City, 1770–1810.* 1991

Wilson, Ben. *Decency and Disorder: The Age of Cant 1789–1837.* 2007

Winfield, Rif. *British Warships in the Age of Sail 1793–1817: Design, Construction, Careers and Fates.* 2005

Winter, William. *The Jeffersons.* 1881

—. *Life and Art of Joseph Jefferson.* 1894

Witham, Barry B. ed. *Theatre in the United States: A Documentary History, Volume I: 1750–1915, Theatre in the Colonies and United States.* 1996

Wood, Marcus. *Slavery, Empathy, and Pornography.* 2002

Zieger, Susan. *The Mediated Mind: Affect, Ephemera, and Consumerism in the Nineteenth Century.* 2018

Zimmerman, J. F. *The Impressment of American Seamen.* 1925

Online Resources

America's Historical Imprints https://www.readex.com/products/americas-historical-imprints

Amputation Foundation https://amputationfoundation.org

Ancestry https://www.ancestry.com

British Library digital collections https://www.bl.uk/collection-items

British Museum digital collections https://www.britishmuseum.org/collection

Broadside Ballads Online http://ballads.bodleian.ox.ac.uk

English Broadside Ballad Archive https://ebba.english.ucsb.edu

The Surprising Adventures of Bampfylde-Moore Carew, King Of The Beggars. 1812 https://www.exclassics.com/carew/carew.pdf

FamilySearch https://familysearch.org

Folk Archive Resource North East http://www.farnearchive.com

https://jeffreygreen.co.uk

Lester S. Levy Sheet Music Collection https://levysheetmusic.mse.jhu.edu

Lomax Digital Archive https://archive.culturalequity.org

MeasuringWorth https://www.measuringworth.com/calculators/ukcompare/relativevalue.php

Minor Victorian Poets and Authors https://minorvictorianwriters.org.uk

https://www.nationalarchives.gov.uk/currency-converter/#currency-result

National Library of Scotland digital collections https://www.nls.uk

New York Public Library digital collections https://digitalcollections.nypl.org

OED Online https://www.oed.com

https://www.oldbaileyonline.org/static/Coinage.jsp#reading

Old Bailey Proceedings Online www.oldbaileyonline.org

Playbill, Thursday 28 March 1822, http://www.arthurlloyd.co.uk/Olympic.htm

https://www.portrait.gov.au/exhibitions/dempseys-people-2017

Royal Museums Greenwich digital collections https://www.rmg.co.uk/collections

Society for the Suppression of Mendicity, Instituted 1818. Broadsides and Ephemera Collection, David M. Rubenstein Rare Book & Manuscript Library, Duke University. https://idn.duke.edu/ark:/87924/r41v5dj3g

The Dear Surprise (naval history resources) https://thedearsurprise.com

The Session https://thesession.org

Three Decks (naval history resources) https://threedecks.org/

Traditional Tune Archive https://tunearch.org/wiki/TTA

Village Music Project https://www.village-music-project.org.uk/

Index

NOTE: Page numbers in italics refer to illustrations. Plates are indicated by Pl. and a number.